MW00935876

# The Personal Academic

A Textbook for English Composition

First Edition

By David William Foulds

Edited by Megan Jameson

Special Thanks to the English Department
at San Francisco State University

Cover Art by David Foulds

# Table of Contents

# CHAPTER ONE

## *Introduction*

Outside of the university, all writing is directed toward a specific audience, yet you've probably all been writing primarily for your teachers for years. It's no wonder you may feel like the whole process is just another hoop you need to jump through in order to get on with your lives.

I can't undo the years you've been taught to write boring five paragraph essays that no one really wants to write nor read. But what I can do is try to help you see writing as a mode of self-expression, as a way to think through complicated ideas, and help you develop skills that will enable you to better articulate your thoughts and feelings.

I can also try to convince you that in order to become a good writer, you also need to develop your skills as a reader. Trying to write without pairing your writing to close reading is like trying to learn to play the guitar without ever listening to music. That would be ridiculous wouldn't it?

Extended reading of articles and short stories online is a very rewarding experience. Sure, watching videos is easy, but when you do so someone else is doing all the fun stuff for you - they make all the casting decisions, choose the lighting, the costumes, the settings. When you read, you are the director, cinematographer, and editor. It's no wonder there's that cliché that 'the book was better than the movie.' When you read a book, *you* create the movie in your mind with the perfect actors, the perfect shots, the perfect edits. Moreover, when you read, more detailed and in-depth information is provided than typically provided in a video, which is all too often a sort of "crash course" that merely skims the surface of ideas. Reading helps mental development and keeps your brain sharp while watching videos seems to dull everything. In reading, you are an active participant, but while viewing you are passive, just letting the sounds and pictures wash over you.

Your writing is your calling card to the world. People, rather unfairly, often judge others' intelligence by their writing ability. It has been proven that there is no actual connection between writing and intelligence, yet if you cannot communicate your brilliant and insightful thoughts to others in a clear, cohesive way, some may not trust the ideas behind the writing. It's a sort of "first impression." Once made, hard to change.

In addition, writing actually helps you clarify your thoughts. If you stop and pay attention to your thinking for a few minutes, you may be startled at how your brain jumps from thought to thought so rapidly. If you were to write down what actually came out of your brain spontaneously, no one would be able to make much sense out of it. Writing is a way to quiet and focus your mind on one central idea. It is a way to think through and organize your thoughts, often leading you down paths you didn't even know existed. It is a way to make you see clearly what assumptions you carry that are grounded in fact, and which are actually in desperate need of further research and reassessment.

Writing can direct your reading, and vice versa.

Writing can help you make connections.

Writing is actually very freeing. Through writing you are able to create whole new worlds or incite much needed social change. Through writing you can connect not only to those directly around you, but to those across the globe and even through time.

In this text, I want you to write for an actual audience: your peers. Which means the stakes are higher, but it also means that there's a reason to write beyond getting a grade.

## Practice 1-1: Introductions

*Say hello to your fellow classmates. Here, you will have a space to write, and write often. Post your responses to the practice prompts in this book as well as to the larger essay prompts on your course web page.*

## The Hero's Journey

We often think of heroes as people who accomplish extraordinary feats against insurmountable odds. They are often the 'good guys' (and by 'guys' I mean all people) who are brave, often risking their lives for others. Or we may think of superheroes, like Batman or Wonder Woman, who spend much of their energy making the world a better place by defeating evil villains.

Joseph Campbell, in his book *Hero with a Thousand Faces*, expands our understanding of a hero by saying that essentially anyone is a hero when they go on a 'hero's journey.' Briefly, the hero's journey is broken down to 12 steps: ordinary world; call to adventure; refusal of the call; meeting the mentor; crossing the first threshold; tests, allies and enemies; approach to the inmost cave; ordeal; reward; the road back; resurrection; and return with the elixir.

If you've seen *Star Wars Episode IV: A New Hope* (or *Lord of the Rings*) you're already familiar with the hero's journey. Luke is, at first, a pretty ordinary guy, living in his ordinary world of Tatooine, nephew of his Uncle Owen and Aunt Beru, working on their moisture farm. Then, when he discovers the hologram of Princess Leia pleading "Help me Obi- Wan Kenobi, you're my only hope" hidden in R2-D2 (the call to adventure), he seeks out Obi-Wan, who ends up being his mentor. At first, he is reluctant to train as a Jedi because he doesn't want to let his Aunt and Uncle down (refusal of the call), but then when they are killed by the Imperial Army, he decides to join. They go to Mos Isley and meet Han Solo (an ally), and cross the threshold with him into the Death Star. They face many enemies, but end up in the trash compactor (the inmost cave). They make it out with the help of C-3PO and R2-D2, but then Obi-Wan is struck down by Darth Vader (ordeal). However, they have rescued the princess and importantly, the plans to destroy the Death Star (reward), they travel back to the rebel base and regroup, and Obi-Wan returns as a voice from the Force (resurrection) to guide Luke to destroy the Death Star (return with the elixir).

According to Campbell, all myths from all time have

traces of these stages. He calls it the "monomyth." In the prologue to *Hero With A Thousand Faces*, Campbell writes:

*Throughout the inhabited world, in all times and under every circumstance, [the hero's journey] ha[s] flourished; and [it has] been the living inspiration of whatever else may have appeared out of the activities of the human body and mind. It would not be too much to say that [the hero's journey] is the secret opening through which the inexhaustible energies of the cosmos pour into the human cultural manifestation. Religions, philosophies, arts, the social forms of primitive and historic man, prime discoveries in science and technology, the very dreams that blister sleep, boil up from the basic, magic ring of [the hero's journey] (Campbell 1).*

He's basically saying that we can look at human culture through the hero's journey construct as a lens to understanding ourselves.

"What does any of this have to do with writing?" you are probably asking. Quite a bit it turns out. Would you believe me when I say that all good writing has aspects of the hero's journey in it?

Okay, this may seem like a stretch, but bear with me. According to Campbell, a hero, as we saw above with Luke, begins in his 'ordinary world.' Look at any Hollywood film and you'll notice that this is a fairly uniform convention. Luke starts on Tatooine. Frodo starts in the Shire. Even Juno starts as an 'ordinary teen' before she finds out she is pregnant. These characters undergo an 'call to adventure' that propels them into a new situation: the message from Leia, the appearance of the Ring Wraiths, the positive pregnancy test. And during their adventure, they often meet a mentor, encounter allies and enemies, overcome obstacles, and 'return with the elixir,' which is actually a lesson learned. Through their experiences, they grow. They become more knowledgeable and wise about their worlds. Luke learns to 'use the force,' Frodo overcomes incredible odds and his own doubts and insecurities to destroy The One Ring in Mount Doom, Juno realizes that she's in love with Paulie.

When we write, whether it is a narrative story or an academic article, we undergo a hero's journey. We begin in our 'ordinary worlds' of knowledge and understanding, then, there's an inciting incident. We come across a new bit of data that makes us question our previous assumptions. We then 'cross the threshold' into adventure, seeking out mentors to teach us more. We encounter difficulties and even contradictions. Things get complicated. We make discoveries. We follow paths. Finally, we come to a new understanding through our adventure with a multitude of texts and discussions with experts. We return with the elixir of new knowledge. We are wiser about our world than when we began, just like Luke, Frodo, and Juno.

Good writers don't just write the results of this quest for knowledge, but take readers through the journey with them. Through the practices in this text, and the major essay assignments, you will learn to use writing as a tool to help you sort through new information, and learn how to communicate this process of discovery to your readers in a compelling and personal way.

To better understand and apply the hero's journey to your own writing and storytelling, let's first take a look at some stories that you regularly tell to friends, and see how you can use Campbell's theories as a lens to understand how your stories are constructed.

## Practice 1-2: Your personal favorite story

*Think about stories you tell your friends. There are likely stories that you tell over and over to new friends as you make them. Why do you tell these particular stories? What is so compelling about these stories? Write a list of the top 3-5 stories you tell often.*

*Choose one and make an outline of the story.*

*Now, see how your story uses the hero's journey as its structure. Can you map the steps of the journey onto your story? Link as many as you can - you may not have all of them and they may be in a slightly different order.*

In the next unit, you will develop this story into a full narrative autobiographical essay after we have read some examples of the personal narrative essay from *the appendix of this text.* Reading examples of each genre of writing that you will undertake in this text will give you models to learn about structure and other conventions and expectations. This is much like listening to rock music to learn how to play it. You have to know what the destination looks like in order to get there.

In the narrative essay, we write our stories the same way people write fiction stories. In other words, we use specific, concrete details and usually tell the story in order of how things happened. We will tell it in the first person, and our story will have the structure of the hero's journey when done properly. We will look at narrative structure in more detail in the next chapter.

We are starting with story because some of the best academic and journalistic essays are framed by a personal story. When we write from our personal experience, and then come up with a central question that needs further research, we provide the reader context as to why we care about the subject, and thus asserting why they should too.

By connecting to ideas on a personal level, we imply that these ideas and arguments are important to understand for psychological, sociological, cultural, or even spiritual reasons. So, as we begin our writing journey, a solid understanding of how you can use narrative devices in practically any essay is paramount to writing in a compelling way.

Quick note on *your voice:* We will discuss a writer's voice, or more appropriately, 'voices,' in this text, but for now, think of your voice as the voice you use in conversation. Students' writing actually often suffers the most not from their inability to write well, but from their desire to sound 'academic.' This has the unfortunate side effect of sounding not like yourself. When you are pretending to be someone else, chances are good that you will sound a bit silly and your prose will get all twisted and go in circles. After all, would you say aloud, "I find it most fascinating that heroes of all time have been historically understood as wanting to have self-esteem because of their need to hunt for food for their families giving them a feeling of being proud." I hope not. So, just hear the voice in your head talking simply, clearly, and resist the desire to sound official or academic. Academic writing isn't about sounding smart, it's about communicating complex ideas *clearly*.

## On Citation

You've certainly heard that plagiarism is a serious no-no, but then you are asked to use sources all the time. Hmm. I know, confusing. Citation is basically a way of saying, 'hey, I looked this up - cool right? You should check it out.'

This text uses the MLA (Modern Language Association) style, which is the North American convention for the humanities. The sciences use APA (American Psychological Association) style. The best guide for both of these styles is to go to the Purdue OWL (Online Writing Lab) page, where you will find detailed instructions and examples of both the MLA and APA styles. Just Google "Purdue OWL" and click on "MLA formatting and Style Guide." For now, check out "MLA In-Text Citations: The Basics" and "MLA Formatting Quotations" and "MLA Works Cited Page: Basic Format."

Note that at the end of each chapter of this book, the works I have referred to are under a 'works cited' section in proper MLA format. Use this as a template for how you should cite your sources.

## Practice 1-3: Citations

*Pick up the closest book to you, see what it is about or who wrote it, then find an article on the internet that is about the same subject. Write up MLA style bibliographies for both sources using what you learned from the Purdue MLA website and write a short paragraph using quotes from each source and use proper in-text citations. Add to your blog.*

After completing practice 1-1, you probably noticed a few things about your story. It likely revealed something about you that is personal - maybe something you are proud of, or even a moment that caused you shame at the time. There was most certainly conflict, and difficulty or struggle, and some sort of outcome. Chances are, something about you changed as a result of what happened. You may have even concluded the story with some sort of moral: "and that's why I will never... again." We will talk in a moment why you shouldn't do this. Professionals rarely write conclusions and summaries of what they've learned at the end of their autobiographies. This feels too didactic (forced instruction) and insulting to readers. When writing stories, as you will examine in class, it is best to stick with the story and leave the interpretation to your reader. Readers, believe it or not, love to interpret. People love to 'fill in the blanks' with their own experiences so that what they're reading resonates with their individual reality.

In this text, I want you to write about what you find fascinating. All good writing happens because the writer is engaged with the idea. That means personally engaged. You've certainly read texts in your academic careers that appear to have been written by someone who seemed as uninterested in the subject as you are. It is like the text was written by the economics professor who sleepily takes roll (as portrayed by the inimitable Ben Stein): "Bueller? Bueller?" in John Hughes' *Ferris Bueller's Day Off*.

Yes, you will certainly be asked to write about topics in your coming academic careers that make you drool and stare off into space, but, eventually, you can find almost any topic interesting once you've cultivated a mad desire for knowledge. Once you've discovered that the joy of writing isn't about telling us what you know, but about a dive into the shark infested waters of what you don't know, then, you will find *any* dive exciting. But that takes practice. You've probably been trained with that 5 paragraph formula: Thesis, evidence x 3, conclusion. Yawn. Nobody writes like that outside of high school classrooms; if it's boring to write, you damn well better believe it's boring to read.

So, we will first have to unlearn our past writing habits, as Richard E. Miller and Ann Jurecic posit in their brilliant text *Habits of the Creative Mind*. They write:

*Why does writing remain an exercise in trussing up banalities for almost all who produce it in school? The short answer to this question is that students today are trained to follow a recipe-based approach to writing and have been rewarded (or punished) by the standardized testing system for their ability (or inability) to produce writing that is clear and concise.*

They then go on to argue that "the best writing is curiosity driven and is carried forward by creative acts of connecting and thinking" (Miller and Jurecic 8).

I agree.

Good writers all know one thing: you don't write to just state what you already know. Writing is a process of discovery, not simply a mind dump. This is true of good novels, good films, and good academic essays.

Yes, academic writing is a hero's journey - we strike out from 'the ordinary world' to discover new and exciting things. We don't know what is coming. We must discover it along the way. And when we do so, so do our readers. It is a journey we all take together; it is a journey into the mind and into the world and back again. We have a thought that is based on our assumptions or our experiences. We talk about it. We think about it. Then we look to others. "What do you think?" we ask. They provide their answers based on their own experiences, which are different than your own. We question their assumptions, and they question ours. We perhaps look to a third. Or go to the internet. We are curious, we are engaged, we are open to new ideas. We look at things from new angles, we are flexible and creative, and we are faced with thinking about our own thinking, wondering how we learned what we did the way we did, where our ideas came from, and how they were shaped. We wonder about our childhoods and our parents and our cultures. Everything is connected.

It turns out that these very concepts: curiosity, engagement, openness, creativity, persistence, responsibility, flexibility, and metacognition (thinking about thinking) are the very "habits of mind" that are called for in the *Framework for Success in Postsecondary (College) Writing* as stated by the Council of Writing Program Administrators, the National Council of Teachers of English, and the National Writing Project.

You mean our goal isn't to write five paragraph essays that argue a specific point and stick to it? Our goal isn't to win?

Don't take this to mean that your experience with five paragraph essay argumentation was a waste of time. Indeed, it is a necessary step for clearing your thinking and learning to use evidence. So, let's say, "thank you for that lesson," and now use writing to learn, to discover. Write for passion and interaction and engagement and surprise.

Let's conclude this first chapter with a graduation commencement speech. Maybe it seems a bit weird to use a speech given when you are done with college in a course that you take the first semester of college. Or perhaps that's the very reason to use it. You may feel like there is a long road ahead of you. It may, at times, feel insurmountable. But know that your first year, indeed your first semester, is the hardest. A lot is being asked of you. You are likely away from home for the first time.

You are buried in books and essays to write. Your roommate won't turn off their horrible music or always has their partner over. You miss your friends and family. You have regrets. You worry about student loans, or the burden your parents are taking on financially to put you through this grind.

Being in college is both, as Charles Dickens writes in *A Tale of Two Cities*, "the best of times, the worst of times." So, think about your first year composition course as a sort of homeroom. A place to settle into this new world: the threshold, if you will, of your own hero's journey into college. We will spend the first few chapters to give you space to think about your past, to talk to fellow classmates about college life, and to prepare you for this new 'extraordinary world' of college.

## Practice 1-4: This is Water

*Now, Google "This is Water" by David Foster Wallace. Ideally, find a page with both an audio recording and the transcript of the speech. Read along as you listen.*

*Choose three of the following prompts and write responses to add to your blog. Write at least two to three paragraphs on each. The goal here is to use writing to think, not to construct a 'perfect essay.' Just think and write and see what happens.*

*1) Wallace says "The point of the fish story is merely that the most obvious, important realities are often the ones that are hardest to see and talk about." Think about this statement as it relates to the "parable-ish" story he tells about the fish in water. What "obvious, important realities" is he referring to? Can you think of any from your own life and experience that fall into this category?*

*2) What is the purpose of a liberal arts education to you? What does Wallace say? Do you agree? Why are you in college? What do you hope to get out of the experience?*

3) What does Wallace mean by "belief templates?" Think about some of your "belief templates." Where did they come from?

4) What is something that you have "blind certainty" about? Free-write about your assumptions. Then, question them. Do you think there is room to change your mind? Or even better, complicate the issue so that you no longer are so certain about your position.

5) What evidence is there that we are indeed "the center of our own universe?" How can you truly know another's reality? Can you really understand anyone outside of yourself?

6) Spend 10 minutes just sitting quiet and noticing what you are thinking. Put yourself somewhere as quiet as possible to do so. Then, spend 10 minutes writing about what you were thinking. How many subjects came into your head? How many were emotionally charged? Were there <u>segues</u> from one thought to the next? What surprised you the most when you were doing nothing but noticing your mind buzzing away?

7) Think about the last time you were frustrated and it seemed like "everyone was just in my way." Write it out as a story. Use the kind of details that Wallace does in his speech. Then, do some 'metacognition' - think about your thinking. Was your assessment fair? Are you more important than anyone else? Write an analysis of your feelings in that moment. How can you re-think the experience so that the experience isn't as horrible and dramatic as you first thought? Think about how others around you during that moment in time might have seen you? What do you see? Were you being inconsiderate to others?

8) Sit in a crowded space - a coffee shop, the quad, the cafeteria, a bus stop. Pick at least 2-3 people and invent a story about each. What do you think their lives are like? What are you basing these assumptions on? Did you use stereotypes? Where did you get these assumptions?

9) What does Wallace mean that we learn to get to choose what to worship? What does he mean that what you worship will "eat you alive?" What do you worship? How might that worship cause you

*pain? Use some of Wallace's examples and apply them to your own experience.*

## **Works Cited**

Campbell, Joseph. *Hero With A Thousand Faces.* Novato, California: New World Library, 2008. Print.

Dickens, Charles. A *Tale of Two Cities.* Project Gutenberg. 2004. https://www.gutenberg.org/files/98/98-h/98-h.htm#link2H_4_0002 Accessed 19 July 2018.

Foster Wallace, David. "This is Water." Farnham Street. https://fs.blog/2012/04/david-foster-wallace-this-is-water/ Accessed 17 July 2018.

Council of Writing Program Administrators. *Framework for Success in Postsecondary Writing.* http://wpacouncil.org/framework. Accessed 14 July 2018.

Miller, Richard E. and Jurecic, Ann. *Habits of the Creative Mind.* New York: Bedford/St. Martin's. 2016. Print.

# CHAPTER TWO

## *Autobiography*

You know stories. You are surrounded by stories all day long. We consume stories as much as, or more than, we consume food. Why are stories so compelling to us? In the academic text *Narrative* by Paul Cobley, he begins by quoting Bryan Appleyard, a writer for the *Sunday Times:*

"We tell stories to ourselves; of our journey from birth to death, friends, families, who we are and who we want to be. Or public stories about history and politics, about our country, our race or our religion. At each moment of our lives these stories place us in space and time. They console us, making our lives meaningful by placing us in something bigger than ourselves. Maybe the story is just that we are in love, that we have to feed the cat or educate our children. Or maybe it is about a lifelong struggle for salvation or liberation. Either way - however large or small the story - the human impulse is to make sense of each moment by referring it to a larger narrative. We need to live in a world not of our own making."

## Practice 2-1: On Stories

*Stories, Appleyard seems to be saying, are the way we make sense out of our world. Why do you think this is so? Take five minutes and free-write about the purpose of story. Specifically, think about a few of your favorite stories, whether they be films, television shows, or novels. Why is this (or are these) stories so compelling to you? What do they say about the world that you find fascinating? Do they help you understand your world? Go beyond thinking of stories as mere entertainment and escapism. Everyone has different tastes. Why do you like the types of stories that you do? What do these stories say about you or your outlook on life?*

*Add your response* to the discussion board.

More than simply lining up 'this happened and then this and then this,' the purpose of telling stories seems to be an attempt to find cause and effect. It is our attempt to make sense out of our world. To problem solve. To wonder. Ernest Becker observes that we are indeed the only creatures on the planet who seem capable of true language. So perhaps it makes sense to first start with a look at what exactly we mean by language.

## Language

Where did our capacity for language come from? Becker points us to a few different theories. One, as posited by anthropologist Charles Hockett, is that language grew from the need for hunters to communicate with one another. To work together to bring down large game, the hunters needed to be able to say "the deer is over there. You go left, I go right," and so on.

Anthropologist Weston La Barre, on the other hand, believes that language likely formed within the family unit, from the child's necessity to communicate with her mother about her needs. Sociologist Lewis Mumford asserts that language was part of play, that we started to use language during playtime in order to communicate the rules of the game (Becker 14).

Language, brought down to its essence, is the use of symbols and signs to communicate about the concrete world. Basically, both symbols and signs mean *this* points to *that*. They are something on the page or on screen that represent something in the real world. The word "tree" is a sign for tree, as is a picture of a tree. However, language isn't just that simple. You've probably heard of symbolism in literature or heard someone talk about something being "symbolic." A picture of a bird in a cage is a sign of a bird in a cage, but it may also be symbolic of the idea of feeling trapped. So, language works on many levels. First, what the word *points to*, and what the word *represents*.

This brings us back to story. We say this happened and then this happened, but when we ask "but what does it all mean?" we are asking about symbolism. Even a simple argument with someone about leaving the butter out will actually be symbolic of a larger issue in the relationship. "I do all the work around here. I wish you'd help out," might be the unspoken communication. So, when we read, and when we write, we first focus on content and structure - what the book says or how we write the words to be clear. But then we need to go the next step and ask "what does it mean?"

Which leads us to a thought experiment. What is life like without language? Can you have thoughts that aren't symbolic? If you eliminate language from your thinking, is all that is left instinct?

Becker ties language to the ego. This is that sense of self that psychologist Sigmund Freud talks about. Language, says Becker, gives us this sense of self, this ego, because it is only through language that we can say "I" or "me" as opposed to "you." It is through through words and pictures in our minds that we remember yesterday, and last year, and think about what may happen tomorrow, or five years from now. Language places us in a specific space and time as part of a larger whole.

As opposed to the ego, Freud says there is an "id," which is "a world of pictures, emotions, sensory meanings stamped on the animal in confusion - 'confusion' because it takes an ego to sort memories and sensations, to separate and classify and cognitively hold events steady in awareness" (Becker 16). Becker goes on to talk about a deer's experience of the world. To the deer, who does not possess language, the "world is a flow of 'eternal' sensations, punctuated only by a fearfully pounding pulse, a flavorful berry, and the unanticipated annihilation of sudden death" (16). We, on the other hand, are 'time bound' because we are aware of the difference between today, yesterday, and tomorrow, but the deer, as far as we can tell, is not.

So language seems to be pretty central, perhaps the most central and important aspect, of being human. Think back to what David Foster Wallace said in "This is Water." Our thoughts define our realities, and our thoughts are in our language. "Learning to think" is really "learning to control thinking" because thinking is how we exist in the world. What we think defines our lives. We can think ourselves into a world of despair, or a world of beauty. We can think things through by carefully weighing facts, or we can jump to conclusions based on limited data. We can hold dearly onto beliefs that are wrong, or we can be open to new ideas and experiences, and thus grow and change and evolve.

However, it is important to note here that thinking is an organic, physiological process as well. It is not merely conceptual, but based on actual chemistry happening inside of our brains and bodies (Dougherty). So, it is important not to jump to the conclusion that someone who is depressed can just think themselves out of depression. It has been scientifically proven that a lot of our thinking, and our emotional lives, can be created by chemical imbalances in the body, so if you do find that your thinking is troubling or your emotions are not under your control, there are ways to help rebalance your physiology, and you might consider seeking psychological and medical experts to help you do so.

## On Reading

However, language is actually fairly limited. Certainly, you've heard the expression 'a picture is worth a thousand words.' That is because a picture of a tree seems more accurate than the word 'tree' or even the word 'maple tree.' Think about it. How difficult would it be to render a tree that you see in front of you in words so that the hearer or reader sees the *exact* tree that you see? It's basically impossible. How could you describe every branch, every leaf, exactly how the light falls through, the subtle movement of the leaves each time the wind blows? The texture and variation of colors in the bark, the surrounding grass and all of its mottled specificity? Even as you read this, each of you are picturing a slightly different tree. This is what Wolfgang Iser calls 'filling in the gaps' (Iser 959). When we read, we picture in our minds a more complete picture than that of what we are actually reading.

This picture in our minds is what some call "envisionment." This is the film that runs in our minds as we read - what we picture. Our cultures have become extremely visual, which is perhaps why many students would rather watch a film or YouTube video than read a written text. This is understandable. Visual information is more complete. We can see clearly the characters on the screen. They have been fully embodied for us. We often link stories with recreation, and who wants to work when they are relaxing?

Okay, well it's not as simple as that. As I also teach film, I have a strong argument for the fact that we 'read' films and all visual media in similar ways that we read words. Visual images have symbolic levels of meaning that we 'fill in' with our own experiences just as we do with words. However, written language leaves more gaps, and as such, requires more of our imagination. I think, even though I am an avid lover and teacher of films, that because of this, reading written words is more fulfilling and engaging than watching a film. As I stated in the last chapter, when we read we get to be the directors, casting agents, actors, set designers, and editors. We enter into a relationship with the author, and each of us fills our part in telling the story.

Okay, so now with some philosophy about language and the purpose of story and even a few thoughts about the reading process under our belts, let's return to the task at hand: writing the personal narrative essay.

It has been a trend in recent years for composition courses to throw out narrative as unnecessary instruction. Lucky for you that phase is coming to an end. As I've asserted above, narrative is how we understand our world. It is how we make meaning, find cause and effect. When your parents have asked you in the past "how was your day?" they were hoping for a story, by the way, not the usual "fine" response. They wanted to hear about how you interacted with your friends, they wanted to hear what you learned about in class, they wanted to know about your life because stories connect us to one another.

When you tell a story to your friends, what are you hoping for? You are likely hoping they will lean in, eyes wide, and say "oh my god!" You hope that your audience will be fascinated by what you are telling them, and that through your storytelling, they will connect with you. "That same thing happened to me!" they may respond. Storytelling is how we create bonds to one another by finding out that we have similar experiences in the world. It is a way to make us feel less lonely. It is a way to form groups that want to meet again and again.

Think about groups of friends you have had, or if you were like me and were more of a one-on-one kind of person, think about your BFF that you now have or had in the past. What drew you together? If you were to 'invent' a best friend, what qualities would they have? Chances are you'd want to spend time with someone who you feel understands you, and again, this understanding comes through storytelling.

At the heart of storytelling is the ego. The 'I.' Your experience in the world. This not only goes for narrative writing but for all writing. Again, going back to Wallace, whether we admit it or not, all our experiences, all our thoughts, start right here in our bodies. Whether we are telling an autobiographical story, as we will be doing shortly, or writing about a new scientific discovery, or pitching an idea for a startup business or new app, it all starts with you.

Through this text, we will build from you and move outward. If you look at all good writing, and by this I mean compelling writing, it is writing that is created with desire and engagement. It is writing that has clearly shown those 'habits of mind' we talked about last chapter: curiosity, openness, engagement, creativity, persistence, responsibility, flexibility, and metacognition. These habits of mind are all really based on your own particular point of view, and using that as a place to start, to explore, to write to learn and share your process. It is, again, that hero's journey into the unknown.

## The Hero's Journey and Essay Writing

We've already seen the backbone of narrative structure - the hero's journey as written by Joseph Campbell. Not all aspects of the hero's journey need to be in every story, or every essay. Nor do they have to be in the very same order. But you can use the hero's journey as a scaffold, an organizing principle, to build your own story, and indeed your academic essays. But keep in mind that it is just a starting point. A guide. Write in order to discover you own thinking, and to develop that thinking in relation to others. It is to learn and to expand our minds through writing, rather than sticking to any particular structural formula like that that awful five paragraph essay. That being said, each discipline does have its conventions and through your writing later in this textbook, you will explore some of the specific expectations of a few of these disciplines: literature, visual media, science, and economics. But, regardless, all should start with you, in your 'ordinary world,' who then comes across some sort of question or difficulty, and then your journey through that difficulty to a new understanding (the return with the elixir).

Rather than going directly through Campbell's *Hero With A Thousand Faces*, which is a fascinating but incredibly dense text that warrants its own course, we will be better served thinking about it through Linda Seger's "Creating The Myth." According to Seger, the goal of the protagonist/hero (the main character, who in this case is you) is trying to "find some kind of rare and wonderful treasure" (1). She states that these can be external rewards like "job[s], relationship[s], or success" or inner rewards like "respect, security, self-expression, love, or home." While Hollywood films specifically, and indeed American society in general, tend to emphasize the former, it is really the latter which connects to audiences. Think about it. Were you more deeply moved by Michael Bay's *Transformers* (2007) or Walt Disney's *Bambi* (1942)? Why is this? Because Bambi's journey is largely internal, it is a bildungsroman, a 'coming of age' story wherein the character learns the harsh realities of growing up. Bambi doesn't literally come back with a 'holy grail' or win the war, but instead suffers great loss through the death of his mother, and through this loss is transformed and takes on a new understanding of the world as an adult. Bambi connects to us because it is honest about the difficulties of an inner journey. The only way through to the other side is by going into a metaphorical special world, a place where your ideas and beliefs are challenged and even changed.

This is the goal of a story, and this is the goal of excellent academic writing. As you will see as we progress through this text, and as I've already reiterated, our goal in writing isn't to convince someone that we already know everything, that we are right. While there is an art to rhetoric, or 'argument' as you are likely more familiar, we largely do it incorrectly. To argue isn't to hold fast and use metaphors of war, it is to engage and develop. It is to participate in an ongoing conversation with others about ideas that change both viewpoints. It is to undergo a journey, not to conquest.

Now, this may seem at first confusing. If I say that writing is a hero's journey, and often we think of heroes as those who indeed 'win the war,' how is winning the war not the goal of writing?

Fair point.

And this is exactly why our use of language is so important to how we understand our worlds. What we need to do here is continue to redefine what we mean by hero. As stated in the last chapter, a hero isn't necessarily the strongest, bravest, or deadliest on the field. The hero is the one who overcomes obstacles despite their inherent difficulties. A hero is one who takes risks *to help others* mentally and physically. *A hero is someone who dares to change on the inside to become a better person.*

You can use both an inner and an outer journey in your narrative autobiography essay. In the last chapter, you thought about a few stories you tell people often, and traced your own hero's journey through one of them, writing an outline of it in preparation for your first big essay. For your essay, be sure when you write to use specific, concrete details as often as you can to help your audience envision the scene in their minds.

## Writing Space

When you write, it is important to have a space and time to write that works for you. Some people, like me, find it necessary to have 'a room of one's own' as Virginia Woolf states and as reiterated by Miller and Jurecic in *Habits of the Creative Mind*. By this, Woolf means that in order to write, you need a quiet space and time where you will remain undistracted from any and all outside events. This means, as Miller and Jurecic point out, closing both the physical door and your virtual door: turn off your cell phone, stay off the internet, keep away from the television, lock up the iPad. Of course, this can be tricky business, as you will certainly need access to the internet while writing. So perhaps have a dedicated browser that includes tabs just for academic references. Create one browser that is your virtual room for thinking - no Facebook (I know, that's already out anyway), no social media, no text messages, etc.

Okay, so now that you've said "forget it, never going to happen," we can move on. I'm telling you, just give it a shot. That text message can wait. You can even set up your phone and email to auto reply so that people won't take it personally when you don't respond immediately. If you are able to set time and space specifically for writing, your writing will be (1) way better, and (2) completed in half the time. When you learn to fall into the groove of writing, when you are truly writing from your own passions, your own curiosity, you will likely find it to be terribly addicting. I mean, you get to sit there and talk and no-one will interrupt you! How great is that?

While many need this quiet space, others find it too isolating, which is why there are so many coffee shops. If this is your bag, go for it. Try writing in a coffee shop on campus if there is one, or one nearby. Or in the library. If you need to be around other people working to keep you working, then do that. Sometimes it can feel more social just to be out, or maybe those darned roommates won't let you work. Whatever the case, if writing in a public space works better for you, try out a few spots and pick your favorite.

## Practice 2-2: Your Writing Space

*Now that you've chosen your writing space, take a picture of it and post it to your blog. Write a few paragraphs about your writing space. Why does it work for you? What makes it a good writing space? What about your writing space would you recommend for others? What isn't perfect about your space? What would you change if you could?*

## The Autobiographic Narrative Essay

Before you write your discovery draft of your personal narrative, it is a good idea to read a few examples. Refer to the autobiography essays in *the appendix* as models. We can't know where we are going without some sort of map, right? Essentially, a short narrative essay is very much like a short story, only it is a story about something that you actually experienced. Remember, you cannot tell your reader everything so pick key details that represent the space and the people.

Writing a narrative can help us as writers in many ways. We learn that (1) our voices are important, (2) our experiences are important, (3) concrete facts and images are important, (4) writing from a personal place, with our own voice, is important. We will talk later about how we actually have 'voices,' not just one voice, but for now let's stick with the one you use most often - in conversation with your peers.

While some writing teachers dictate that you should never use "I" in your writing, I find this very problematic. If you aren't writing from your experience, who is the one doing the writing? Does the writing exist without a writer? And further, if we are to pretend that there is no individual, just ideas, why? Why are we trying to erase ourselves from the process? Reading writing by someone who doesn't seem to appear at all in the work is extraordinarily boring. And, indeed, why insist that undergraduates eliminate themselves from their academic writing when graduate level students and professional academics use "I" all the time?

## Practice 2-3: Reading as a Writer

*Read all the autobiography essays in the appendix.*

*Be prepared to discuss your findings with your group and the class. After you read all of the essays, choose your favorite to analyze.*

*First, look at the story in terms of the hero's journey. Is the writer a hero of their story? What is heroic about their journey? What is their ordinary world? What was the threshold they crossed? What is the extraordinary world? Who were allies? Who were enemies? What is the 'elixir' they come back with? In other words, what have they learned through this journey? Find some specific, concrete details. Use quotes from the essay as evidence of your thoughts. Now, write a response to your reading using the hero's journey as a lens to understand the story's structure. As you re-read your chosen story, be sure to annotate the text. Write in the margins, noting how the story uses the steps and characters of the hero's journey in it.*

*Now, look at how description is used. Note how they use specific images to put the reader in a specific place and time. Using concrete details, whether in narrative or academic writing, is paramount in both engaging your reader and convincing them that you have real, concrete facts as part of your discussion. Writing specifically rather than in general, vague, and abstract terms is the best way to draw a reader in and let them see your vision of your world or ideas. Write a few of your favorite sentences and state how the details helped you understand the setting, the story, and the writer's emotional journey.*

*Finally, free write about what in your life these stories reminded you of. What connections did you make? Use quotes from the story and say, "when she said 'xxxx', it reminded me of…" Note that this is how a conversation is built. You tell a story from your life, or talk about something you read or watched, and then the other person chimes in with their related experience. Writing, as you will see and as discussed in Graff and Birkenstein's They Say/I Say, is all about entering a conversation. Add your observations to your blog.*

## Major Essay Assignment: Autobiography Essay

Now, at last, it is your turn to type away. Worry not about the blinking cursor and blank page. The lovely thing about writing is that it isn't like a tattoo - it isn't permanent. Just write. Edit later. Don't worry about sentence structure or anything. The first thing you want to do is be spontaneous and let the story lead you. Tell it like you tell your friends, but now that you've learned a few things about the genre of the narrative autobiography, use those tools as much as you can in your discovery draft. Even if you can't remember exactly what people said, you can 'put words in their mouths' so that we get the essence of what they said. Autobiography can be, and often is, partially invented. You don't have to remember everything, but act as if you did. Put us there in the moment that everything happened. Use a unity of time and place. Sit down and write 1000 words as quickly as you can. Your final essay should be between 1000-1250 words. Tell your story!

## On Rewriting and Workshops

Okay, let's get one thing clear from the outset. Most of you have a completely wrong idea of what rewriting is. I get it. You wrote it, it's done. You have a ton of other things to do. This is likely your first year in college, so you are overwhelmed physically and mentally. One and done. After all, your math teacher doesn't let you redo your math problems.

Well, they should.

There is a cliché in the writing world that "all writing is rewriting." Anne Lamott says that everyone writes "shitty first drafts" (1). Back in the days of typewriters, or stone tablets, to rewrite meant literally that you had to write it all over from the beginning. There was no easy rewording of sentences, restructuring of chapters, etc. You had to write it and then write it again and again until you were happy with it.

Rewriting is not editing. Editing is fixing. Rewriting is exactly that: *re*-writing.

Do you always have to rewrite? Yes and no.

Sometimes, rarely, the first draft is indeed the best draft. Notice the word 'rarely.' Even if what you wrote is terrific, if you rewrote it, it would be fantastic. Award winning. Pulitzer prize material. But since you thought it was 'good enough,' no Pulitzer for you. Too bad. That would have been nice.

The best way to figure out what is working and what isn't is through workshopping. So, if you are reading this text as part of your freshman composition course, I encourage you to get into groups, trade essays, and talk about what you read. Compare your essays to the student essays in *the appendix*. What do they have in common? What is different? What feels right and what is confusing?

It is amazing how much you learn about your own work from having an audience. As such, I encourage you to read your essay aloud to your group. You will be amazed at how many times you will stop yourself and say "oh that doesn't work, gotta change that" even before any of your colleagues say a thing. Just reading your essay through a reader's eyes, which is revealed through reading aloud, is a miraculous thing.

Help each other out. Give encouragement and guidance, but don't try to make the other's writing your own. Avoid saying "I'd write…" because it isn't your writing. It is theirs. Instead, use questions to help them figure out what they should write instead. Be inquisitive. Note where you are lost, where it doesn't make sense.

Remember those "gaps" we talked about that we fill while reading as per Wolfgang Iser? Well, when we are writing, we fill in those gaps with our own experience automatically, but that can result in leaving gaps that are too large for the reader to fill in. We won't notice that we are missing information until someone says "I don't know what's happening here," or "wait, I thought that...." Listen to your readers, they are trying to tell you what *is there*, not what you think is there. After all, without paying attention to your audience, your reader, writing is just self-reflexive. While there is value to that, and I highly encourage you keep a regular journal just to record your own thoughts about your life - again writing helps you think! - here our goal is to write both to think and to communicate.

So, in your first draft, your discovery draft, you are discovering your thinking. Then, in your second draft, your re-vision, you are paying attention to communicating so that your reader understands your writing.

Also, when you workshop early drafts, refrain from giving each other tips on grammar and syntax unless they are requested. Some of your colleagues will be eager to have you help with these more technical aspects of craft, but to others this kind of feedback feels disheartening and discouraging. Editing and grammar are best to be worked on after your last draft is complete. No sense spending a ton of time editing a paragraph that ends up getting deleted!

Writing is a sensitive business. Since it comes from a personal place it feels like it is an extension of us. Indeed, Marshall McLuhan, in *Understanding Media: The Extensions of Man* writes that all media is an extension of ourselves. It is a way of making us feel somehow immortal. If you've seen the television show *Futurama*, I am reminded of season 3 episode 17 "A Pharaoh to Remember," where the robot Bender has a giant statue erected of himself that chants "Remember me!" and flames shoot out of its eyes. Isn't that really what we all want, a giant statue of ourselves to live on forever in the public square?

Maybe not. But you get the point.

So, be kind, but helpful. You should rework and rewrite the essay until you are happy with it. As Malcolm Gladwell asserts, your writing is done when you move on to the next project.

As you rewrite, see where you can take general words like "tree" and be more specific. Describe the tree. First, what kind of tree was it? And importantly, what did you feel about the tree? Okay, maybe you aren't passionate about trees, but look at those settings that are in your story and see if you can use words to make it more visual for the reader. This means specific, concrete details.

—

Now, after you've written your discovery draft of your essay, let's look at a professional writer's approach to a short narrative autobiography. Find Annie Dillard's "American Childhood" online. Look specifically at Dillard's use of concrete details. For this exercise, pay attention to her word choice, and find and post a few sentences that you thought were particularly creative and vivid. Discuss these sentences in your blog.

Look at this example from Anne Dillard's story:

"Best, you got to throw yourself mightily at someone's running legs. Either you brought him down or you hit the ground flat out on your chin, with your arms empty before you. It was all or nothing. If you hesitated in fear, you would miss and get hurt: you would take a hard fall while the kid got away, or you would get kicked in the face while the kid got away."

Now, Dillard could have, and may have first written, "I really liked to play football when I was a kid."

Was that as much fun to read? Note how Dillard uses both concrete detail and an analysis of the moment: "It was all or nothing…"

Look at all the places in your story where you can open up the scene visually, emotionally, and analytically for the reader. Slow down time. Take things blow by blow. Try to include those feelings you had at that time just as Dillard did. All the concrete, specific details make us feel her passion for the sport, put us on the field with her, and, super-duper importantly, call up our own memories of playing football.

You can also employ metaphors and similes to further enrich your writing. These are tools that you can use to make abstract ideas more concrete. For example, again from Dillard's story:

"It was cloudy but cold. The cars' tires laid behind them on the snowy street a complex trail of beige chunks like crenellated castle walls."

In this case you might have to look up the word 'crenellated' in order to make sense of the image, but once you do, or if you already knew the word or could figure it out through context, you can see how this simile "like crenellate castle walls" makes vivid the "complex trail" of marks in the snow laid by the cars in a way otherwise impossible to describe.

Notice that Dillard's story doesn't have the hero end up essentially succeeding in some external, physical quest. Indeed, she is caught! But, she has realized something true about the world, and shared it with her readers. It is their specific experience that is also universal. We have all felt that heart pounding fear that we are 'dead' if someone catches us or if we get in trouble as kids, but that fear turns out to be just that, only a fear.

Writing is about being honest, above all else. It is about connecting our own experiences with others so that our readers, like our new friends, can say "oh my god, that happened to me!" And we bond.

## On Peer Review Workshops

Yes, sharing your work, especially early drafts, can be tough. That's why it's important to be considerate but helpful. Allow the writer to make their own realizations about changes to be made by reading their own work aloud. Again, this is the most eye-opening activity a writer can do because here is where they really sense their audience. It may even be subconscious, but while reading aloud, the writer senses subtle changes in the mood of their audience, and from these non-verbal cues can learn a great deal about how their work is being received.

To prepare for peer review, I suggest you read Peter Elbow and Pat Belanoff's "Summary of Ways of Responding". They open their essay stating that there are two paradoxes of responding: (1) both the reader and writer are "always right" and (2) the writer must keep control of their own writing but must quietly receive feedback.

So, how do we deal with these paradoxes? I agree with Elbow and Belanoff, these are the key reasons why people struggle with peer review, and indeed even with getting feedback on writing from their professors. This is why we (and I include myself here) are so hesitant to make changes to our writing. It is why we resist rewriting even when it is necessary.

Elbow and Belanoff give us a set of guidelines, options really, for how to choose to receive your feedback so that it will be most useful to you. Even if the feedback you receive is exactly what the writing needs, it may not be what the writer, in their development (we are always and forever developing writers, by the way) is ready to hear. Indeed, feedback that is too forceful, that demands the writer stretch too far beyond their abilities, will have the opposite of its intended effect. Instead of helping the writer it will be so discouraging as to make them all but throw their writing in the trashcan, sometimes for good.

To understand why this is so, let's compare writing to learning to play the piano. The funny thing about writing is that since we can all "write," as in put down words on paper, we assume it is easy. It is not. But when we sit down in front of a piano keyboard and look at the squiggly lines on the sheet music in front of us for the first time, we understand that this is a whole new world, and won't be easy. But we dig in, start to learn the rules, and eventually out comes "Hot Cross Buns" after a lot of hard work. We feel proud. Then someone comes along, listens to our rendition, and demands we play Beethoven's Moonlight Sonata and anything less isn't good enough. We get up and leave and say, "forget piano, I can't do it!"

This isn't to say that your writing is at the level of Hot Cross Buns as a freshman in college. This is just an analogy to say that learning to write is a lifelong process that occurs in steps, and you must continue to practice and practice if you want your writing to get better. So be mindful that we all come from different backgrounds, and have different levels of experience with writing as we come into our college classrooms. Encouragement with perhaps a single suggestion for the 'next step,' is helpful.

Saying all the things you find 'wrong' with one of your peer's writing is not.

Elbow and Belanoff suggest that the writer choose from what is essentially a menu of options for how they want to hear their feedback and what sorts of feedback they wish to hear. They also give the writer the option to raise their hand if they suddenly feel the feedback they are receiving is making them discouraged, indicating for the responder to cease speaking. This way, the writer can tread in waters that feel comfortable, stay encouraged, stay in control and yet hear what they need to hear in order to improve the writing of the piece at hand, and their writing in general.

Okay, happy writing and rewriting!

## Works Cited

Dillard, Annie. "American Childhood." www.jonescollegeprep.org/.../An%20American%20Childhood-Annie%20Dillard.pdf Accessed 19 July 2018.

Dougherty, Elizabeth. "The Chemistry of Thought." MIT School of Engineering. https://engineering.mit.edu/engage/ask-an-engineer/what-are-thoughts-made-of/ Accessed 8 August, 2018.

Elbow, Peter and Belanoff, Pat. "Summary of Ways of Responding." https://www.usi.edu/media/2962444/summary-of-ways-of-responding.pdf Accessed 19 July, 2018.

Foulds, David. *Crossing the Threshold: Student Essays.* Columbia, SC: Amazon. 2018. Print.

Graff, Gerald and Birkenstein, Cathy. *They Say/I Say: The Moves That Matter in Academic Writing.* Chicago: Norton. 2017. Print.

Groening, Matt. *Futurama.* "A Pharaoh to Remember." Season 3, Episode 17. Video.

Iser, Wolfgang "The reading process: a phenomenological approach", *Modern Criticism and Thought: A Reader ed.* David Lodge. London: Longman. 1988.

Lamott, Anne. "Shitty First Drafts." Bird by Bird. *https://wrd.as.uky.edu/sites/default/files/1-Shitty%20First%20Drafts.pdf.* Accessed 19 July, 2018.

McLuhan, Marshall. *Understanding Media: The Extensions of Man.* Boston: MIT Press. 1994. Print.

Miller, Richard E. and Jurecic, Ann. *Habits of the Creative Mind.* New York: Bedford/St. Martin's. 2016. Print.

Seger, Linda. "Creating The Myth" on iLearn.

Woolf, Virginia. *A Room of One's Own.* Cambridge: Hogarth Press. 1929. Print.

# CHAPTER THREE

## Autobiography Book Club:
## Honing Your Voice

A lot of students in my courses state that they 'don't like reading.' I get it. I wasn't a big reader for a long time either. I was raised in front of the 'boob-tube' as we used to call it. I went to the movies all the time, but rarely picked up a book. It was, simply, easier to watch a film or television show than to read. Reading seemed to hurt my eyes. If the book wasn't really engaging, right away, I found my mind drifting, thinking about all the things I'd rather be doing. Thinking about my day. Conversations I had. Things I wanted to do later, tomorrow, when I grew up.

Yes, I guess I was a bit of a daydreamer. When I was a kid I'd lie in bed and close my eyes and make up stories. But these weren't stories built with words; these were stories built with images. My favorite story to make up was that my uncle gave me a big rig truck for my tenth birthday. And since it was a present, obviously I'd get to drive it even though I wasn't old enough. I drove it to school and all the kids thought I was pretty amazing, you know, being a ten-year-old pulling up to elementary school in an 18-wheeler.

So, it definitely wasn't that I didn't like stories. I loved stories. In fact, I loved them so much I was often lost in my daydreams and not really focusing on what was happening right in front of me.

And what was right in front of me was piles of school work. Reading that I didn't want to do. My grades started to slide, and my dad punished me by locking me in the study for an hour a day so that I'd actually do my schoolwork.

At first I would just stubbornly stare at the wall, or out the window, refusing to be cajoled into reading.

Then, soon enough, and bored enough, I found myself browsing the shelves of the study, which were lined with classic books. There were names I recognized but never read: Charles Dickens, Jules Verne, Herman Melville, Jane Austen, Bram Stoker, Mary Shelly, Mark Twain, F. Scott Fitzgerald, Robert Louis Stevenson... Then, I came across a title that stuck out. *Island of the Blue Dolphins* by Scott O'Dell. I had this fascination with scuba diving, so the next thing you know I slid the book out, opened it, and was magically transported... I know, you are already thinking 'here we go again, reading is so great, blah blah blah,' and picking up your phone and playing whatever the heck is the game of the season.

So, I won't try to convince you that reading will change your life and all those clichés. All too often, reading is put out there as this amazing thing that makes you a great person, and if you don't read then you must be intellectually inferior. There is this attitude about reading that is pretty off-putting. Again, I get it. I find it pretty annoying too. The idea that reading makes you so much better than everyone else is utter BS. It doesn't. This idea has more to do with what is called 'cultural capital,' which is really just jargon for things that make you seem snooty, than the truth. You can learn plenty through film and video. We are very visual people.

So let's forget all of that. Let's forget that 'reading is good for you' like Brussels Sprouts.

Let's just start over. What I realized was that reading, if you choose the right book, is a better experience than a great video. Yes, the book is better than the movie. It's true. You know why? Because, like I've already said, when you read, you are the director, casting agent, set designer, etc. When you envision in your mind what is written on the page, the story you are reading becomes partly *your* story. You make up exactly what the characters look like. You decide from minimal description what rooms, houses, even cities look like. You put voices in the characters' throats, clothes on their backs, even the stride in their step. Yes, the reader creates much of the experience while reading.

In the text *Writing Fiction*, Amanda Boulter, writes about the history of the idea of voice in writing. Although her book is about fictional works, her discussion works for any narrative, like the autobiographies you wrote and the one you will read in this chapter. Voice, she says, is a confusing concept because identity is also a confusing concept.

It has been argued that because we are products of our social worlds, there is no such thing as a truly unique individual. She cites the work of Louis Althusser, who states that we "live according to the rules and rituals of society: we work as we are supposed to; bring up children as we are supposed to…" and so on. We cannot find any part of ourselves that is not a product of our social and biological construction.

An interesting idea. What do you think? Are we unique individuals or are we simply "automata" that behave in ways that are essentially programmed by our circumstances? Is there free will?

Yes, we can categorize ourselves, and each other, all day long. We use these words to finish the sentence "I am…" and "You are…" and then make assumptions based on these categories.

But, are we truly exactly like anyone else? Certainly not. Even identical twins are different in many ways. When someone talks about your "voice," this is what they mean. That way of being, and talking, and writing, that is uniquely your own.

However, when we really look closely at identity, the way we are in the world is not totally unique, but rather an amalgam of our experiences and our genetics. We are all unique, but from within the bounds of the requirements of our society and biology. We can speak freely, but what we say, and how we say it, is a product of our experiences. We have different accents if we grew up in different parts of the country. We have different expressions, and the content of our conversation depends largely on where we grew up, who we talked to, what media we watched, and so on.

If we were to truly communicate in a way that is uniquely our own, no one would understand us. We have to follow agreed-upon rules of communication in order to get the message through. What we say is not only a series of linguistic signs (the alphabet, words), but also symbolic. When I talk a certain way, there are other messages being sent than just the words themselves. "I am powerful," "I am smart," "I am insecure," and so on. How we communicate on paper communicates a lot to our readers.

Have you ever found yourself accidentally saying something just as one of your caregivers did? Have you said "oh my god, I sound just like my mom." Have you ever repeated something you heard in the media? Have you ever started to sound a bit like your best friend? Or like your favorite celebrity?

My point is this: voice is something that is created by a unique individual given their social circumstances. Voice thus changes as situations change. We learn to craft our voice through time based on what we hear and read that resonates with us. As Boulter points out, every writer is a product of all of their reading. As you read more, you will pick up on some of your favorite ways of writing just as you pick up on expressions and even accents of those you spend your time with. So, in this textbook, I ask you to hone that voice as you broaden your reading.

Voice isn't static; it is fluid.

It is supposed to grow and change through time and experience. Yes, there will always be that core "you" in how you speak and write, but you can use influences to change your voice and still be true to who you are.

Check out the following books. I suggest autobiographies since you will use your text to help you rewrite your own autobiography from the last chapter. These are the ones I use in my book club:

**Tweak** by **Nic Sheff**
**The Glass Castle** by **Jeannette Walls**
**Buck** by **M.K. Asante**

My students could not put these down. But be warned, these books are pretty raw and honest. This is, of course, what makes them so compelling. So, I highly suggest starting a book club in class, either with these books or with books that you choose together.

The remainder of the chapter mostly contains specific questions to use with the books above. Regardless of the text you choose, your book clubs should meet several times with guided questions provided by your instructor, and should culminate in a 'book report' as well as a 'writer's report' thinking about how the 'voice' of the writing can be used to help you hone your own voice.

## Practice 3-1

*Form book clubs of about 4-5 students who all meet regularly during class time to discuss their chosen texts.*

Book Club meeting questions for discussion:

### The Glass Castle by Jeannette Walls (to page 90)

1. What stereotypes of homelessness are broken down in the very first chapter "A Woman on the Street?" Would you be embarrassed if you parents were homeless? Do you think that some homeless people could choose to not be homeless but instead actually make that a life choice? Why would someone make that choice?

2. Were her parents negligent when they ignored Brian's head injury on page 13? What is it to be a negligent parent?

3. When they check out of the hospital on p. 14 "Rex Walls Style," what are they doing? What is your moral

judgment about this? Do you think that he is making a political statement about socialized health care or cheating the system? Somewhere in between?

4. Did dad really think "henchmen, bloodsuckers, the Gustapo" were after them? Why were they always "doing the skedaddle?"

5. Find a description of the desert that you found appealing. Share it with the group. What
is it about the writing that is so vivid?

6. Do you believe Rex Walls is legitimately trying to make 'the prospector'?

7. Why are they moving around so much?

8. Locate, look up, and share at least 3-5 new vocabulary words from your reading.

9. Describe mom – what are her passions? Why doesn't she like teaching?

10. When they left their cat behind – is this animal abuse?

11. Describe Battle Mountain. Find some vivid sentences that give us a sense of the place.

12. Discuss any other issue, moment, character that jumped out at you during your reading.

## Tweak by Nic Sheff (to page 130)

1. Nick says "I drank some and then I just had to drink more until the whole glass was drained empty. I'm not sure why. Something was driving me that I couldn't and still don't comprehend. Some say it's in the genes" (2). Look up addiction and genetics. Is there a correlation? What would cause someone to drink so much so quickly that it poisoned them? Have you ever known anyone to go

through this? If you feel comfortable relating the story, do so.

2. Share some vivid quotes from Sheff's writing. Take a sentence or two and dissect it. What makes it such compelling writing at the sentence level?

3. Why do you think someone would give up so much for a 'high?' Sheff writes, "I guess I've spent the last four years chasing that first high. I wanted desperately to feel that wholeness again. It was like, I don't know, like everything else faded out" (5). And later "it was like I was being held captive by some insatiable monster that will not let me go" (6). Do you believe that addiction is out of the addict's hands? Is it a true illness? How could a drug make you feel "wholeness?"

4. So far, how has your view of methamphetamine users changed? Do you feel less empathy, more empathy? About the same? Why?

5. Does your view of Nick change when he starts dealing?

6. Describe Gack. Is he a real friend to Nick? Why or why not?

7. Describe Lauren. Are they in love? After her OD, why does she not want to go to the hospital? (p. 68)

8. Are there parts of the book that you find offensive? What is the purpose of art / literature? Should some be censored?

9. Predict the end of the book. What do you think it will take for Nick to overcome his addiction?

10. Pull 3-5 vocabulary words, look them up, and share them with the class.

11. Discuss any other issue, moment, character that jumped out at you during your reading.

## Buck by MK Asante (to page 105)

1. Talk about Asante's writing style, his 'voice.' What are some rules that he breaks in order for his personality to come through? How might you break these rules in your own writing in order to sound uniquely like yourself?

2. What does he mean by the line "Change hangs in the air like the sneaks on the live wires behind my crib" (3)?

3. Why does Asante include lyrics to (mostly) hip-hop songs? Pick one of the lyrics and relate it to what is happening in the story at the time. What is he saying about hip-hop and it's connection to his real life?

4. Who is Uzi? What's he like? How do you know? Pick out some lines that describe Uzi and show him in action as evidence.

5. Why does Uzi go to Arizona?

6. Why does Uzi go to jail? How long is he put in jail? Do you think he deserves to be there?

7. Are you offended by some of the language that Asante uses in the book? Is it necessary? What makes language offensive? Why do you think some people are offended by certain words and phrases while others aren't?

8. Is the book offensive to women? How are women represented in the book so far? Name a few (or a few moments in the book women are described) and discuss.

9. Do you "like" Asante as a 'character' Malo in this book so far? Why or why not? What is compelling about him? What does he want? What is in his way?

10. Describe Asante's mom Amina. Why does Asante use the invasion of the diary in order for us to learn about her? What does she want? What are her main concerns?

11. How are stereotypes about the African American community in an urban center complicated through the

book? In other words, if you see stereotypes portrayed, how does your understanding of what seems to be stereotypes deepen through your look at these individual people living their lives?

12. Discuss any other issue, moment, character that jumped out at you during your reading.

More book club meeting questions after reading completed.

## Tweak

1) Nic's body goes through a lot when he is in detox. Research what happens to the body when drugs are being used, and the physiology of detoxification.

2) Nic finds strength to stay sober in his family, his writing and other aspects of his life. Identify the people, hobbies and beliefs in your own life that you rely on for strength when going through a tough time.

3) What causes Nic to get help each time he relapsed? What does hitting bottom look like for him? Why is his stay at Safe Passage more effective than his other attempts at rehab? Do you think it's because of what they do there, or what led up to his going there...or both?

4) Nic mentions many times that he feels worthless, and that his addiction has caused him to irreparably damage his relationships with others. Do the actions of his friends and family back this up? Do they treat him as though he has no worth? Does anyone give him unconditional love?

5) What does it mean for Nic to give himself over to a higher power? Why is it so difficult for him to do this?

## Glass Castle

1) What character traits -- both good and bad -- do you think that Jeannette inherited from her parents? And how do you think those traits shaped Jeannette's life?

2) The two major pieces of the memoir -- one half set in the desert and one half in West Virginia -- feel distinct. What effect did such a big move have on the family -- and on your reading of the story? How would you describe the shift in the book's tone?

3) In college, Jeannette is singled out by a professor for not understanding the plight of homeless people; instead of defending herself, she keeps quiet. Why do you think she does this?

4) Do you think Jeannette should have been more insistent on getting her parents off the streets? Why or why not?

5) Picture living without running water, reliable electricity, or heat (other than from a wood stove) in the middle of a hard east coast winter. How does that make you feel? Describe your state of mind. Would you be mad at your parents for not giving you better shelter?

## Buck

1) Analyze the rap that Malo performs at the end of the book.

    a) Pull 5 different stanzas and discuss how they relate to what happened in the book.

    b) Read 5 different lines and analyze what they mean, word for word

2) Discuss why Malo turns to writing and reading to make sense of his world (chapter 40). What are some of the books he turns to?

3) Read the Whitman quote on page 226. What does it mean? Why is Malo moved and inspired by the quote?

4) Read the Ginsberg quote on page 227. What does it mean? Why is Malo moved and inspired by the quote?

5) Pick 3 of the quotes on pages 228 and 229 and analyze them. Relate them to Malo and his world.

## Practice 3-2: Writing Mashup

*Book Club - Writing Mashup*
*1) Read your book club text silently for 20 minutes.*
*2) Then write for 20 minutes.*
·      *Choose one paragraph from your autobiography essay*
·      *Rewrite it completely using your book club text as a reference*
·      *Use what you just read as a style guide*
·      *Try to mimic the author's voice and use it to write your paragraph*
·      *Steal phrases from your book club text if you wish, particularly vivid phrases of description*
·      *Can you integrate their style into yours? Can you do a mashup of their approach to writing and your own?*
*3) Then reflect for 10 minutes.*
·      *What has this activity done to help you understand the idea of 'voice' in writing?*
·      *Did you feel like you were co-opting the author's voice? Were you not being an authentic you? Or did you feel more "you?"*
*4) Post the original paragraph, the new paragraph, and the analysis to your blogs.*

Here's a mashup one of my students, Alejandro Carranza, did, using Nic Sheff's *Tweak* as his source.

**Original**: Right when I got hit I heard this pop in my knee. I rolled around the ground in the agonizing pain in my knee, screaming and crying. I'm not one to show emotion let alone cry, so if I cried it meant that I was really in pain. I have never experienced a pain like this in my 18 years of living and the countless other injuries I've had. All the players stood around me looking, wondering what happened, trying to help me out and grab me to calm down.

**Mashup**: Right when I got hit I heard my knee pop. As I was rolling around the ground screaming, crying sounding like a wounded animal because of the agonizing knee pain, I felt my leg get colder. It was as if my leg was freezing starting from my knee down to my toes. I felt the swelling in my knee rise, the blood slowing down, the coldness just taking over. It was as if my leg had its own heart beat, and I could see and feel the throbbing. It felt like the lower part of my leg wasn't there anymore, I couldn't feel it there, yet I still felt the pain. There was this numbness and tingling feeling like being poked a thousand times by needles all over my leg. It was a feeling like no other, nothing like any of the injuries I sustained the past 17 years of my life. All the players were surrounding me, with blank expressions, lost, confused, not knowing what to do. A few tried to help by trying to hold me in one position to stop me from moving.

**Reflection**: This idea did help understand the "voice" in writing. Nic Sheff uses a lot of imagery; he goes into great detail when experiencing a feeling, or emotion. While reading his book, with description like that, I felt as if it were happening to me, as if I were the one actually experiencing it. I hope that with incorporating his "voice" in my writing will give the readers a better understanding of feeling what I did.

———

Note that some of you will find this to be a fun, insightful exercise that helps you loosen up your voice, helps you let go of that old, stuffy, boring 'college essay' writing to your teacher kind of writing. Others will find this incredibly frustrating and feel like trying to write like someone else is stealing your voice, making you write in a way that feels false and ridiculous. Some may even get angry.

This is all fine. This writing mashup practice will not help everyone. But for those who find that it helps them, it can really change their writing and their approach to both reading and writing. I've seen latent writers suddenly spring forth colorful, vivid, surprising and honest prose as Carranza did above.

Maybe you're a poet and you don't even know it.

But also note that you don't have to actually mimic the particular voice of the author. Instead, you can use them as a mentor to help you write with more vivid descriptions, or have your own voice come closer to how you speak.

If this activity was helpful to you, use it to assist you as you rewrite your autobiography essays.

When you finish your book club texts, write an individual review of the book. Then read a review of the book posted online and respond to it.

## Practice 3-3: Book Review

Write a review of your book including:

1) Your direct reading of the book.

- Your analysis of the book as engaging or not – do you recommend it?
- Your analysis of themes brought up in the book: psychological illness, drug and alcohol abuse, parental neglect, inner-city life…

2) A literary review of your book. Look up 1 or 2 articles reviewing your book.

- How does the review help shape your understanding of your reading?
- What points do you agree with?
- What points do you disagree with?

## Works Cited

Althusser, Louis. "Ideology and the State." *Modern Literary Theory,* 2ⁿᵈ Edition. London: Edward Arnold, 1992.

Asante, M.K. *Buck.* New York: Spiegel and Grau, 2014.

Boulter, Amanda. *Writing Fiction.* New York: Palgrave, 2007.

Sheff, Nic. *Tweak.* New York: Atheneum, 2009.

Walls, Jeanette. *The Glass Castle.* New York: Scribner, 2006.

# CHAPTER FOUR

## *The Dreaded Grammar Chapter*

There's a lot of debate about whether or not there is value in teaching college students grammar. Grammar, though it is made of rules, is something that is not set in stone, but develops and evolves over time. There is plenty of evidence that students learn grammar best by reading and writing rather than filling out workbooks. So, no worksheets will be included in this chapter.

However, I have found that there are some basic grammar issues that students commonly struggle with, and I couldn't in good conscience write a textbook about English composition without including some sentence level instruction and work.

Yes, ideas are our focus. But there are conventions to know so that your brilliant ideas are communicated as intended to your readers. A lot of my students say "Hey, no one will teach us grammar! I don't remember it, so come on!" Okay, you've been heard.

I do, however, want to reiterate that there's no one way to write well. It depends on so much - situation, audience, purpose, writing style, voice... Just look at this sentence from one of my favorite books, *The Dharma Bums*, by Jack Kerouac:

"The woods do that to you, they always look familiar, long lost, like the face of a long-dead relative, like an old dream, like a piece of forgotten song drifting across the water, most of all like golden eternities of past childhood or past manhood and all the living and the dying and the heartbreak that went on a million years ago and the clouds as they pass overhead seem to testify (by their own lonesome familiarity) to this feeling."

A hardcore copy editor might be horribly offended at this sentence. Indeed, Truman Capote is said to have exclaimed "that's not writing; that's typewriting!" Let's edit this piece according to the following guidelines:

1) You should have only one thought per sentence.
2) You should eliminate all unnecessary words.

Here's an edited version:

"The woods always look familiar yet long lost, like the face of a long-dead relative. They are like an old dream or a piece of forgotten song drifting across the water. The clouds overhead testify to the loss of memories from long ago, of millions of years passing, and of heartache."

Okay, admittedly it is hard to screw up Kerouac's prose no matter what you do since he is such a vivid writer. Maybe even some of you prefer the edit to the original. However, I feel like the original has an energy and spontaneity that is lacking in the latter. The sentence is complex, it builds, it moves in unexpected ways yet remains cohesive and focused. It also sounds more uniquely "Kerouac." It retains his voice - no one else could have written that sentence, it seems. What this proves is that writing 'rules' can and should be broken *on the right occasion.*

Writing is about context. It isn't about a thesis and perfect syntax and topic sentences and bing bang boom, one two three, here's your essay. It is about writing in a way that conveys meaning to your reader based on what you want to say and how you want to say it. To paraphrase Marshall McLuhan, it is about using the medium of writing as part of the message of writing.

All languages are constantly evolving. Just look at the beginning of the prologue from Geoffrey Chaucer's *The Canterbury Tales*:

Whan that Aprille with his shoures soote,
The droghte of March hath perced to the roote,
And bathed every veyne in swich licóur
Of which vertú engendred is the flour;
Whan Zephirus eek with his swete breeth
Inspired hath in every holt and heeth
The tendre croppes, and the yonge sonne
Hath in the Ram his halfe cours y-ronne,
And smale foweles maken melodye,
That slepen al the nyght with open ye,
So priketh hem Natúre in hir corages,
Thanne longen folk to goon on pilgrimages,
And palmeres for to seken straunge strondes,
To ferne halwes, kowthe in sondry londes;
And specially, from every shires ende
Of Engelond, to Caunterbury they wende,

The hooly blisful martir for to sek**e**,
That hem hath holpen whan that they were seek**e**.

English grammar and spelling have changed quite a bit through the centuries. Language is alive; it evolves and changes over time. As the United States becomes wonderfully more diverse, our language is going to continue to change, like a magpie picking up sayings and words from our diverse population, creating a new English over the hundreds and thousands of years to come.

In addition, it is a sad truth that even though it has been proven that there is zero connection between someone's grammar ability and their intellectual ability, the man on the street (or worse, your potential employer) may, and often will, judge you for not following standard English conventions before they even get to your ideas. So, for now, it will help to learn a few of these conventions so that some people don't misjudge you. Plus, as you saw from Kerouac's prose above, having power over grammar and punctuation gives you more control over how you use your words to convey meaning. Control means knowing when to stay in key, and when to break out of it, like Kerouac does with his Jazz-like be-bop prose.

### Practice 4-1: Picasso

*Google Pablo Picasso's "Les Demoiselles d'Avignon" painting. We will talk about how to think and write about art in a later chapter; but for now, take a few minutes to look at the painting and write down some notes. Anything goes. Whatever comes to mind. This can be what you see, what you think you see, and of course, your reaction. Lastly, ask yourself if you think this is 'good' art or 'bad' art. Does it take skill or is it a haphazard mishmash? Does Picasso know how to paint or is this a big scam?*

*Next, Google Pablo Picasso's "Science and Charity." Do the same as above. Take a few minutes to look at the painting. What is your reaction? Most importantly, now compare it to "Les Demoiselles." Which is better? How do you define "better?" Which took more talent? If you didn't note the dates, which would you think was done first?*

*Finally, think, and write, about the term "talent." Look back at the first painting and reanalyze your thoughts about what talent is. Write about how Picasso broke the 'rules' with "Les Desmoiselles." Could, as some people argue, "a child paint that?" If so, why did Picasso paint this way when he could have painted it the way he painted "Science and Charity?"*

*Why would you write in a conventional way and why would you break the rules? Is there, then, good writing and bad writing?*

Picasso learned all the rules before he broke them. He learned about form and color. He learned about proportions. He learned all the classical moves a painter should know so that they can make choices as to how, when, or when not to use them. It may surprise you to know that Picasso painstakingly worked and reworked the composition of "Les Desmoiselles" before he painted the final version.

Unsurprisingly, when painters broke the classical rules, like the impressionists did in the late 1800s, (Google "impressionist painting" if you don't know what it is), they were laughed out of The Salon, chastised for being terribly unskilled. Now these are arguably some of the most beloved and most valuable paintings in the world.

Likewise, Kerouac learned all the basics of writing before he played with and broke the rules. His earlier work is more contained, more 'proper' in terms of syntax, and yet it doesn't feel as alive. But it is clear when one reads *The Dharma Bums* that Kerouac has a deep understanding of the language. He also is writing fiction, and his storylines were about spontaneity, about living life in the moment, about 'carpe diem,' seizing the day.

In other words, form followed function.

An unconventional, casual style would not sit well if you were trying to convince readers that your genetic experiments with fruit flies prove that you have discovered a new gene implicated in the cause of cancer. Can you imagine a scientist writing, "So I just popped those genes there in that bad boy, did some serious kick-ass PCR on that sucker, and then when I used all that shit like I learned in graduate school, I was like, "woh, this is killer."

Right time, right voice.

Again, while we write our early drafts to think through our ideas, to just get ideas on the page, we need to redraft thinking of the reader. Once our ideas feel fairly solid, we need to double check that the sentences we wrote will actually make sense to your readers. This is where peer review can be particularly useful.

Maybe you don't like peer review. It's a mixed bag to be sure. Not all feedback is created equal. Yet peer review is the basis, believe it or not, of all academic writing. Academic journals, before they are published, are "peer-reviewed" so that other experts in your field can question, analyze, and discuss whether what you have written is valid, clear, and actually contributes to the ongoing conversation taking place in your field. As I've said before, in college, you are no longer required to just spew out facts you researched through a five paragraph essay. Now, your purpose for writing is to join academic conversations, to write into areas that are unclear, to question and connect and discuss.

Just as Picasso learned how to paint through an understanding of the basics of color and composition, you need to have a firm command of some of the basics of writing in order to decide, consciously, when to break away from those rules and when to use them.

The most common issues I have found in students' writing are the following:

1) Comma usage - often put where people pause when they speak. There are actually a few specific rules for proper comma placement. Most people overuse commas or use them to splice together multiple sentences.

2) Tense agreements - staying in the proper tense (past, present, future) throughout a piece of writing often proves difficult. Rereading your essay just looking to make sure that your tenses make sense can really help.

3) Coordinating and subordinating conjunctions - These are those connectors between ideas in a sentence: for, and, nor, but, or, yet, so. We often use the acronym FANBOYS to remember these.

4) Parallel construction - using a base verb for a series of actions so that they make sense individually.

5) Dangling modifiers - who did what to whom?

6) Passive structure - having a way to say a thing in a roundabout way. Usually not a good approach.

7) Sentence boundaries - when to stop and start a new sentence versus using a comma and "splicing" them together like Frankenstein.

In this text, we won't go into great detail about grammar. If you find that you'd like a full grammar review, my favorite quick texts are *The Only Grammar Book You'll Ever Need* by Susan Thurman and *It was the best of sentences, it was the worst of sentences* by June Casagrande. You don't really need to know what an appositive is or really even what an adjective is in order to write standard academic English (but it helps). It really just takes time and practice and most importantly, reading.

Lots of reading.

The more you read the more you realize that good writing, and by that I mean writing that keeps your interest, isn't stuffy and academic. It's personal and engaging. And academic. Yes, you can do both.

Okay, on to our grammar lesson.

Beware: a lot of these terms act like a natural sedative. But since they can help you understand how to construct sentences that make sense, let's go over a few definitions:

## Nouns

Person, place, thing, or idea. You need a noun in order to have an action. You need a noun in order to have a sentence.

"Chandra ran." This is a sentence because it has a noun and an action.

## Pronouns

Stand in for nouns. My name is David. Once you know that you can say "he." Likewise, "the table" becomes "it."

## Verbs

The action that a noun takes.
In "I ran," ran is the verb.

Verbs can be "tense." In other words, when we talk about tenses (past, present, future), we are talking about verbs. "I ran" is in past tense. "I run" is present. "I will run" is future.

## Adjectives

A word that modifies a noun. What do we mean by "modify?"

"The table" is a noun with no adjective. "The red table" is modified by the adjective "red." Think of it as someone taking a plain wood table and modifying it by adding paint.

But adjectives don't have to just be concrete terms like "red." They can be feelings like "delightful." For example, in: "The delightful barista gave us extra whipped cream," "Delightful" is the adjective modifying the noun "barista." "Gave" is the verb.

Adjectives answer one of the following questions:

1) What kind?
2) How many?
3) Which one?

## Adverbs

Adverbs seem very much like adjectives, but they modify a verb or adjective, not the noun. Many adverbs can be recognized by their "-ly" ending.

"I will run to the store quickly." Here, "quickly" is the adverb.

Adverbs give the following information:

1) degree - very, almost, a bit, slightly, extremely...
2) frequency - daily, hourly, sometimes, always, often, usually...
3) manner - quickly, slowly, fast, well...

4) place - outside, down, up, over...
5) time - tomorrow, eventually, all day...

## Prepositions

Think "position."
Up, over, on, under...

## Phrases

A phrase is a group of words that do a job of one of the above. They have either a subject (like in noun phrases) or a verb (as in verb phrases).

1) A prepositional phrase, for example, starts with a preposition:

"...on the dresser." "...over the hill."

2) A noun phrase is "the boy in the car." The whole phrase essentially acts like a noun in the sentence "The boy in the car was hot."

3) A verb phrase is "was walking fast." The whole phrase is the action the noun is taking: "She was walking fast."

4) An adverb phrase is "very quickly." "She was walking very quickly."

5) An adjective phrase is "smarter than me," as in "She is smarter than me." Smarter than me modifies "she."

## Clauses

A clause is either independent or dependent.

An independent clause can stand on its own: "Lazy students whine."

A dependent clause starts with a coordinating or subordinating conjunction, so it is also known as a subordinate clause. coordinating conjunctions are the FANBOYS, as mentioned above: for, and, nor, but, or, yet, so.

Some dependent clauses:

"…so there were only two left."

"…nor did they remember the balls."

"…but I hadn't even started."

These are dependent on the rest of the sentence:

"I sold four bicycles, so there were only two left."

"They didn't remember the clubs, nor did they remember the balls."

"They had been running for an hour, but I hadn't even started."

You might be noticing that sometimes people write sentences that begin with coordinating conjunctions. I use them sometimes in this textbook. These are technically sentence fragments or "incomplete sentences." Since they are technically incorrect, you shouldn't use them very often, if at all, in formal academic essays. But they can be used to bring home a key point. (That was an incomplete sentence because it started with "But.") So, again, we see that rules aren't hard and fast.

Subordinate clauses are similar to coordinate clauses, but they start with subordinating conjunctions. Some often used subordinating conjunctions are: because, whenever, as, after, once, until, whereas…

For example:

"Because the kitchen is too hot…"

"Whenever we go to the drive through…"

"Once I had enough eggs…"

Notice that these cannot stand alone because they don't make any sense. They are clearly incomplete thoughts.

Phew! Okay, hopefully some of that stuck. If not, worry not. Like I said, you don't need to know all these parts of speech, but the better you know them the more control you will have with your writing.

## Writing Simply

Many people, like William Zinsser in his book *On Writing Well*, believe that the best writing is when it is concise. Zinsser writes that "clutter is the disease of American writing. We are a society strangling in unnecessary words, circular constructions, pompous frills and meaningless jargon" (7). June Casagrande agrees, stating that "This sentence rocks. It's concise. It's powerful. It knows what it wants to say, and it says it in clear, bold terms" (1). I agree with both, to a degree. Yes, if you strip your sentences down to the basic level, try to keep them as clear and straightforward as possible, you are heading in the right direction. A lot of beginning writers get muddled when they write longer sentences, forgetting what the sentence was actually supposed to be about. Then they ask their readers to figure it out, not bothering to re-read their own writing.

If you don't re-read your own writing to make sure it makes sense, why are you asking someone else to read it?

Many, if not most, errors can probably be caught by simply proofreading before you submit your work. That is the great thing about writing compared to speaking. Writing has a delete key. You can take the time to be sure that you say what you mean to say. So please, proofread. Asking someone to proofread for you when you have not done so yourself is a bit selfish. It's like banging out something from your throne and then tossing it to the peasant and saying "fix this up for me. I can't be bothered. I have more important things to do."

Writing simply, as Zinsser says, is a great place to start. Does that mean all your sentences should be short? No. You want to change things up so it doesn't get boring for the reader. As long as you are clear, and your sentence additions add color through the use of phrases and clauses, then you should take on some compound or complex sentences. But be careful! A lot of the confusing writing I come across is because students string together multiple sentences into one sentence, losing track of the central subject and action.

The first thing you can do is trim the fat. Where have you repeated yourself? Are all sentences clear? Does one thought lead to the next?

In *They Say/I Say*, Graff and Birkenstein urge us to think of each sentence as both looking backward and looking forward. They write, "The best compositions establish a sense of momentum and direction by making explicit connections among their different parts, so that what is said in one sentence (or paragraph) both sets up what is to come and is clearly informed by what has already been said" (107). In other words, your writing should continue to build and move. If you find that you are often repeating yourself, then you probably have run out of ideas. So, time to stop, think, and then write.

Word counts aren't about filling space. Ideally, they are actually a limitation, not a minimum. Sort of like the speed limit. It says 65 but we all agree that 65 is the minimum, not the maximum - we want to go 75! If you are engaged with your writing, you will always have somewhere to go. One thought will lead to the next, and the next. You will curse your word count and email your professor asking if you can go over it.

In order to keep this momentum going, Graff and Birkenstein argue that using "transitions" will help fuel that car. This really is a great, easy to read and in-depth guide to writing argumentation, so I highly recommend it.

These are words that keep your writing brain, and the reader's brain, connecting old thoughts to new ideas.

Here's a few **transitions** that you can use to make your writing flow:

Additions: also, and, furthermore, indeed, moreover…
Elaboration: actually, in other words, to put it another way…
Examples: for example, for instance, specifically…
Cause and Effect: so, thus, therefore, since…
Comparison: likewise…
Contrast: although, but, however, whereas, despite…
Concession: of course, admittedly…
Conclusion: thus, therefore, to summarize…

Use these transitions to get your brain thinking about where your writing will go next. How does each sentence relate to the one before and the one after? How does each paragraph relate to one another?

## Commas

There are only a few basic rules on comma usage:

### 1) Separate items in a list:
"I will go to the store and get jam, peanut butter, and Wonder Bread."

You probably already know this one and am wondering why I even bothered to mention it. Well, because there's a thing called the Oxford comma. That's the comma at the end of the list that is just before the 'and.' Do we need it? Some argue that we don't since the 'and' tells us that it is another item of the list, so it is redundant.

"I will go to the store and get jam, peanut butter and Wonder Bread."

Does this still make sense? Sure it does. We are going to get these three items. But before you say "well then forget the last comma, I don't need it," look at this sentence:

"We invited the strippers, JFK, and Stalin."

And now this one:

"We invited the strippers, JFK and Stalin."

Google this on the internet and see what comes up. This meme started when a Dallas, Texas high school English teacher used it to illustrate the point.

See what a difference an Oxford comma makes?

In the former, it is clear that this very strange party is going to include strippers, JFK, and Stalin. The latter sentence is saying that we are inviting JFK and Stalin, who are strippers.

**(2) When you use two words in a row to describe something (aka two adjectives to describe a noun).**

"That is an old, weather-beaten fence."

Here, we have described the fence as both old and weather-beaten, so we need a comma to separate out the two descriptors (adjectives).

**(3) To separate two discrete but connected ideas (complete thoughts aka independent clauses) that are joined by the coordinating conjunctions (as you learned above): for, and, nor, but, or, yet, so_(FANBOYS).**

"I have listened to all of the band's songs, and I conclude that they suck."
"I went to the store for eggs, but they were out of stock."

Each of these clauses could be stand-alone sentences:

"I have listened to all of the band's songs. I conclude that they suck."
"I went to the store for eggs. They were out of stock."

By using **coordinating conjunctions** (FANBOYS), we are able to show how the two thoughts connect (aka conjoin). Think of conjoined twins. They are connected. Conjunctions conjoin.

Actually, here's a good place to talk about **semicolons.** Some people are very anti-semicolon. They figure the semicolon isn't committed enough, so they just don't use them. Indeed, semicolons aren't necessary in most situations. However, there is one condition, the super comma, as will be discussed below, in which it is imperative to use the semicolon. In fact, when used correctly, semicolons work quite nicely.

All you have to do to use a semicolon is use it instead of the coordinating conjunction/comma or period in the above examples.

In other words, you could write:

"I have listened to all of the band's songs, and I conclude that they suck."

"I have listened to all of the band's songs. I conclude that they suck."

OR

"I have listened to all of the band's songs; I conclude that they suck."

What is nice about the semicolon is that it shows that two thoughts are related, but doesn't require the coordinating conjunction. It thus has a slightly different feel, and is perhaps better than merely separating the two thoughts with a period, for they are directly related.

And, going back to using commas to separate items out in a list, what if the list has commas within it?

For example:

"On my trip, I went to Paris, France, Milan, Italy, and New York, USA."

Since we know that Paris is in France and Milan is in Italy, perhaps we aren't too confused. But look at all those commas! What if we didn't know that Paris was in France or Milan was in Italy? We'd think the writer went to Paris and France and Milan and Italy and New York and The US.

Enter the **super comma**!

"On my trip, I went to Paris, France; Milan, Italy; and New York, USA."

The semicolon acts as a comma in between items that already have commas, thus its name, super comma.

### Back to commas...

### (4) To separate out descriptors of something (appositives).

For example:

"My professor, the one who is so boring I can't even stand it, wore a top hat today for no apparent reason."

Note that you can remove 'the one who is so boring I can't even stand it' from the sentence and it would still make sense. My professor wore a top hat today for no apparent reason. The phrase that can be removed isn't necessary for the sentence to make sense, but further defines the professor (a noun). This is called an appositive, and needs to be set apart from the sentence using commas on either end.

You may have heard that you use a comma before "which" but not "that." Again, this is about context, not an absolute. Your word processing program probably underlines your lack of comma before which every time you write it. Here's the scoop:

When a clause starts with "which," and further defines or modifies the subject, then use a comma, like this:

"The ski chalet, which is now open for the season, is two miles up the road."

Note that, like above, you can remove the relative clause "which is now open for the season" from the sentence and it still makes sense.

"The ski chalet is two miles up the road."

However, you cannot always remove a clause from a sentence and have it make sense. For example:

"The house that burned down was my sister's."

If you remove "that burned down" from the sentence, we won't know which house you are talking about, so it is not separated out by commas. It is also the main subject of the sentence. "The house that burned down" is a noun phrase.

If you use "which" instead of "that," you get:

"The house, which burned down, was my sisters."

The subtext here is that that information that the house burned down is just a side note, a parenthetical. In other words, that the house burned down is an afterthought not the main bit of information in the sentence.

"The house, which just so happened to have burned down, was my sister's."

or

"The house (which burned down) was my sisters."

See how meaning and structure go together?

## (5) Use commas to separate introductory words or expletives.

"My, what a beautiful hairdo you have!"

"Holy crap, that's a big wave."

"However, it is a good idea to let the food cool down before you eat it."

"Basically, I have no idea what you are talking about."

## (6) Use commas to separate out dependent clauses.

"If you go to the store, get some cat food."

"Because it is storming outside, you must wear your raincoat."

Note that if you wrote "If you go to the store" only, that would be an incomplete thought, thus it is a dependent clause as we talked about above. It has no meaning until you finish your thought. It's dependent like your cat is on you for food. Again, phrases become dependent or 'subordinate' when they are subordinated with a **subordinating conjunction**:

because, since, as, although, while, whereas, before, etc.

When you *add* a subordinating conjunction to a phrase, it becomes dependent, subordinate, on the rest of the sentence.

A complete sentence:

"Go to the store." (Note here that 'you' is implied). Since this is read as a command, it is called an imperative.

An incomplete sentence (dependent clause):

"If you go to the store."

To make these phrases complete, you need a comma.

"If you go to the store, get some cat food."
"It is raining outside, so you must wear your raincoat."

Note that if you reverse the order of the phrases, you do not need a comma:

"Get some cat food if you go to the store."
"You must wear your raincoat because it is storming outside."

**(7) Use commas when someone is speaking and you put their words in quotes.**

Dryer said, "I am so tired of going to the store for eggs."

Note that you do not necessarily need to use a comma when you are using a quote from a source.

Applegood stated that "we are better off than we were two years ago."

That's really about it for commas. Sure, there's other places like in addresses etc, but that should clear up some of the biggest confusions.

## Practice 4-2: Comma drama

*Okay, I said no worksheets but maybe a little practice finding and placing commas isn't such a bad idea.*

*1) Write an example (a new one, not a copy and paste job from the examples given) for each of the seven rules for comma usage, as well as the two rules for semicolon usage. State the rule and give an example. I really want you to get this.*

*2) Here's some writing with no commas or semicolons. Put 'em in!*

*The snowstorm came quickly so quickly it was like a dam burst in the sky. I wasn't prepared. All I had on were my regular old red Reebok tennis shoes striped socks and blue jeans but the snow drifts came in so powerfully they practically knocked you over if you tried to go outside.*

*"I don't know" I said looking through the shards of ice that had crawled up the window in minutes.*

*"You can't stay here" Ivan said. "My mom will kill me she still calls you the 'bad influence'."*

*"Can I borrow your boots?" I said.*

*I only have one pair he said.*

*It looked like it was me and the storm. I looked Ian up and down. He just shrugged. Sure shrug all you want. You don't have to go out in this horrible horrible storm. You don't have to walk 2 miles the sleet driving through your wet shirt and into your bone marrow. No you get to curl up by the fire with some hot cocoa and maybe cuddle up with Chauncey the orange white and rather fat kitty cat. I thought we were friends apparently not.*

## Why so tense?

Students struggle with tenses. Yes, we all are pretty clear about past, present, and future, but you might not notice when you accidentally slip from one to the other while you are writing.

You aren't the only one.

The easiest fix for most tense issues is to proofread. Go back and make sure that you are consistent throughout. A common issue is to switch tenses when you start to talk about action. If you are writing a story, it is usually in the past tense because it already happened. But, as you are describing what happened, you may get so absorbed in telling your story that you feel like you are there again, and you switch to present tense. So, actually, switching tenses is a sign that you are really involved in writing your story! However, you still need to go back and fix it so that you don't confuse your readers.

That said, a review of tenses is probably a good idea. So, here goes…

Remember that verbs are the action of a sentence, and their *infinitive* form starts with "to." Like "to go," or "to sit." Well, when you use action verbs, you can indicate through them what time a particular action took place: in the past, present, or future.

"I went to the store."
"I go to the store."
"I will go to the store."

However, there is more than just past, present, and future tense. Above are the "simple" forms of each tense. But past, present, and future can actually be broken down into 4 forms: simple, continuous, perfect, and perfect continuous.

Oh boy.

A note about the "perfect" tense. Does this mean it is the best tense? No. It is called "perfect" because it comes from Latin "perfectus" which means "completed, achieved, finished." So, when thinking about perfect tenses, they are ones that have "had" in them. In other words, you "had done" the action.

Instead of trying to memorize each of these, I find it makes more sense to think of all the tenses on a timeline. Past is on the left, present in the middle, and future on the right. As we move from left to right, we move through all the forms of the tenses.

---

| Past | Present | Future |

Now let's zoom into just one section and break that down into its four forms.

————————————————PAST————————————————

| Perfect | Perfect Continuous | Simple | Continuous |
| had walked | had been walking | walked | was walking |

78

## Past Perfect = Two things finished in the past.

Example: "I had walked to the store when I realized that I forgot my grocery list."

Past Perfect is the farthest back in time. Why? Because you are saying that two different things happened in the past:

1) you had walked to the store
2) you realized that you forgot your grocery list

In other words, you had already finished walking to the store and then you realized that you forgot your list. When you use "had" before a past tense "walked," you are stating two frames of time: first, you walked to the store, **then** you realized that you didn't have your list. The walking occurred farther back in time than the realization, so in this sentence you are referring to two moments in the past.

Another example: "I had already run all the way to school when I realized that I forgot my shoes."

## Past Perfect Continuous = Was doing something when...

Example: "I had been walking to the store when I realized that I forgot my list."

The past perfect progressive isn't as far back in time. Why? Because you were still doing one action when the second happened. Above, the first action was completed: you had finished walking. In the past perfect progressive tense, you were still walking when you realized you forgot your list, thus this is not as far back in time.

## Simple past = one point in the past.
Example: "I walked to the store last night."

Here, you are talking about last night as the past, and you have already completed the task. Question: "What did you do last night?" Answer: "I walked to the store."

## Past Continuous = was happening then...

Example: "I was walking to the store when you called."

Here, you are talking about something that was happening last night. This might be in answer to a question "Where were you last night when I called?" Answer: "I was walking to the store." Unlike simple past, it indicates that you were doing an action at a time in the past, rather than completed an action at a time in the past. You are answering a question of "what were you doing?" as opposed to "what did you do?" as above in the simple past.

―――――――――PRESENT―――――――――

| Perfect | Perfect Continuous | Simple | Continuous |
|---|---|---|---|
| have walked | have been walking | walk | walking |

**Present Perfect:**

Example: "I have walked five miles."

Notice that since it is a perfect tense, it has "have" in it since "perfectus" means finished. Notice the slight difference between this and past perfect. In past perfect, you "had walked," in present perfect you "have walked." "Had" is in the past, "have" is in the present.

You may walk another mile, or you may quit. But at this moment, you have walked five miles.

**Present Perfect continuous:**

Example: "I have been walking for five miles and I still am."

Since it is continuous it is ongoing.

**Present continuous:**

Example: "I am walking."

This is presently happening at this moment. It doesn't mean that you always walk, but that you are walking right now.

**Simple present:**

Example: "I walk."

This is present tense, but it doesn't mean it is happening at this very second. Confused? Simple present tense actually means that it is something that you do.

## Practice 4-3: Tense Forms

*Now that you've seen how to make the four forms of the past tense and present tenses, it's your turn to do the same with the future tense. Do this for the example above and add to your blog.*

Let's look at an excerpt from John Updike's *Rabbit, Run,* which is written in the present tense:

Boys are playing basketball around a telephone pole with a backboard bolted to it....The scrape and snap of Keds on loose alley pebbles seems to catapult their voices high into the moist March air blue above the wires. Rabbit Angstrom, coming up the alley in a business suit, stops and watches, though he's twenty-six and six three. So tall, he seems an unlikely rabbit, but the breadth of white face, the pallor of his blue irises, and a nervous flutter under his brief nose as he stabs a cigarette into his mouth partially explain the nickname, which was given to him when he too was a boy. He stands there thinking, the kids keep coming, they keep crowding you up.

## Practice 4-4: Editing Tenses

*Since we have an example of Updike's prose all in present tense above, let's assume that, as an editor, you've decided that his story should be in past tense. So, rewrite the the paragraph all in past tense and post.*

## Parallel Construction

Parallel construction means that you have created a sentence where each adjective or adverb has the same form. The best way to understand this is through an example:

"I work quickly, quietly, and efficiently."

Here, the **stem verb** is "work," so each of the adverbs that modify the verb need to match so that each could be its own sentence.

1) "I work quickly."
2) "I work quietly."
3) "I work carefully."

Example of non-parallel construction: "I work quickly and am careful."

Looks okay? Nope. It's confusing. What this sentence is really saying is:

1) "I work quickly."
2) "I work am careful."

Again, remember, when you are writing about multiple actions, you need to go back to the **stem verb,** in this case "I work," to make sure that each item in the list of actions matches the stem.

If all the actions in the list don't actually have the same verb, they need to have the same verb form.

Example of non-parallel construction: "I watched television and then was listening to the radio."

Again, seems okay, but it cold be better. Using parallel construction, you want the two actions "watch," and "listening" to match.

Fixed: "I watched television and then listened to the radio."

### Practice 4-5: Parallel Construction

*Okay, now your turn. Try to fix up some of these sentences so that they have parallel construction.*
*1) Henry enjoys walking, running, and to ride his bicycle.*
*2) Sung-ho goes shopping, then walks, and finally to swim.*
*3) Louie listens to records, tapes, and watching television.*
*4) The salesperson was expecting to make a sale, earn a commission, and questions would be asked about his sales for the day.*
*5) I have learned a lot of grammar, punctuation, and looking up information on the internet.*

### Sentence Boundaries and Comma Splices

Now let's look at sentence boundaries. Knowing when a sentence should stop and a new one should start is a sentence boundary. You might have heard of the term "comma splice." This is when you "splice" (connect) two sentences together with a comma instead of separating them.

Example of a sentence with a comma splice:
"I have been working here for seven months, I can't stand my boss at all!"
Do you see why it is a comma splice? These are two complete thoughts. They are related, so there are multiple ways to fix it.

1) Coordinating conjunction: "I have been working here for seven months, and I can't stand my boss at all."
2) Semicolon: "I have been working here for seven months; I can't stand my boss at all."
3) Two sentences: "I have been working here for seven months. I can't stand my boss at all."

Here's an example from a very talented writer in my class, Makaio Lawley:

"10-year-old me was sitting in the back of my moms van in the cushy seats at 6:30 in the morning, barely awake with the heaters on full blast, the inside of the car windows still foggy from it, I was wrapped up in a blanket still shivering, although I was wearing a hoodie, sweatpants and a beanie."

This is an awesome sentence! Kind of reminds me of Kerouac! But there's a comma spice in there. Do you see it? Here's an edit with proper sentence boundaries:

"10-year-old me was sitting in the back of my mom's van in the cushy seats at 6:30 in the morning, barely awake with the heaters on full blast, the inside of the car windows still foggy from the morning dew. I was wrapped up in a blanket, but still shivering although I was wearing a hoodie, sweatpants, and beanie."

The point of sentence boundaries is to make sure that each thought is complete and connects properly to the other thoughts. I like how Lawley here wrote the nice, long compound sentence "10-year-old me was sitting in the back my mom's van in the cushy seats at 6:30 in the morning, barely awake with the heaters on full blast, the inside of the car windows still foggy from it." It is very visceral, so we can see and feel the writer's situation. So here, all I did was add a required apostrophe on "mom's" for "mom's van" because it is her van, not the van of multiple moms. Then I added a period instead of a comma after "foggy from it." The newly-created second sentence needed a bit more work. We have a blanket he was wrapped in, as well as the hoodie, sweatpants, and beanie, yet he was still shivering. I elected to leave the writer's voice more intact and just add words to make the sentence read a bit more fluidly. I added the coordinating conjunction "but" with its required comma since it makes clear that even though he was wrapped up in a blanket, he was still shivering. I cut the comma before "although" because it wasn't needed, since subordinating conjunctions only need commas if they are at the front of a sentence, not at the end.

Another, and perhaps clearer version, would be:

"Although I was wrapped up in a blanket, wearing a hoodie, sweatpants and a beanie, I was still shivering."

However, note that some of the spark has gone from this latter rewrite. It is 'proper,' yet it is less exciting to read. So, again, think of the 'rules' as strong suggestions that will often help your writing, but following all the rules does not make good writing. Yes, you know what I'm going to say here.

Passion and engagement make good writing.

## Apostrophes

A few other things to look for in your and your peer's writing. Look for the use of apostrophes. They are used on two occasions: to make a contraction and to show possession.

Example of a contraction: "That is" = "That's"

Example of possession: "Ellie's ball" = Ellie owns the ball.

Example of plural possessive: "The teams' uniforms" = the uniforms that the team owns.

## Quotation Marks

When someone speaks in a narrative, you need a new paragraph:

"Hey Ted, how's it going?"

"Great," said Kai. "I just got my football scholarship."

"Gee that's super."

A big question that comes up is: when do you need to put a comma when using quotation marks?

I'm glad you asked.

When someone is talking and you use their name or a pronoun (he, she, I, they…) use a comma.

Example: "Great," said Kai. "I just got my football scholarship."

Example: In the article, Torres says, "Quotations are awesome."

When you are writing your own words and then you need to "add a quote," you don't need to put a comma before it.

Example: The study said that "four out of five dentists recommend our product."

We will go into more details about sources and how to quote sources in the next chapter.

## There, They're, Their

There still seems some confusion about the three different ways to spell this word and when to do so. I know, sometimes it just comes out wrong even when you know the rules. I've done it. But, just to be sure, here are the rules:

There = in that place.
Look over there.

Their = the things that they own.
Those dolls are theirs.

They're = contraction of "they are"
They're going to be late to school.

## More on Writing for your Audience

A formal academic paper filled with slang and curse words would be off-putting, and moreover, it would communicate to the reader that you aren't taking the subject seriously. It would be unprofessional and land you with a very poor grade. Likewise, a grant proposal for developing a new app that was written sloppily and with poor grammar and slang would communicate to the CEO that you aren't to be trusted.

Likewise, an email to a professor like this is inappropriate: "hey Larry so when's the paper due?"

Think of your audience. Be the more formal version of yourself to show respect and make yourself seem more credible. This will go a long way in the working world. In England, where I did a lot of my education, emails are very formal:

Dear Professor Langstrom,

I cannot locate on the syllabus when the next paper is due. Could you please let me know the date and time so that I can plan accordingly?

Many Thanks,

Oswald

In America, we aren't quite as formal, but you should still lean more toward formality than overly familiar, even if you believe the professor is rather laid back. When you are more formal you communicate quite a bit about how you respect the professor's time and all the work they put in to help you get a good education.

## Works Cited

Casagrande, June. *It was the best of sentences, it was the worst of sentences."* New York: Random House, 2010. Print.

Chaucer, Jefferey. *The Canterbury Tales*. New York: Penguin Classics, 2005. Print.

Graff, Gerald and Birkenstein, Cathy. *They Say/I Say: The Moves That Matter in Academic Writing.* Chicago: Norton. 2017. Print

Kerouac, Jack. *The Dharma Bums.* New York: Penguin Classics, 1971. Print.

Thurman, Susan. *The Only Grammar Book You'll Ever Need."* Massachusetts: F+M Media, 2003. Print.

# CHAPTER FIVE
## *Quotes Don't Talk*

Take a look at the following examples of student writing using quotes. Which is correct and which are incorrect?

1) "Every human existence is a life in search of a narrative." This quote implies that humans use narrative in order to define themselves...

2) The quote "every human existence is a life in search of a narrative" says that humans use narrative in order to define themselves...

3) The article says, "every human existence is a life in search of a narrative."

4) Richard Kearney, in his book *On Stories*, writes that "every human existence is a life in search of a narrative." Here, he asserts that humans use narrative in order to define themselves...

They may all seem correct, so what's the difference? Many students use the first three quite often, but think about it logically. Which one gives credit to the author? Which one makes the most logical sense?

Number 4. Why? Because Kearney is the one who says it. Not the article, not the quote, but the author.

When you use quotes, you are taking thoughts that others have had and then reacting to them. You use them as springboards to think further about ideas. As such, calling something a "quote" in your paper is technically incorrect. It is an assertion, a claim, a statement, a thought... by a real person who you need to credit.

Think of writing as a form of speaking. It is a communication from the speaker to the listener, but it takes place on the page. So, instead of writing "the paper says," or "the quote says," it is "the author says."

There are several ways we can talk about what someone has written. We can summarize their article or book, stating their main points or their key ideas or even their main argument. We can paraphrase sections of their writing, or we can use direct quotations from their writing.

In most academic papers, you will do all of the above.

Much of the purpose of your essay writing in college is to process and then evaluate what you've read and viewed and discussed. It is, as I've stated many times already, writing to think. If you want to get passing grades on your papers in college, you will usually need to show your thinking, not just regurgitate facts. You need to work with sources and *react* to them. Reacting to your reading doesn't mean just using quotes to show that you've done the reading. It means entering a dialogue with your sources, stating if you agree or disagree with their assertions and why. It is using summary so that the reader knows what the source is about and discussing who wrote it and why they are credible.

Much of this will be covered in chapter 7 on academic writing. In this chapter, I want to clarify something that students often struggle with as illustrated by the examples that opened the chapter: how to actually incorporate quotes, and summaries, into your writing.

In the next chapter, you will be asked to write a paper about your college experience. Specifically, it will be a paper wherein you reflect on what difficulties you are having adjusting to college life. You will do research to find some answers and be expected to integrate that research into a paper about your own experience in a fluid way.

You will be asked to refer to your sources in almost every paper you will write in college because while your opinion is valuable, it is only valid if you can back it with data. You can't just write anything and call it true just because you wrote it. We live in a society where the scientific method rules the way we think because for something to be true it must be repeatable.

## The Hit and Run Quote vs. Quote Sandwich

Many students use what Graff and Birkenstein, in their text *They Say/I Say*, call a "hit and run" quote. This is where the student has been told to "use quotes," so they go to the text, grab a sentence, copy and paste that sucker into their essay, and then they are out of there. Like a hit and run.

Example of a hit and run quote:

Humans are interesting creatures. "Every human existence is a life in search of a narrative" (Kearny 7). They also really care about bonding...

Notice how the writer above drops the quote in and lets it speak for itself, not introducing it nor analyzing it afterwards.

It is a 'hit and run.'

Instead, use a 'quote sandwich.'

When using thoughts, ideas, or statements from authors that are on paper or on the internet, aka 'quotes,' we need to put them in context. Assume that the reader of your essay has not read your sources, so you need to tell us enough about the source so that we understand why you decided to use those exact words to enhance what *you* are trying to say. When someone has your back, they can't just be anyone. They have to be respected, interesting, and contribute to your discussion. It is a conversation, not just evidence that you read the source you are using. You are entering a conversation with the other author's ideas, synthesizing them to create a new piece of work.

A quote sandwich means you give us context for why you will use the statement from the source. What is your point? So, you need to start with *your* thinking before we move to the source. Then, who is this person who is going to have your back? Why should we trust them?

When you first introduce a source, tell the reader some or all of the following:

1) Who they are. Name, job title, organization, etc.

2) Name of the article or book

3) Brief summary of what the article or book was about. This can be just a sentence or two. What was their research? What is their focus? What is their point?

4) How the author's work relates to your work.

5) A specific quote that really backs up the point you are making in that paragraph.

6) Your analysis of the quote and the author's ideas in general. State it in your own words. Say how it furthers your discussion. This should be the majority of your paragraph.

However, before you move on to using sources, you need to start with your own independent thoughts. Then, you need to introduce and then subsequently explain why a source should be trusted. If you just say "According to Jones, blah blah blah..." the reader will likely be wondering who the heck this Jones character is and why they should believe what they say is valid. Think of your source as someone you are bringing on a stage to talk about their research. You wouldn't let them just randomly walk up to the mike, spew one line, drop the mike and walk away, right? It wouldn't make any sense to the audience. Before allowing your source on stage, you would give a short introduction stating their qualifications, so the audience has some context as to why your source should be trusted. That's the key idea here; context.

Then, and only then, can you use your quote.

Be sure you finish your quote sandwich by tying together your initial point with the quote you used so that we now see why you used it. What does it add to your discussion? Moreover, you might be best off starting by stating what the quote means by using the words, "in other words." Define the quote in your own words so that it is clear how you interpret and integrate it into your own ideas.

Let's take a look at a paragraph from Brandon Acuna Embriz. This is an extract from page 151 of my text *Crossing the Threshold: Student Essays.*

He writes:

In the article "The Dumbing of America" by Susan Jacoby, she introduces the topic of adults reading much less. Using information reported by the National Endowment for the Arts, she reports "in 1982, 82 percent of college graduates read novels or poems for pleasure; two decades later, only 67 percent did" (6). We can connect this to the growing usage of technology, but we cannot blame the people. As technology grows, people build an interest for it. They start to wonder how to use it, play with all the features and they tell their friends about it. The interest keeps growing, and people forget about casual reading of simple ink on paper…

Notice how Embriz states who wrote the article, what the article was about, why the data is valid, and then jumps off the quote he pulled to think about why there is this massive drop in college students' reading habits over two decades.

## Practice 5-1: Quote Sandwich

*Take a look at these examples and improve them by using the quote sandwich as described above.*

*I have often thought that you need to pace yourself and take breaks while you are studying. "With all this hard work happening outside of class time, it's important to make sure students take proper study breaks." You also need to go on walks to get your blood flowing….*

*What is wrong with the way the student used this quote?*

*Yes, it is a hit and run quote, sort of the worst kind. It may seem okay logically; the quote itself does indeed add to the argument, but we have no idea who said it, and then the writer just moves on to the next point without processing it for the reader. It is a classic hit and run quote.*

*Okay, now I'll give you the source: Google "Study Break Tips and Oxford Learning." The direct web address is:*

   *https://www.oxfordlearning.com/study-break-tips/*

*How would you write it so that the reader has all the information they need and the paragraph flows better?*

*Here's another one:*

*The quote "Making the decision to work while in college is not a decision that should be made without understanding fully how that may impact your experience" is right on point. As a college student, you already have a lot of work to do. College should be your top priority, but if you need money, you may not have a choice…*

*What are the problems here?*

*Google "Pros and cons of working while in college" and "Ashford." Here's the source: https://www.ashford.edu/online-degrees/student-lifestyle/the-pros-and-cons-of-working-while-in-college*

*Now, rewrite the paragraph using the guidance outlined above. What elements are missing? How can you make the reader understand more about the source? And yes, how can you prove that you actually read the article rather than simply did a Google search, found a line, copied and pasted, and moved on?*

When using quotes, you can certainly write "Sanchez said", but it is better if you can be more specific. Are they arguing a point? Then write "Sanchez argues that..." Are they making a claim? "Sanchez claims..." or "Sanchez asserts..." Is she theorizing? Then "Sanchez posits..."

You can also write so that the writers argue with one another. If Montoya claims that "most errors in composition papers are made from lack of proofreading," but a study by Lawrence finds that the errors are actually due to lack of understanding grammatical principles, you can say that "Lawrence disagrees. According to her research..."

## P.I.E. Paragraphs

Another way to look at writing paragraphs is to use P.I.E. as a guideline. I think the people who came up with these must have been hungry. A P.I.E. paragraph is basically this: Point, Information, Explanation. This is a more general way of looking at constructing paragraphs. You start a paragraph by stating what the point is you will be discussing in this particular paragraph. After all, paragraphs are separated because they have a unity that ties them together. This is their point. You can think of them as idea chunks or even as 'scenes.' A paragraph is a bit different in an academic paper than in journalism and autobiography narrative. In narrative writing, including journalism, you differentiate paragraphs based more on emotion than on logic.

In academic papers, you want each paragraph to really hold some weight. And that weight consists of your point, the information that backs up your point (your quote sandwich, summary or paraphrasing) and then an explanation of how your research deepens your, and our (the reader's), understanding of the point you are making in the paragraph. Most of your paragraph should be your explanation. Your analysis makes it clear how the information you provided actually supports your beliefs.

I cannot emphasize this enough. Most of your writing should be your thinking. It should be your analysis. That is what you are here to do. So, be sure to read your sources carefully, and then take the time to integrate the ideas of the author with your own ideas. Then decide how to convey this new information to create a deeper understanding of the topic at hand.

Here's an example of a P.I.E. paragraph from The University of Nevada, Reno, written by Logan Miller. Miller has put his main point in bold, his information in italics, and his explanation is underlined.

**Jim is introduced through cinematic techniques that feminize him, which lays the foundation for the reclamation of his own masculinity.** *After the title card, the audience first see Jim through an extreme close-up of his face. His eye is closed, centered on screen. The next shot shows Jim lying on a hospital bed naked, his covers cast off. The following shots show extreme close-ups of his elbow, neck, shoulders, and back. As he rises, his body is obscured by plastic sheeting or partially hidden by medical equipment.* <u>These cinematic decisions result in Jim's feminization. By opening the scene on an eye, the film presents the possibility that the character might be female. While Jim's full body is revealed soon after, during most of this scene it is shot close or obscured behind detritus on set. Instead of Jim, we see parts of him. These obscuring and fragmenting techniques are identical to those used in film noir to eroticize and objectify female characters. By filming this scene using such techniques, audiences are</u>

given clues into Jim's feminization. In this way, the film sets the stage for Jim's masculine transformation near its conclusion.

Notice how the majority of the paragraph is Miller's analysis: the underlined part. You should aim for this type of balance in your writing as well. Introduce the point, provide information from your source, then analyze why this information proves your point.

## Practice 5-2 P.I.E. Paragraphs

*Your turn. Here's a paragraph from my student Lynnae Dumalo's essay responding to reading the essay "Mother Tongue" by Amy Tan. Can you find the Point, Information, and Explanation? Do the same as above to show which is Point (bold), Information (italics), and Explanation (underline) and post in your blog.*

She wrote:

I even tried hard myself to make sure that I didn't speak with an accent. I was afraid to speak Tagalog because I didn't want to sound "weird." Just like Arthur Chu said in his NPR article about broken English entitled "Breaking out the Broken English," he says "The 'Asian accent' tells the story of [Asian]-American assimilation in a nutshell. Our parents have the accent that white Americans perceive as the most foreign out of all the possible alternatives, so our choices is to have no accent at all," (Chu, Par. 13). I didn't want to be outcast by my white peers. Chu said it right when he said that we "react so viscerally" (Chu, Par. 14) to the taunting because "to attack our language, our ability to sound 'normal,' is to attack our ability to be normal. It's to attack everything we've worked for," (Chu, Par. 14). I always cringed at people who spoke a blend of English and Tagalog because

I saw it as trashy. It was like, you were somehow cooler if you only spoke English and if you spoke Tagalog it was fine- you just couldn't mix the two because it was like you didn't know what you were doing. Unfortunately now, I'm unable to confidently speak Tagalog and it's a regret I hold very strongly. Whenever I go home to visit my family in the Philippines, I feel a sense of disconnect from them. Because of the language barrier, I am unable to eloquently and accurately express myself to them.

## Quality of Sources

When you find sources, you need to be sure that they are valid. This means that they are from a reputable source. This can, of course, be a sticky subject. What is printed on any given website, even those of large corporations, may be affected by special interests. Always ask where their revenue is coming from. Advertisers. Any non-academic source would be foolish to print anything that puts their advertisers in a negative light because this could mean the loss of their contract and thus loss of revenue. So, always be aware that in a capitalist society, the dollar speaks quite a bit louder than perhaps it ought to. So, no, not all sources are objective. In fact, it seems that it is becoming harder and harder to find objectivity rather than opinion and argument, especially when it comes to controversial issues.

As we will discuss in the chapter on rhetorical writing, when someone has a point of view (which is practically always), they can find data that backs that point of view and either eliminate counterpoints from their discussion or discredit them by stating that the source isn't trustworthy. So-called 'right-wing' and 'left-wing' media are specifically catered to appeal to audiences with a particular political POV, so they report use rhetorical appeals so that they seem to be correct. This is, as I will discuss in chapter 8, the danger of rhetoric, and why so many issues seem to be so polarized.

Anything on social media needs to be questioned. Social media is filled with opinions. Facts are hard to come by. What someone posts on any social media platform needs to be scrutinized. If anyone can tweet anything, how can you know they aren't just making it up? Of course, you can look at the credibility of the person sending the tweet. But, regardless, social media is created to place opinion over fact, so should usually be only used if you are clear that you are looking for opinions from people with particular points of view and not for raw, factual data. Is this 100% true all the time? No. But it is a good rule of thumb.

This all is why academics turn to peer-reviewed academic journals. These journals are by and for the academic community whose goal is pure information. You can log in to your school's library to access these journals. At San Francisco State, we have a "One Search" system that allows you to find specific articles in academic journals by scholars in their fields. This is often considered really the only appropriate research for academic papers, especially in your upper division and definitely in your graduate level coursework.

However, a lot of these journals are written for specialists in their fields. Remember how we talked about discourse communities having their own language? Well, when you read these academic articles, which often seem to be bursting with Engfish, you may feel like you don't know what the hell they are talking about.

Unfortunately, too many academics believe that it is more important to show off how intelligent you seem by just gorging their writing with overly complicated words in order to sound smart. But, it is also true that your vocabulary does continue to grow throughout your life, and as you move through college and specialize in your field, a lot of this language actually makes the most sense - they use words that are more specific, more loaded with meaning. This is why, as you move into your specialties (aka your majors), a lot of what you learn will be the language, the actual vocabulary, of your specialty.

We will look at a little of this in the concluding chapters of this text - how to write in specific disciplines. No, you won't become an expert in one paper and a few readings, but it will allow you to sample some different genre conventions and more importantly *ideas* that are important in some of these fields. Who knows, maybe you'll even stumble upon something that you knew little about but grabs your fascination and won't let go.

Set up a discussion on your page. Read and understand your sources rather than skimming them. Be able to summarize their main points or conclusions, and be able to use specific statements, assertions, claims, data, theories, in order to deepen your discussion of a topic.

If some of you are thinking, "this is starting to sound a lot like the five-paragraph essay," be assured that it is not. I am not here arguing for using formulae for your essay. Each essay is its own unique creation. In fact, the term "essay," as coined by Michel de Montaigne, means "to attempt." An essay is a flexible, individual piece of writing crafted from the mind of the writer. However, whenever you use sources your reader will expect the above information. If you do not provide context for the quote you used, and then really discuss what it means in terms of your overall discussion in your paper, your readers may get lost or not believe that what you say in your essay is reliable or accurate.

## Appropriate Secondary Sources

Secondary sources are academic sources. These are essentially articles about the topic you are working on written by specialists in the field. These are not essays from any of those essay mill companies that are so ubiquitous on the internet. Whatever you do, don't use those. Sites such as 123HelpMe or freestudentessays.com are "cheater" websites who offer pre-written essays for money. If you refer to any website that has "student essays" in its title or says that it offers "student help" with essays, you are on a cheater website.

This is a huge problem, and not just if pay for a full essay. Some students think they can just use a sample from one of the free papers or portions of a free paper. This is plagiarism.

This includes Spark Notes or Cliff's Notes. These give quick easy answers without requiring you to even read the text. If I spend my day writing feedback on papers that are assembled from Spark Notes, I have just wasted all my time. You learn nothing, and my notes are meaningless because it isn't your thinking.

You are paying tuition in order to learn how to think critically and become a person of integrity and intelligence. You aren't paying for a piece of paper with your name on it that says to your future employers, "pay me more." So, using these websites undermines all of our efforts, so even if you are under a deadline and full of anxiety about getting work done – don't do it. A majority of your professors will give you an extension on the deadline if you really need it.

If you get caught plagiarizing in your paper, depending on your instructor, you can either get a firm warning, fail the paper, fail the class, or even get kicked out of school. I think many instructors overreact about plagiarism, but I also think that many students, most students, know that you shouldn't copy and paste off of the internet without citing your source. Any ideas you write must be your own, if ideas or words are from a source, just cite it. We want you to do this! This is part of the whole academic process. This is the discussion. If you have questions about plagiarism, do some research online and ask your instructors to clarify.

To find valid secondary sources, your best bet is going through your school's library webpage. To find out how to do this, go to your library or ask your instructor to show you how to use your particular school's library search feature. Through your school you can find and download hundreds of thousands of academic articles from JSTOR and other academic repositories.

Before you read a secondary text, read the title carefully. What do you think the article will be about? Make some guesses first. Activate your schema. What do you already know about the subject? What do you think will be covered? Where did you get these ideas?

Next, skim the work. If there are graphs, take a look at them and try to determine what they mean. Read the information and interpret it. Look at any headings. Look at topic sentences. Get as much of an overview of the work as you can before you start reading. Gather questions that you hope the reading answers. This way, you are already actively engaged with the text before you begin to read.

Find key points. Just like how you read to understand rhetorical devices, so too should you read secondary sources closely and critically. Look at how their argument unfolds. Do you believe their assertions? Does their evidence back up their claim?

You will, in a sense, be writing a 'claim' when you analyze a work of literature, as you saw above. You do your direct reading of the text, come up with some ideas, re-read the text and find the evidence that supports your thesis, do some research through secondary texts that back up and contradict your thesis, and then write your paper.

## Works Cited

Graff, Gerald and Birkenstein, Cathy. *They Say/I Say: The Moves That Matter in Academic Writing.* Chicago: Norton. 2017. Print

Miller, Logan. "PIE Paragraphs: A Model for Body Paragraphs" *University of Nevada, Reno.* March 6, 2014. Accessed January 4, 2019.

# CHAPTER SIX

## *Journal Article: College Life*

Back in the first few chapters, you spent some time reflecting on a moment in your life that was meaningful to you in some way. It is likely that you picked a specific story because it revealed some significant moment that marked a change of some sort: a change in perspective, a change in self-awareness, a change in location or friendships or beliefs. You were asked to start your story in 'an ordinary world' where things were the way they usually are on any given day, but then something happened that pushed you into an 'extraordinary world,' a new experience that challenged you. You faced obstacles and learned something about yourself or your world and are now compelled to tell people about this journey.

Whether you've come to college from far away or are living at home with your parents and attending a local school, you have indeed 'crossed the threshold' into an 'extraordinary world' of college. Things here are decidedly different than in high school. You may be on your own for the first time, living with roommates who you've just met, or perhaps you've found a place with some friends, or have a studio apartment, or like I said, are still living with your parents. You've likely found that regardless of your living situation, the workload you find yourself under is overwhelming. You may have had ideas of what college would be like from television or movies, or from older siblings who have gone before you. You may indeed be the first one in your family ever to come to college. It's not like in high school where you saw the same familiar faces in every class or passing in the hall or at lunch. Here, everyone has a different schedule. You likely don't have many people in more than one class together. It may feel isolating and overwhelming. If you are like most freshmen, you are having doubts about your choice to come to college. Maybe you aren't ready? Maybe you should work for a year or two? Maybe you chose the wrong major? Maybe you just aren't smart enough or strong enough or brave enough?

All these feelings are perfectly normal. I know, banal platitudes like Wallace says in his speech. Saying that feeling depressed and isolated and overwhelmed (as many of my students have reported to me and indeed how I felt when I went away to college) is normal is like shouting out to a drowning person, "Hey, don't worry, panicking when you are drowning is perfectly normal!"

But what can we do about it? Surprise, surprise, I'm going to suggest you write about it. Not only can you write about your feelings in this strange new world, you can also go to others and ask their advice. You can explore and join clubs to find others with similar interests to yours. What is most important is that you find a community. Some colleges have this built-in; they make an effort to gather students together and put you in cohorts so that you get to know each other and feel like you have a new family. Others, many others, are made up of a diverse student body who often commute to campus, work part-time or full-time jobs, and so on, which can lead to a more isolated and fragmented college experience.

## Practice 6-1: College Life Free-write

*For 20 minutes, free-write about your experiences so far in college. Take this time to vent your frustrations, if you are having them. What are the things that are the most difficult for you? What do you wish you could change? What is the most surprising about your first month of college life?*

*Start a new blog page titled "College Life." Enter your free-write, but only enter what you choose to share with the public.*

*In class, get together in groups and talk about what you've written, but again, only share what you feel comfortable sharing. You will certainly find others who have had the same feelings, the same doubts, the same frustrations. Next, talk about what you might do to improve your situation. What do you need to accept about your situation and what can you actually change to make it better? Remember, the hero on their journey makes internal changes (changes in belief or understanding) rather than, or in addition to, external changes (destroying the Death Star). Finding ways of seeing things differently, as Wallace posits, is often the key to success.*

Vicki Nelson, on college parent central, writes that going to college can be a 'culture shock.' This might seem like a strange idea to you. We usually think of the term 'culture' as somehow related to race or ethnicity or location (southern culture etc). Or, you may be familiar with the term 'sub-culture' and think of different sub-groups or even 'cliques' in high school.

So, what is a 'culture?'

A culture is essentially a group of people who have similar ways of seeing the world, of behaving in the world. When you are immersed in your home culture, that in which you grew up, you just think of this as 'the way things are' or as 'normal.' When you encounter people with different approaches to the world, who have different priorities or values, you may have thought of those cultures as 'different' or even 'weird.' Again, this is normal. I know, I know! Not helpful. But think about it. You walk around with a set of assumptions about what is right and wrong. Many of these we can agree on as universal truths, and many of us will turn to our families or our faiths about how we are supposed to interact in the world. This is indeed the goal of growing up. Through family, school, religion, sports, music etc, we learn how to belong.

Often, but certainly not always, we have grown up in a specific place for much of our childhoods. We know our neighborhoods. We know our friends. We watch the same youtubers, the same movies, the same sporting events. We talk about the same things, think about relationships and family in similar ways, and so on. But, even within our home culture there were certainly differences in opinion, differences in beliefs. Perhaps we even moved around a lot as children and thus experienced many different cultures growing up, and so already know that when you change cultures you yourself change a bit in order to fit in.

While there might have been a broad, general culture in which you grew up, you also certainly noticed that you have a family culture that is unique to your own family. Certain sayings and beliefs - even that 'dinner is at 6:30,' whereas your friend may have always had dinner at 7:30 - are specific to your own family's culture. You have certain shared stories about loved ones, certain beliefs about marriage, and social and family roles, that are uniquely your own. You may have friends who came from another country, or perhaps you yourself, or your parents, were immigrants. When you've 'crossed the threshold' into any new culture's space, you've had to negotiate your own feelings of difference.

Henri Tajfel, a Polish social psychologist, has worked extensively on social identity theory, which boils down to 'in-groups' and 'out-groups' (McLeod). Think about these terms for a moment. What do you think he means by 'in-group?' What about an 'out-group?' Tajfel says that we seek out others who are similar to us, form an alliance with them, and doing so helps us understand ourselves. Ernest Becker says that we use language to define ourselves as separate from others and the world. Self-esteem comes from our contributions to our groups. Tajfel extends this argument and agrees with Becker; we do indeed use our sense of belonging in our groups, our cultures, to define us and give us self-esteem. Think about how you might gather together as fans of a particular sports team, or type of music, or even country: "The Pittsburgh Steelers are the best football team in the world!" When we say that "we" are better than "them," we feel better about ourselves. This has the unfortunate side effect of making "them" out to be worse than ourselves, and is the birth of stereotyping and racism.

When we come to college, we are coming to a new culture. This might be readily apparent if you've moved to a new city or state or even country to come to college, but it is equally true even if you have decided to go to your local college. Here, not only is the community likely made up of a diverse set of voices, perhaps far more diverse

111

than that of your local high school, it also has its own culture: the culture of academia. And, of course, each university has its own culture as well. Much to adjust to!

## Practice 6-2: Culture Shock

*Go to collegeparentcentral.com and read Vicki Nelson's article "The Culture Shock of Adjusting to College." What in this article rings true for you? What do you think the author is missing? Does it bother you that the article is written for parents rather than for you? Does this change your feelings about what is stated in the article? Is there anything written here that gives you that "aha!" moment? Anything surprising or informative? Add to your blog.*

## A Note on Using Wikipedia

Wikipedia has a bad reputation in academic circles. You may have been told that you can never use Wikipedia as a reference in your papers. I agree and disagree. Wikipedia is a fantastic starting point in your research, but should rarely be where you stop. If you are using it to clarify ideas, learn basics and importantly, find solid sources, Wikipedia is great. Just make sure that when you use it, the sources are cited and that those sources are credible. You'll note in a Wikipedia article that there are superscript numbers next to claims. If you click on those numbers, the article will jump down to the source where the information was taken. If it is a credible source (and we will talk much more about how to determine this later in the book), then by all means use that information. If, however, there is a superscript that says "citation needed," a claim has been made that has no source attached to it, so cannot be substantiated. In other words, someone has written down their thoughts or understanding of an idea, but have not stated where they got the information from - they lack evidence for their statement - so it cannot be trusted as true. This is the weakness of Wikipedia and why academics never use it in their works, but if you know how to use the resource, it can be quite valuable.

## Discourse Communities

A term that some people use that is similar to culture is "discourse community." This is often attributed to John Swales, who defines it as a community of people who act and speak according to a set of implicit and/or explicit rules. Your family is a discourse community. Your friends are another. You communicate differently with your friends than you do with your family. If you have a job, there are certainly specific rules of communication and behavior that apply there that are different than with your friends or at home. For example, if you are a waiter, you walk up to the table and introduce yourself formally, and perhaps state what the specials are for the day. If you did this to your family or friends, they would think you were weird. "Hello, I'm Javier, I'll be your friend for today. Our specials are talking about Chelsea and eating Chinese take-out."

## Practice 6-3: Your Discourse Communities

*Think about all the different discourse communities you belong to. In your blog, write about how you act and speak differently depending on which community you are currently in. Use examples of how you would talk about your day with each community. Use your different voices to show different parts of your personality that you like to accentuate in each community. Then, think about why you alter your identity for different situations. What are you trying to convey through these subtle changes? Are you trying to fit in to a certain set of expectations: "good friend" or "good employee" or even "fun and nice person" or "strong and powerful person?" Finally, write about a time when you first began a new job, or a new school, and how it was disorienting and perhaps a bit frustrating. Tie this together with the concept of discourse community.*

Okay, Let's get to the task at hand for this chapter: a journalistic essay about college life.

For the full-length essay in this section, we are going to look at the genre of journalism, learn some of the rules of the genre including structure, voice, research, and conducting interviews, and use it to discover how juniors and seniors made it through their tough adjustment to this new discourse community of college. You will find that this genre is very similar to that of narrative. You will begin by writing about your personal experience coming to college and/or that of someone you know (even just a hypothetical someone) who is having a difficult time finding their groove in this new world, and then seek out mentors to help you out. But you aren't just writing this for yourself, your audience is anyone and everyone who is entering college for the first time. You are a pioneer, a trail blazer, for those who will come after you. So, being the first to cross the threshold into college life, you seek out allies (friends, groups, interviewees) and find ways around your enemies (fear, doubt, loneliness, anxiety, homesickness…) so that you can return with the elixir of knowledge - how to survive your first semester of college. And hopefully not only survive, but maybe actually even enjoy.

Now that you've written about some of the difficulties you are having with adjusting to college life and demands, let's go online and see what others have already written. The purpose of our reading here will be twofold: one, to get advice we can use for our own articles in the form of ideas and quotes, and two, to get to understand the genre of journal article or 'op-ed' piece. As you read, note how the author's voice comes through, how they use their own experiences and central question, and then how they interweave their sources, both written and through interviews.

## Practice 6-4: Voice

*Find the article "I've Been In College For One Week And I Hate It!" by Carlota Zimmerman on Huffington Post.*

*Read the article through to the end. Make some notes about her voice. Note that this piece is completely Zimmerman's opinion. She does not interview anyone or seek out expert advice, but her voice is clear as day. Too clear? What do you think of her voice here? Find some quotes and talk about how you can 'hear' her through her words. Note where she breaks grammar conventions. She uses a lot of sentence fragments. Like this. And she uses other non-standard English writing like: \*Shifty eyes.\**

Use this article as one of your references, or not. Look through the HuffPost College Life website and browse the articles. Read a few. Note that some are much more specific than others. Right now, I see an article called "What All First-Generation College Students Must Know" by Christina Berchini. That sounds interesting. Here's another: "Creating Positive Energy in the College

Dorm." Hmmm. Seems like most of these articles are offering advice.

Berchini started with a simple, straight-forward question: "What should first-generation college students know to be successful?" then did some research about the topic, and then wrote the answer: "What All First-Generation College Students Must Know." I'm guessing that Berchini is a first-generation college student, so her article will probably start with that premise. That will be her 'ordinary world.' Then, she will probably set out to discover what she learned as a first-gen student, and hopefully reached out to other first gen students who have already succeeded, and is now sharing their advice. Note: I wrote all of this before clicking on the article. We call this 'priming the pump' or more fancifully 'activating schema' (discussed below).

Now, load up the article by Berchini and read along with me. The following will make much more sense that way.

Okay, so now I click on the article and what is the first sentence? "I began my college career behind the eight ball." She starts with her own personal, passionate investment in the topic. She then writes, "...Like many of you - I was the first in my family to attend college." Here, we see how she directly addresses the reader, "you," in her piece. She knows who she is, why she is writing the article, and who her intended reader is.

Okay, now read the rest of the article.

Note how she blends narrative in here. She puts us in that first moment she walked into her dorm and uses dialogue, like you did when you wrote your autobiographical essays. She brings us to the moment where she was about to quit: "Maybe I'm just not meant to go to college, I remember thinking, in tears." We are hooked, we keep reading. Why? Because there are stakes here. She is sharing her personal experience and we can relate. "Oh my god, that's just like my experience!" The personal taps into the universal. It's like we are having a conversation with her.

She compares her expectations of high school work to that of college. She realizes that success in high school was about memorization, but in college she "actually had to think." This is similar to what David Foster Wallace talks about college in his speech that we read and listened to in the introductory chapter.

She states that the toughest part was feeling like she didn't belong. In other words, adjusting to this new discourse community. She then relates college to learning a new language. She writes, "some people are lucky enough to grow up having several different languages under their belt. Other people, however, are tasked with learning a new language - in this case, the language of college" (Berchini). We know that different discourse communities have different ways of communicating, so are, in a sense, different 'languages.' Berchini notes that as a first generation student, she didn't already have this 'language' since no one in her family had experience in this discourse community, so it felt more difficult for her to adjust and 'learn the language' of college.

## On Reading: Activating Schema

Why do we want to 'activate schema' or 'prime the pump' and what the heck is it? According to Ellin Oliver Keene and Susan Zimmerman in *Mosaic of Thought* (1997), schema is simply "prior knowledge." When you start with what you already know about a subject, you can make predictions about your reading. Then, you can determine what is missing from your knowledge about the subject, and thus form questions you hope the reading will answer. When you go into your reading with questions in hand, you are actively reading. You are engaged, searching, and analyzing rather than simply passively reading.

You can use KWL as a way to structure your reading of any source. KWL is an acronym for:
1) Know
2) Want to Know
3) Learned

You can make a chart for each of your readings. What do you know? Write a brief paragraph about what you already know, or assume, about the subject at hand. Then, formulate questions that you want answered. Finally, after reading, write a quick summary of what you learned in your own words. When you process your reading through reflection you will make connections back to your original beliefs and process the information in a much more integrated and efficient way than if you didn't go through this process.

You've probably heard that old drill: first, look at the title, then scan the article. What do you think it will be about? What do you already know about the subject? What are the assumptions you bring to it? What questions do you believe will be answered by reading the article? Being mindful of schema as you approach any reading, you can think not only about what the article or essay might be about, but what you bring to it as a reader. Again, remember those 'gaps' we talked about that you fill as a reader that Wolfgang Iser talks about? Well, you fill the gaps with your schema.

## Engfish

A problem for many freshman writers is focusing too much on trying to sound "important" or "scholarly." Should you expand your vocabulary? Absolutely. Should you try to write according to the conventions of the particular discipline and be influenced by other writers in that discipline? Again, you bet. That is part of learning the language of any discourse community. But be careful not to focus on trying to sound smart and losing that core voice that is indeed truly you. Your voice will grow and change through time and reading. Don't force it. It will happen naturally. Instead, focus on being concrete and real, not dressing up your prose trying to impress everyone. Write about complex matters in a clear way, not simple matters in a complex way. Now might be a time to introduce the topic of Engfish. No, that's not a typo.

## Practice 6-5: Engfish

*Google "The Poisoned Fish" by Ken Macrorie. Read the article. What is Engfish? Not English, EngFish. How do we avoid it in our writing, according to Macrorie? Write a blog response to the article. Where have you used Engfish in the past? Why? Write a sentence in Engfish and then translate it to non-Engfish. Talk about the difference.*

## Practice 6-6: Reading as a Writer

*Now it's time to read all the student essays in the appendix on College Life. Choose your favorite essay and analyze it for both content and structure. Read as a writer. In other words, read the essays to learn how to write about college life and to get ideas that spark that "Hey, that's what I'm going through!" moment. Note that the essays in the text do not incorporate interviews as I will ask you to do for your own essays.*

*Be prepared to discuss the essay in groups. Write your general observations in your blog: how is it structured? What sentences are particularly powerful? What can you use here in your own writing?*

When we first read something, it is all new material. We won't remember a lot of it. We don't really understand the essay as a whole until we finish it. But once we've gone through and finished it, and now know where we are going, we can go back and re-read (if we re-write, shouldn't we re-read?) and see *how* the writer got us there.

This is a key point, so I will re-state it. When we read something the second time, we can better analyze it as writers and look closely at how the writer crafted their essay. Since we know what the content is from the first read, we can concentrate more on form in the second. We can look at word choice, sentence structure, paragraph structure, and overall flow. We can use the writer, in other words, as a mentor for our own writing.

Your goal in this next essay is to write a journal article that will help you and other incoming freshmen deal with a specific difficulty you have been facing in your first semester in college. You will do research online and find and interview an upperclassman to get advice that you can use and convey to your readers.

## Major Essay Task: College Life Journal Article

For this essay, you will take your first observations about your difficulties with transitioning to college life, and write an article with some recommendations to help out the next incoming class. You should write from your own personal experience as you did with the narrative piece, but here you will reflect on that experience. Then, create a central question you want answered and seek some answers. This question can be as broad as "what are some things you can do to make the first semester or quarter in college easier?" to something more specific like "how to get along with a noisy dorm mate," or "how do you find a group of people to hang out with?" or "how the heck do you do laundry?"

Then, do a bit of research online. See what others have written. Write down a summary of their findings, and pull a few useful quotes. Make sure that you cite your sources properly, put anything anyone else has written in quotation marks, and tell us who wrote it and who they are. What is their experience? Is this a college professor? A psychologist? A sociologist? A student? What kind of college did they go to? Is their experience going to be different because they went to a small private school and you are at a large university or vice versa? Think it all through and be sure you communicate to your readers all *we* need to know in order for the article to make sense. As you draft, write directly to the incoming class. You should even use "you" to address them directly.

Next, you need to find at least 2 juniors or seniors to interview. If you live in the dorms, you can probably ask around. If you can't find any upper division students, at least find a sophomore, maybe in one of your other classes. If you live off campus, this will take a bit more work. You may have to put on a brave face, or get an outgoing friend to help you 'canvas' in the quad and ask people if they wouldn't mind answering a few questions about college life. You can start by just saying, "excuse me, are you a junior or a senior by any chance?" and then tell them about your assignment. Who knows? Maybe you'll even make a new friend.

Conducting an interview isn't too tough, but you should plan ahead. Make a list of questions that you want answered. If you have focused your article on something specific, be sure to ask them if they know anything about the topic before you go on. For example, if you are going to ask someone about dorm life, obviously you'd have to first ask them, "do you live in the dorms?" If you are interested in finding out about their experiences as a first-generation college student, obviously you need to find out if they are a first-generation student. Indeed, asking a specific question to passers-by might be your best 'bait' because if you are asking an interesting question, people will more likely be drawn in to want to talk about it.

Try to keep your interview short and sweet. Only 5-10 questions, so be focused and make sure you get what you want. The easiest way to conduct an interview is by recording their voice using your smartphone if you have one. But be sure to ask permission first! You may even ask them if you can take their picture to include it in your article. You may even want to video record the interview and upload that as part of your article. You should use at least one picture (note how journalism articles usually have at least one picture), but be sure to focus on the writing part of your article as this is what you are trying to master.

After you've collected the interviews, go home and listen to what they say. Take notes. Pull quotes that really jump out at you as you would when reading any source.

Take all your pieces and sit down and write. I like to have a separate page with summaries of articles and quotes on it that I can paste into my own writing. This can be useful for tracking who said what, and who they are. Make an MLA listing at the top of the page, then write a summary of the article and then pull some of the best things they said out of the article. Do the same for your interviews. Then, when you sit down to write, you will begin by writing from your own experience and then you'll think, "Wait! That connects to what my interviewee said, and my article also has information that helps me understand…" and you'll be off and running.

Remember to write from a point of interest. Write about something that you want to know. If you care about your writing, it will be fun to do. If you write about something because you think you should, or it's just easier, it will show in your writing.

Use the Purdue OWL (online writing lab) to learn to properly cite your sources in detail. Use proper in-text citations as well as a works cited page.

Here's a few of the basics on in-text citations to get you started:

1) When you first introduce a new article, use the author's first and last names and the title of the article (articles in quotes, books in *italics*).

2) After that, use the author's last name. When you use their name in your writing, you don't have to put it in the citation at the end of the quote. Example: Johnson said, "this is how you use in-text citations" (24).

3) If you don't use the author's name in the paragraph but refer to their work, either with a direct quote or with paraphrasing or summary, put their last name and page number in your citation. Example: He wrote, "this is how you use in-text citations" (Johnson 24). Example 2: It has been suggested that you should always use in-text citations (Johnson 24). Example 3: Johnson suggests that you should use in-text citations (24).

For works cited, note all the works cited in this textbook. The words "Works Cited" are centered. The format of each work can be seen by looking below. Notice how the second line is indented, not the first. Notice that articles are in quotation marks and books and magazine names are in italics. Notice that websites have the date accessed.

You should also discuss this with your instructor, particularly if you struggle with proper citation. Never copy and paste, or even paraphrase, anything from the internet or elsewhere without attributing the original writer or speaker. To do so is plagiarism.

Think about it. If you paraphrase something you read but don't say where you got the idea from, the reader will assume it is your idea. And since your ideas are supposed to be the heart of your writing, if you are passing off others ideas as your own, you aren't really fulfilling your end of the deal. You are, instead, gathering information that others have worked hard to discover and calling it your own. It's sort of a lie by omission.

As you work through this essay, discuss plagiarism with your instructor if you have questions. Some other good sources about plagiarism are plagiarism.org and Grammerly's plagiarism checker.

## **Works Cited**

Berchini, Christina. "What All First-Generation College Students Must Know." *Huffington Post College Life.* 2016. https://www.huffingtonpost.com/entry/what-all-first-generation-college-students-must-know_us_580b952ce4b0f8715789fb74 Accessed 20 July 2018.

Fritch, John. "Discourse Community." Purdue University Library Guides. 2018. http://guides.lib.purdue.edu/c.php?g=353142&p=2378497 Accessed 20 July 2018.

Keene, Ellen Oliver and Zimmerman, Susan. *Mosaic of Thought.* New York: Heinemann. 2007.

Lauren, Linda. "Creating Positive Energy in the College Dorm." *Huffington Post College Life.* 2016. https://www.huffingtonpost.com/entry/creating-positive-energy-_b_12385948.html Accessed 20 July 2018.

Macrorie, Ken. "The Poisoned Fish." *from Telling Writing.* www.writing.ucsb.edu/faculty/dean/Upload-STEP08/ThePoisonedFish.pdf Accessed 20 July 2018.

Mcleod, Saul. "Social Identity Theory," *Simply Psychology.* 2008. https://www.simplypsychology.org/social-identity-theory.html Accessed 20 July 2018.

Swales, John. *Genre Analysis.* Cambridge: Cambridge University Press. pp. 21-32. 1990. Print.

Nelson, Vicki. "The Culture Shock of Adjusting to College," College Parent Central. 2018. https://www.collegeparentcentral.com/2014/11/the-culture-shock-of-adjusting-to-college/ Accessed 20 July 2018.

Zimmerman, Carlota. "I've Been In College For One Week And I Hate It!" *Huffington Post College Life*. 2016. https://www.huffingtonpost.com/entry/ive-been-in-college-for-one-week-and-i-hate-it_us_57da8c64e4b0d5920b5b258e Accessed 20 July 2018.

# CHAPTER SEVEN

## *Crossing the Threshold: Academic Writing*

So now that you've looked back at a moment from your pre-college life that helps define who you are and have wrestled with some self-doubt about how you will succeed in college, it is time to cross the threshold into academic discourse.

You've already done some research with a key question in mind as you tried to troubleshoot some area of college life that was causing you difficulty. You formed a question that you wanted answered and found that the answer was not simply "do this and you'll be happy," but that any question that you have can be answered in multiple ways depending on who you ask. And, importantly, you thought about how valid those opinions were, or if indeed the answers you found went past opinion and into actual data. If, for example, you wanted to know how to get along with a difficult roommate, there were many different sources of information. Obviously, you could ask those who have been in a similar situation and find out what they did in order to make life more livable. These are known as 'case studies.' You could turn to psychologists and find out what they know about conflict resolution or life transitions. You could read what sociologists say about group dynamics, or even what physicians say about anxiety and irritability. A seemingly simple question then leads you on a quest which takes you from place to place, from person to person, as you gather information that you and your reader can use.

What hopefully made writing the last essay interesting to you, and to your readers, is that you were driven to solve a problem that you needed to fix. Finding the answer could indeed change the quality of your life, and that of your readers.

This is essentially academic writing. Any topic you choose should be because you are driven to find the answer. If you are passionate and connected to the topic in a personal way, your readers will be drawn in.

Notice that you didn't just write about what you knew. Instead, you used research to learn new information and then synthesize it with your own experience and then relate your findings.

You went on a quest and came back with the elixir of knowledge.

When you write academically, you write to think. Every time you sit down to work on a paper, you should begin by writing what you already know or think you know. What are your assumptions? Then, ask what you want to know. What is unclear to you? What question do you want answered? Then, think about who you could turn to in order to find those answers. What will be your sources?

Writing to think is using writing to focus your mind. It's sort of like a meditation. Instead of letting your mind wander, you are able to think through the concept to realize what you know and what you don't know. This is why the first draft is called the discovery draft. You are writing to discover what your paper will be about. Or, more specifically, you are writing to figure out what you really find interesting. You first write to make connections between the topic at hand and your own experience, then you move to research.

It is important in college, and in life, to put your ideas first. In this age of information, anyone can look things up. Anyone can copy and paste. But a true thinker, innovator, artist, entrepreneur, and scientist make their living by coming up with new ideas rather than simply following instructions or memorizing facts. Through the exercises in this chapter, you will go through the process of starting with a narrative about your life, and then using that to figure out what you are interested in learning about, and thus drive your research.

As we move forward, I encourage you to take on topics that perhaps don't seem so obviously 'on your radar.' Who knows, maybe you'll discover that you are really into post-modern art when before you thought it was just junk your kid brother could do. I know it's hard to think about college as a place to experiment and take risks and explore these days. With tuition being so high, it is no wonder students are concerned that they need to make a return on their investment, which leads you to picking fields that are employment-prep rather than simply intellectual and emotional pursuits. But you can, as was advised in the article you read in Chapter Four by Carlota Zimmerman, slip in a poetry class or an art class. Join clubs that you truly find fascinating, not because they will get you employment. Think of these activities as necessary parts of becoming a more interesting conversationalist, engaged and informed about the world around you. Being able to enjoy music and art and theatre really are part of being a whole person in the 21st century. And, of course the more you know about your political and social world, the more you are able to make educated decisions and not be swayed by advertising and propaganda (more on this in the chapter on rhetoric). And, let's face it, many employment opportunities come up because you 'click' with someone over certain interests (hey, you're in my discourse community!) and bingo! There's a job offer.

This means taking what we've worked on so far, your emotional and intellectual engagement in a topic based on your personal thoughts and experiences (your schema), and then jumping across into a 'special world' of the unknown and making some discoveries about your own preconceptions. It means taking on ideas and then using some 'tools' as Malcolm Gladwell, resident author at The New Yorker and brilliant essayist calls them, or as I think of them, 'lenses' in which to look at an idea.

What does it mean to look at something through a lens? This is basically a metaphor for 'seeing something more clearly.' When you look at something through a lens, you are able to see details that you weren't able to before. And not only can you see those details, but you can analyze their meaning.

Think of it in terms of a telescope. You can look up and see the moon okay. You think you have a pretty good idea what it looks like from your observations just looking up in the sky on a full moon. But then someone gives you a telescope and you can make out the Sea of Tranquility, the craters Grimaldi, Plato, and Tycho. Where once you had a general idea and could talk about the moon in general terms, once you zoom in with the assistance of a lens, you are able to see details you could not see before. When you learn new information, the world around you changes because you understand it in new and even surprising ways.

## Practice 7-1: You daredevil you.

*Time for another narrative. This time, write about something you did as a teenager that was a bit daring. Of course, only write about something that you are willing to share, as all in the class will be able to read it. But the best writing is honest, and open, and daring. So, use your best judgment (don't write about anything that will get you in trouble!). But do try to write about a time when you took a chance or a risk that maybe in hindsight didn't seem too smart. Something perhaps that was based on a dare, or at least had some element of peer pressure. Get in groups and talk about your stories. What do they have in common? Why do you think you did these things in your adolescence? Were you out to prove something to your peers? To yourself?*

*If you cannot think of anything that you did that felt particularly daring, you may use an experience of someone you knew or read about.*

Okay, now that you've done some thinking and writing about your own experience as a teenager taking risks, let's read an article in National Geographic on Teenage Brains written by David Dobbs. He introduces the article with this hook: "Moody. Impulsive. Maddening. Why do teenagers act the way they do? Viewed through the eyes of evolution, their most exasperating traits may be the key to success as adults."

Are you hooked? Do you want to read more? I know I do. Note that the introduction tells us exactly what he's going to do: use evolution as a lens ("view through the eyes of evolution," he says) to understand teenage behavior. Hmm. That's unusual. I haven't heard of that approach. We wonder, could teenage 'risky' behavior actually be an evolutionary trait that is helpful? Weird. And fascinating.

So let's all go to the National Geographic website and read the article. Then we will reconvene and look at how we can use the article itself as a lens to understand *our own* teenaged behaviors. Be sure to read all the way through the article to the end, and watch how Dobbs' thinking and understanding of this topic evolves as he writes.

## Practice 7-2: Teenagers evolved

*After reading the article "Teenage Brains" by David Dobbs on the National Geographic website, write a one paragraph summary of the article. Now, pull some specific lines from the article that really jump out at you and serve as evidence of the summary you just wrote. Post to your blog. Get in groups and discuss.*

*There are some sections of the article that may be a bit difficult. Find some areas that you found the most difficult and write through them. Take one particularly difficult paragraph and respond to it directly. What is confusing to you? Think through the difficulty. What might help you understand the paragraph better? Look up words you don't already know. Define them and add them to your vocabulary section of your blog. After going through this process, revisit the paragraph and think about it in terms of the whole article. Does it make more sense now? Can you summarize the paragraph now? It's okay if it is still confusing to you - just try your best to think through your difficulties with it.*

## Practice 7-3: A lens on the self.

*Now, it's time to use Dobbs' article as a lens to understand your teenaged angst narrative. Think of yourself as your own psychologist. Put yourself on the couch for some deep analysis. Now that you know about some of the latest research on why teens act in ways we label as 'impulsive, moody, and maddening,'' use these theories to analyze your behaviors in your story. Now, interject your analysis of your story into the story itself. In other words, you started writing about what happened, likely in the order that the events and decisions occurred. As you are reading back through your story, any time you have an 'aha!' moment that reminds you of the article, bring up what Dobbs wrote and talk about how it applies to your decision making and actions. Use some of those quotes you pulled from the article as evidence that your summary and application of these ideas to your story actually is based on what Dobbs wrote.*

*Post to your blog and discuss with your groups.*

As you read back your finished essay, hopefully you are having a feeling like "hey, this sounds pretty darned smart!" You bet it does. And not because you were trying to be some sort of stodgy academic, but because it was written both from personal experience and then analyzed using an intellectual lens.

This is essentially the heart of all writing, both academic and professional. Hopefully you found this to be a fun activity. Better than calculus, right! Okay, no offense to math lovers. Calculus does have its rewards. In fact, this is a common complaint I hear for those more scientific minded types about English courses. "It seems so arbitrary. There's no single right answer!" You're right. There isn't. And I think this is the point and the reason it is so valuable. If you do go on into advanced mathematics or the sciences or really any STEM fields (science, technology, engineering, mathematics), you will get to a point of the unknown. New, unforged territories. This is where the money is. Invention. Trial and error. Reworking. Rethinking. Analyzing and discovering. This is what college is about. This is what professional life is about. This is what life itself is about.

*"The unexamined life is not worth living"* - Socrates

We just did that didn't we? Examined our own lives. Pretty interesting stuff I'd say. If you are like me, you may have previously felt guilty or ashamed of some of your teenaged actions - certainly our parents and our society, like Dobbs points out, like to make the teen out to be a 'problem.' But now, after reading that article and applying it to our own experiences, we can see that our actions were perfectly normal, and, more than that, made us stronger and more capable human beings.

Let's now go even deeper and make an unexpected connection. Doing so is why we should read broadly and deeply, according to Malcolm Gladwell in his Masterclass series. I've recently been reading Ernest Becker's *The Birth and Death of Meaning* and found some surprising connections to the hero's journey, and even to Dobb's article. According to Becker, the Pulitzer prize winning social theorist and teacher of anthropology, sociology, and social psychology, self-esteem is the 'food' that humans need most to survive (2). The hunter is in his 'ordinary world' of the home. His wife and children look at him. "We're hungry," their eyes say. The hunter rises up. "They need my help. Food is scarce, but I can do it." He grabs his spear and gathers his fellow men, they each use their own unique skills to bring back the kill. One may be the best tracker. Another, the strongest, yet another, the best with a slingshot, and so on. Each finds their strength and uses it because they have confidence they can do it. And also because that confidence is built on experience and practice and especially a need to be the hero for their family and tribe. They work through the forest, and finally track down an antelope or a bison or a lion. Cooperatively, they defeat their prey and return to their families and distribute the food. "You're my hero!" their eyes say. And the hunter is proud.

Think about how this idea ties into Dobbs' argument. Dobbs talks about how we are such social creatures, how we need one another to survive, so doing group activities with our peers where the social rewards are high is important to our survival. Dobbs writes, "teens gravitate toward peers for another, more powerful reason: to invest in the future rather than the past... Knowing, understanding, and building relationships with them bears critically on success." Going back to Becker, who wrote that, "the main reward of the one who kills the big animal... is the prestige of being able to distribute it to his family and to others," we might argue that this risk taking, these acts of bravery, like the example Dobbs uses of his son who drove 113 miles per hour, is exactly this, a creation of pride, of self-esteem at being able to go out in the world and take risks - to be creative and individual, so that you are admired. As Dobbs points out, this can have some adverse side effects. The hunt is risky business. Bringing down large game is not easy nor safe. Coming back and feeding your family and tribe is the reward that is worth it. That is why risk taking behavior, according to

Dobbs' research, has stood the test of time in terms of evolution.

## Practice 7-4: Gladwell the Mentor

*Now, read an article by Gladwell and look at how he uses a specific lens, or as he calls it, "tool," to understand a, sadly, very contemporary issue in society: school gun violence. Find and read the article "Thresholds of Violence" by Malcolm Gladwell on The New Yorker magazine website (October 19, 2015 issue). You should read the article twice. Read first for content, and second as a writer.*

*Your goal in this activity isn't to argue for or against gun laws, or debate the meaning of the Second Amendment and the "right to bear arms." Instead, I want you to focus on the structure of Gladwell's discussion. Does he come to any solid conclusions? Is it a thesis, body, body, body, conclusion structure? What are some elements of surprise he used in the unfolding of the story?*

*Also, as you read, note any specific sentences that you find particularly interesting. Write them down and analyze them. What makes a good sentence?*

Note how Gladwell alternates short and long sentences, as I do in this text. Note that some sentences feel more formal and others more conversational. This is part of writing to engage: knowing when it is appropriate to lay out information in a formal way, and when to digress and talk about that information in a more passionate, individual way. When you change your writing style within a single essay, to a degree, you keep the reader engaged because the writing feels more dynamic.

Also, notice where Gladwell complicates matters by the usage of 'turns.' These are places where you are going in one direction, but then are taken into new terrain. These turns are indicated by what I call "blinkers" or "indicator lights" if you want to be more formal in your driving terms. Blinkers are words like "but," "although," and "however," those transition words we spoke about earlier. Look for these words as they are places where Gladwell is complicating his discussion. He will state "you think this is happening, that is what we all assume, *but* it turns out…" These turns, these 'blinkers,' are what keep the landscape interesting. If you've ever driven on an endlessly straight road, you know what I mean. When you finally turn, you find new territory, new terrain. You can finally concentrate on something other than not falling asleep. You can look out your window and say "Hey, I've never seen that before!" as you pass through an exciting new town.

## Practice 7-5: Analyze Gladwell's article as a writer.

*Write a summary of Gladwell's article and then write an analysis of craft. Write a response analyzing the structure of the article. Get in groups in class and talk about it.*

## Review of Using Sources

Notice how Gladwell uses his sources. For example, he writes:

"In a famous essay published four decades ago, the Stanford sociologist Mark Granovetter set out to explain a paradox: 'situations where outcomes do not seem intuitively consistent with the underlying individual preferences.' What explains a person or group of people doing things that seem at odds with who they are or what

137

they think is right? Granovetter took riots as one of his main examples, because a riot is a case of destructive violence that involves a great number of otherwise quite normal people who would not usually be disposed to violence."

How has Gladwell framed Granovetter's article? Gladwell gives us the reference's full name, Mark Granovetter, and told us very briefly who he is and why his overall knowledge is helpful to the task at hand. He is a sociologist, one who studies societies and social structures, and he is from Stanford, clearly an institution that lends him some credibility. Moreover, Gladwell notes that the essay is famous. We may, if we are so inclined, use this information to look up both Granovetter and the essay Gladwell is referring to (see works cited at end of chapter). Gladwell then uses a quote that is appropriate to his overall discussion and the specific section of this article: "situations where outcomes do not seem intuitively consistent with the underlying individual preferences," and then, most importantly, he explains *why* and *how* this idea, this 'quote,' fits into his discussion by asking the reader "what explains a person or group of people doing things that seem at odds with who they are or what they think is right?" He has reframed and reworded and extended the quote he has used, which is a little dense. He 'unpacks' the quote for us. Then, he adds more evidence by a brief summary of one of Granovetter's observations.

When you are using sources, this is a great template to use, as we covered in chapter five. First, give us a quick note about who they are and why we should listen to them. When you bring up someone else's ideas and specific words, don't just cite them, but give us an introduction to who they are. This is a person's 'ethos' as per Aristotle.

Then, write a very brief summary about their work as it applies to your own writing and thoughts. Here, Gladwell just says that he wrote about riots because it is an excellent example of otherwise trustworthy, law abiding citizens, doing things they wouldn't otherwise do. Instead of just reading the article by Granovetter and then saying "riots are a good example," he gives Granovetter his kudos for coming up with the thought, rather than (by omission) claiming it as his own.

It is tempting, or perhaps it has already happened in class, to springboard from the article to talk about guns and gun control, as this is often the first place our minds go when confronting the issue of school shootings. But let's notice that Gladwell has taken on this issue and not mentioned guns even once in the article.

The best writing is not writing about the obvious. It is not reiterating things that have been said over and over. It is about making new, surprising connections.

It is about thinking and complicating, not arguing that you are right.

Arguing an issue, defending a side, is a pretty narrow way of thinking, and I believe that this just encourages a simplistic, dual way of looking of our world. I might even argue that this type of thinking is the cause of many of the world's problems, and urge you through your reading and writing in your English courses, and indeed through all of your courses in college, to look beyond this way of thinking and realize that it is not about winning an argument, but about using and understanding academic discussions to complicate, question, and deepen our thinking.

Does Gladwell have an argument that we should do X or Y to stop this problem? No.

Instead, he uses the writings of Granovetter to better help us understand, to complicate our binary notions of, the horrific problem of school shootings.

Notice that he begins with an image - with the moment that the police show up at the storage facility, and then he reveals all the information we need to know in order to understand his later analysis through the phenomena of riots as posited by Granovetter.

In your own writing, keep in mind how Gladwell has given us all the information we require to fully understand the idea rather than just jumping to the idea. In other words, we all know about the frequency of school shootings, sadly, so he could have just gone straight to how he is using Granovetter's writing as a lens to view the phenomenon, but instead he gives us details that serve as evidence as to why this lens works. By giving us a brief, but specific, look at what differentiates each shooter, we are able to think through the process that Gladwell himself underwent as he realized that this issue isn't just a black and white, guns or no guns, issue.

Academic writing is, as Gerald Graff and Cathy Birkenstein write about in *They Say/I Say*, about "entering a conversation." Above, Gladwell entered a conversation about school shootings. You will be entering many conversations though this text and in your college careers.

We are still crossing the threshold into academic writing. But this does not mean that you show up tabula rasa (an empty slate), with nothing to contribute from your 18+ (maybe even 30+) years on the planet. You've had experiences. You've had thoughts. You've had conversations. You've read. You've watched. You have *schema*. You enter the conversation with a lot of knowledge already under your belt. You have opinions that matter, and they aren't just based on feelings. You have data to back up your assertions. When someone asks you about a topic that you know well and are passionate about, you have information to share that comes from reading about it, and often doing it. If you love tennis, you can probably teach someone who hasn't played the basics of the forehand and backhand, how to volley, how to hold the racket, who the best players are and why… If you are really into mixing beats, you can surely teach someone about digital audio workstations (DAWs) like Reaper, Reason, Fruity Loops, Cakewalk, and Logic. You know about VSTs and AUs. You know how to use Maschine and Trigger Finger, you know all about midi channels and using effects. Or if you are a filmmaker you probably can tell someone all about Premiere Pro and After Effects. You know about using drones and the value of 4K footage. You can use framing and the rule of thirds to keep the composition in balance. But to people who don't know about these things, many or all of the words I just wrote sound just like gobbledygook.

Which brings us back to discourse communities. Note how there is certain jargon, words specific to each community that those within the community understand, and those outside of it do not. Saying the score is 40-love means nothing to someone who has no clue about tennis.

So what do you do when you cross over into a new discourse community with information from another one? Well, you teach them. That is, if your audience is interested in learning.

Teaching, believe it or not, is actually the best way to learn something. Why would this be? Don't you only teach things you already know really well? Yes and no. Yes, we need to already have background knowledge in order to teach a subject, this is why professors need to have degrees in the subjects they teach - to prove that they know enough about the subject to teach it. However, beginning teachers often feel, believe it or not, very overwhelmed. Do they remember everything they were taught as undergraduates and in graduate school? Absolutely not. Perhaps they've been selected to teach a course in, say, Freshman English for the first time. How long has it been since they actually took this course? At the minimum, 6 years. For many, up to 10 years or more. That's a long time. And yet they are thrown in front of a classroom and are told 'teach it!' They may not even remember what the heck they did in their own course, and in any subject, including writing, ideas and 'fashions' move quickly, so it is likely that they way they were taught 10 years ago is vastly different than the way it is taught today.

Teaching is like writing, writing like teaching.

Think about it. A central assertion of this textbook is that we write primarily to think, and then we rewrite to communicate what we've learned.

## Practice 7-6: Explain what you know

*Think about a time when you had to explain something you know well to someone. When you have to explain something you already know, you realize exactly what you do and do not know, and most importantly, you make realizations that you perhaps had not even made conscious before.*

*Write about a time when you had to explain (teach) something to someone and how the act of teaching it made you understand the topic better. Perhaps even as you were explaining it you realized,*

*"Hey, I'm not sure, I thought I knew but since I'm not sure let's look it up."*

*This should not be an argument trying to convince your reader you are right. It should be about teaching the reader about something you care about. Is it horses? Is it finance? Is it dancing? Is it soccer? Is it cooking? Is it comic-con? Write about that.*

Our essay writing goal for this chapter is for you to start with your experience in the world (your schema) and then brainstorm about ideas to write about. Do some research and learn more. And then think the idea through, explaining your understanding of it, to your readers. Practice using MLA style for citation as in all the examples you've read and how it is presented to you throughout this textbook. Work on integrating quotes into your own thinking and sentences. At first, don't worry about structure. The goal here is for you to show us your journey through the topic. Then, use that narrative structure (the hero's journey of chapters 1 and 2) that we have used in the previous chapters. Give us specific examples of why you are writing about the topic, how it relates to you. Then talk us through your thinking as you discover these mentors, these allies and enemies, through your research. Who agrees with you? Who disagrees? If they disagree, how do you feel about what they say? Does this change your initial belief? Does it at least complicate it?

The topics you choose should be controversial issues that are 'in the air' amongst your friends and / or family. In other words, what do you talk about? What do you care about? It doesn't matter if it doesn't seem like an 'academic' topic. Being academic isn't about topics, it's about using these lenses, the insights of other writers in multiple disciplines, to help you understand these topics on a deeper level as you did in your college life essay.

So, what's on your mind? What are you thinking about? What would you like to understand better? If you pop onto Google, what do you search for? Write about that.

## Practice 7-7: Invention

*Pick 3-5 topics that you'd like to write about. Free-write for 5 minutes per topic, trying to convince yourself why you should write about each one.*

*Is the topic simply a how-to or academic (a discussion to be had)? We want you to use this essay to build your confidence as a writer, but also want to push you toward academic approaches to any topic. So, if your topic is indeed about tennis, or music making, or filmmaking, how can you complicate the topic? Think about its social value. Is it available to everyone? Why or why not? What is the value of learning how to do what it is you do? Why do you think it is important socially, psychologically, morally, ethically?*

*Then, go to your classmates blogs and provide some feedback. Which topics sounded the most interesting to you? Which do you want to read about?*

Your essay on college life may have been a bit along these lines - an explanation about how to get through your first semester, or how to get along with dorm-mates, or how to do laundry or juggle work and school etc. Here, I am asking you to think more in terms of something specific that will require you to take on a voice of authority about a topic and teach us something new.

## Practice 7-8: Reading Reflection

*Take something that resonated with you from the students'
essays in the appenix and say why it did. Use specific
examples from your own life and use quotes from the essay.*

## Major Essay Assignment: Explaining a Concept

After you've chosen your topic, write it out as
a discovery draft first. See what you already know and
think about a topic. It need not be as complex as
Fine's philosophical essay above, but if you want to
write about some central question about the meaning of
life or work or love or family, this is a great opportunity to
do so. What is something that you find yourself
contemplating often? What is something you've wrestled
with in your own life that you'd like to explore and
analyze? What personally do you think would help you if
you looked at it through a new 'lens' in order to
understand it better? Get in groups and talk about
ideas. Write them out before-hand and bring them to
class. Be sure to do full rewrites after you get feedback
from your peers and professor.

## Works Cited

Becker, Ernest. *The Birth and Death of Meaning*. New York:
    Free Press, 1971. Print.
Dobbs, David. "Teenage Brains." National Geographic.

   https://www.nationalgeographic.com/magazine/201
   1/10/beautiful-brains/ Accessed 20 July 2018.

Gladwell, Malcolm. "On Writing Well." *Dorm Room Tycoon.* https://drt.fm/malcolm-gladwell Accessed 20 July 2018.

Gladwell, Malcolm. "Thresholds of Violence." *The New Yorker* (October 19, 2015 issue). https://www.newyorker.com/magazine/2015/10/19/thresholds-of-violence Accessed 20 July 2018.

Graff, Gerald and Birkenstein, Cathy. *They Say/I Say: The Moves That Matter in Academic Writing.* Chicago: Norton. 2017. Print

Gransovetter, Mark. "Threshold Models of Collective Behavior." The American Journal of Sociology, Vol. 83, No. 6 (May, 1978), pp. 1420-1443 https://pdfs.semanticscholar.org/f29c/cfe347779740ae5cf0c7401c9b8973052983.pdf Accessed 20 July 2018.

# CHAPTER EIGHT

## *Rhetorical Writing*

Find 'Monty Python's argument clinic' on YouTube. Here's an excerpt from the script:

Man: (Knock)
Mr. Vibrating: Come in.
Man: Ah, Is this the right room for an argument?
Mr. Vibrating: I told you once.
Man: No you haven't.
Mr. Vibrating: Yes I have.
Man: When?
Mr. Vibrating: Just now.
Man: No you didn't.
Mr. Vibrating: Yes I did.
Man: You didn't
Mr. Vibrating: I did!
Man: You didn't!
Mr. Vibrating: I'm telling you I did!
Man: You did not!!
The two continue on for a while, then finally...
Man: An argument isn't just contradiction.
Mr. Vibrating: It can be.

Man: No it can't. An argument is a connected series of statements intended to establish a proposition.

Mr. Vibrating: No it isn't.

Man: Yes it is! It's not just contradiction.

Mr. Vibrating: Look, if I argue with you, I must take up a contrary position.

Man: Yes, but that's not just saying 'No it isn't.'

Mr. Vibrating: Yes it is!

Man: No it isn't!

Man: Argument is an intellectual process. Contradiction is just the automatic gainsaying of any statement the other person makes.

*(short pause)*

Mr. Vibrating: No it isn't.


In this sketch, the lads from England poke fun at what we think of as an argument. It is largely thought of as disagreement, or as they say in the sketch, "contradiction" and "gainsaying." While an argument may have some elements of disagreement, and indeed a well-written argument needs to take these disagreements into account, an argument is really "a connected series of statements intended to establish a proposition."

There are plenty of topics that seem to have two sides because those talking about these topics each wants to be right. They simply want to be able to argue. They want there not to be any doubt. Life, my friends, is full of doubt. There are no easy answers. So first, instead of arguing a side, we will take a topic that is usually divided into this simple binary system and research both sides to really find out what each is stating are the facts that back up their position. This is called 'argument synthesis.' Perhaps you remember the word synthesis from science class or chemistry. It means creating something new from building blocks. In this case, the building blocks are ideas. By synthesizing seemingly contradictory ideas, you come to a place of agreement and understanding rather than escalating conflict.

This is a key lesson in writing in general. It isn't about being right or wrong, it isn't about sounding smart and decisive. It is about presenting your reader with a new way to look at an issue so that they walk away feeling like they have a deeper understanding than they did before. You want them to respect your intelligence and insight, not make them feel like you just ranted your feelings about a topic.

Even if (especially if) you are trying to prove a point, you need to be sure to take as many perspectives in as you can, and respect them, before you refute them and argue your point. If you simply insult other points of view, you will change no one's mind. Indeed, you will just further polarize the discussion and make negotiation and agreement more difficult.

Remember, when you are writing an argument, it is pointless to only "preach to the choir." If your intended reader already agrees with you, your writing didn't serve much purpose.

## Writing for your Reader

As June Casagrande writes so cleverly in her text *It was the best of sentences, it was the worst of sentences*, "The Reader is King. You are his servant. You serve the Reader information. You serve the Reader entertainment" (3). Casagrande goes on to ask, "ever read a memoir that sounded too self-pitying? Ever read an op-ed that sounded too preachy or self-important? Ever read a memo that sounded smothered in jargon or unnecessary details? Ever read a blog entry that talked about people you've never met as if you'd known them all your life? These things happened because the writer forgot her place" (4). And finally she concludes "Readers don't read memoirs because Frank McCourt needs pity or because Jeannette Walls needs you to know that her parents are unstable or because Mary Carr wants to get some stuff off her chest. In each these memoirists' amazing stories, the Reader (note how she keeps capitalizing 'Reader') finds not just entertainment but themes that touch on his own life - themes of hope, perseverance, suffering, and the power to overcome" (4). In other words, the writer gives us specific details about their own beliefs, their own lives, their own research, their own points of view in order to talk about universal ideas, problems, fears, loves, worries, in our own lives.

The Reader is King and Queen. You are their servant. You want to make them engage with your writing: that is your ultimate goal.

So, write to think in your first draft, write to communicate in your second, third, and fourth drafts.

Use the first draft to get your thoughts and research together, then rewrite to make sure you are *clear*.

For more help with writing clearly, let's again turn to the work of William Zinsser. In his book *On Writing Well*, Zinsser says two things that back up my assertions that good writing is both personal and clear. First he says:

Ultimately the product that any writer has to sell is not the subject being written about, but who he or she is. I often find myself reading with interest about a topic I never thought would interest me—some scientific quest, perhaps. What holds me is the enthusiasm of the writer for his field. How was he drawn into it? What emotional baggage did he bring along? How did it change his life? It's not necessary to want to spend a year alone at Walden Pond to become involved with a writer who did" (11).

But then he goes on to say:

But the secret of good writing is to strip every sentence to its cleanest components. Every word that serves no function, every long word that could be a short word, every adverb that carries the same meaning that's already in the verb, every passive construction that leaves the reader unsure of who is doing what—these are the thousand and one adulterants that weaken the strength of a sentence. And they usually occur in proportion to education and rank.

Zinnser's point is that while we do need to use our originality and personality in our work we also need to be concise. Every word should count. Does this mean your writing should be plain? Absolutely not. But it does mean it should be focused. It should always move forward from one idea to the next, and not stray too often into digressions or vaguely related subjects. You must remain focused to keep your readers interest.

This is a reminder, again, that you need to redraft your essays to be sure that you communicate clearly to your readers. What assumptions do you have about what they already know and what they don't know? Are these assumptions correct? Be sure you fill in all the information that we need to know. Writing clearly doesn't necessarily mean short, simple sentences. Remember how we discussed in the grammar chapter that you can use phrases within your sentences to vary sentence length and keep the reader interested? Do that. So, our goal is to be complex in our thinking, but clear in our language. As in most things in life, find the middle way.

Let's look at an example paper to see what I mean. Let's go to SFSU student Nathan Stafford, who wrote about the conundrum of what to do when we find out that entertainers do bad things. Note here how he thinks through the debate, complicating it with those blinker words 'but,' 'however,' 'on the other hand,' and hedges like 'perhaps.' Rather than crafting his essay so that he takes and defends a position about 'evil entertainers,' he presents the debate as a whole, working through it on a personal level, trying, even wanting to find a simple solution, but in the end is only able to offer thoughts for us to ponder for ourselves. Note his complex thinking yet clear, fluid prose. We hear his voice clearly throughout, yet we understand what he is saying because he has written with the reader in mind.

## Practice 8-1: Reading as a Writer

*Read through Stafford's essay twice - it is on iLearn. First, to just feel the flow of his prose and how it all fits together to give the reader all the information that he is pondering. Then, on your second read through, make an outline of the points he makes. Note how each point is complicated rather than answered in a simple way. Note anytime he uses a blinker word. Write your response in your blog.*

*Then, write your own personal response to the topic. Do you have an opinion about it that feels strong and clear? If so, find quotes that Stafford has used that counter your certain opinion and go to the end of his essay and look up the article. Read it and write about how their argument complicates and counters your own. In other words, take what seems like an obvious point of view or preconceived notion and complicate it. If, however, you are already convinced that there is no easy answer to the topic, write why this is so using quotes from Stafford's essay.*

To think about argument, we need to look at what is known as rhetoric. According to Christof Rapp at Stanford University, Aristotle stated that persuasion is caused by three things - the character of the speaker (ethos), the emotional response of the listener (pathos) and the logic of the argument (logos). In other words, we can use these three appeals in order to make a point. Perhaps this was covered in your high school English courses. Perhaps you have even been told that this is *the* correct way to write a paper. You pick a topic of controversy, choose a side, and then argue the point with concrete evidence, and take into account counterarguments, rebutting them with the swiftness and mental dexterity of a ninja warrior. You use ethos (your reputation), logos (logic), and pathos (emotional appeals) to convince everyone that you are a wicked genius.

While we may want to keep things simple and feel secure that there are clear answers to complicated problems, this just isn't the case. Does this mean that you shouldn't ever argue a point? Does this mean that there are no clear answers and we are doomed to wander in the grey fog bank of uncertainty and indecision?

No. However, we do have to make decisions based on the data at hand. We do have to make hard choices and be able to argue that the path we have chosen is indeed the best path. But it also means that we need to carefully weigh not *both* sides of an argument, but instead reframe black or white as a continuum, a smooth gradient from black to white. Where we land on the continuum is where we make our decision, knowing that it is not some ultimate truth, but that it is the best case scenario based on facts, some of which may be contradictory to our position yet equally valid.

Yes, there can be a paradox - two seemingly opposing points of view can both be (somewhat or conditionally) valid. This is what Peter Elbow calls "embracing contraries." It is a matter of degree, not kind. In other words, while there may be a discernible point at which we say something is true versus false, we say that because that something is statistically more true than other statements.

You can't simply make assumptions and say they are true just because someone told you they are. You have to base your statements on statistically significant evidence. Science means that results are repeatable and predictable. People seem to lately be debating what 'truth' really is. More often than not, it seems to depend on whose side you are on. Most academics, rightfully, state that science is the source of truth. Neil Degrasse Tyson and Bill Nye are two very vocal and pretty awesome guys who spend tireless and countless hours working to get 'the ordinary Joe' to 'believe' in science. Having an undergraduate degree in Biology from U.C. Berkeley, I am very convinced, if one even needs convincing, that truth isn't opinion, but is based on empirical data through the scientific method.

Therefore, any statement you make when you write has to be based on (1) things that you've observed or experienced, (2) things that have been studied and analyzed by experts, and (3) the two have to agree. If you believe something to be true because you experienced it that way and yet all the research you do states that you are incorrect, you must take this into account and change your mind if the sources you find are valid.

Yes, writing is actually best not when you change someone else's mind, but when you change your own. When you take an assumption you have about the world, put it to the test and find out that your information and understanding was incomplete, even incorrect, then you are really cooking with gas. That's when you are learning.

College is about joining in the big conversations that help us make meaning in our world. It is about questioning assumptions, finding out that what we don't know is vastly larger than what we do, it is about finding out, perhaps, that we've been basing decisions and ideas we have about the world on false presumptions.

So, again, it was not actually a mistake to teach you the five paragraph essay in high school. This organizational form is made to get you to state a thesis and then back it up with facts, take on the counter-argument, and come to a conclusion.

This is fine, clear thinking.

But it is also a bit simplistic. We cannot take into account all the variables. We cannot take into account how ideas are interconnected and complicated. In the five paragraph essay, we don't really have a lot of room to think. Instead, it is built to find facts from reliable sources and then spit them out.

Now that you are in college, you are being asked to add to the conversation, as Graff and Birkenstein state in their text *They Say/I Say.*

You need to be able to weigh out the 'sides' of an argument, take a position, and be able to use facts to support that position. This is hugely important in life and in most careers. If we are always seeing both sides, always saying there is no ultimate clear answer, action cannot be taken one way or the other. Our political system itself constantly argues for this dichotomous thinking, this or that, Republican or Democrat. To vote for a third party is to 'throw your vote away.' Because much of the world likes to think in these black and white ways, it is important to be able to analyze such thinking and be able to use it when necessary. In order to make change in the world you do have to convince others that what you are saying makes sense and is based on sound reasoning and data. And, importantly, you need to weigh the multiple (not just the two) sides of an argument and make a case for a decision or solution.

## Practice 8-2: Picking a topic

*In order to figure out what you'd like to write about, it might be best to get in a group and just start shooting ideas out there. If you were just hanging out at a party or at a coffee shop, what would you talk about? If, for example, you found relationships foremost on your mind, you might come up with some theories that you've formulated, assumptions that you operate under, about relationships, be they romantic or platonic. Write down those assumptions. Talk about them. Do others in your group immediately say, "Oh, yeah, that's been my experience too!" or do they make a face and say "Uh, that's crazy." Well, try not to do the latter because that isn't nice. But you get my point. Come up with a topic that is, by its nature, controversial. Then ask why there are multiple points of view. Think about who might have studied it in a more scientific way. Where can you gather more data? Perhaps, if you are talking about relationships, you could do your own study by asking people in your dorm their thoughts about your subject.*

*In fact, this would be a good way to collect new data about a topic that is important to you and your community. You could poll college students, dorm mates, family, friends, etc. You could even do a few case studies.*

*The important thing is to find multiple points of view on your topic so you know that it is one that is worth debating. If everyone is in agreement about it, like "Is there gravity?", it's not much of a debate topic.*

*However, it will be easier for you to write a fair and balanced argument synthesis of your topic if it is one that you yourself don't already have a strong opinion about. It should be something that you are able to be open minded about.*

*Write down your topics, your thoughts about your topic, the multiple points of view on this topic, and what your thesis is going to be.*

Notice how above that I wanted you to state your assumption and then immediately question it. In other words, writing an argument paper shouldn't be about confirming your assumptions. The data may go any which way. It is about taking your assumptions and putting them to the test. Gathering data and then analyzing the data. Then, either your assumption is confirmed, denied, partially confirmed and partially denied, or outright changed.

If you really want to jump into rhetoric, it is a rich and exciting field. So much of our world is better understood when you look at the messages that you are being bombarded with on a constant basis and understand the difference between what you actually believe and what you've been told to believe. This is the value, perhaps one of the highest values, of getting an education. A great start is to grab *Understanding Rhetoric* by Elizabeth Losh and Jonathan Alexander. This book is in the form of a graphic 'novel,' except it's not a novel, obviously. I guess you'd call it a graphic textbook. Very cool actually.

We will look more at visual rhetorical analysis, specifically how to read and analyze visual media in a later chapter. For now, let's dip into rhetoric and see how you can both understand when it's being used on you and understand how to use it yourself.

Rhetoric basically just means "to say." This is to posit, to position, to argue. But, as noted above, it is not simply to state facts; indeed facts are only part of the way to persuade someone that you are correct. Aristotle (384-322 BCE) thought that rhetorical argument was necessary for politics to work. Indeed, it is ideally the cornerstone of our political system when used correctly. Rhetoric isn't just about the facts (logos = logic), but about who is stating the facts (ethos = persona) and about why you should care about the facts (pathos = empathy). We simply do not operate on a solely logical level. We are not Spock. We make a lot of decisions based on how much we trust and like the speaker and on our emotions, perhaps even more so than we do on logic. Think of how many assumptions you carry around with you because your parents (huge ethos) made appeals to your emotions that their beliefs should be your beliefs. These may even fly in the face of logic and facts that you see in front of you, but because of the power of rhetoric, you find that you cannot change your belief even if you know, in your heart, that you are wrong. Beliefs can become so firmly held that they seem like 'you.' They define who you are. So to have them questioned, or to be daring enough to question them yourself, is dangerous and scary ground.

But that is the only way forward.

Question your assumptions.

Plato, Aristotle's teacher (427-347 BCE), thought that rhetoric was dangerous for this very reason. He argued that using rhetorical devices against your opponent in a discussion is to be devious and dishonest. He believed that facts should be facts, period. But, people don't operate that way. In fact, Plato was so against emotional appeals he felt that plays and poets should be banished! As we will discuss in writing about literature and visual media, the arts operate primarily on an emotional level; they connect to us through our 'hearts.' Thus, they are very powerful in influencing how we view our world. Plato thought this was dangerous stuff. As I will argue in these later chapters, this is exactly why the arts are so important. We use them to experiment with our social and personal worlds. They are necessary places of play and experiment.

The structure of a rhetorical argument is, as Losh and Alexander put it, much like a sandwich (160). So, you have your assumption, you did research, you found out multiple sides to the story, and now, perhaps you can stake a solid claim and then use your research to back you up.

So, here's how you can organize your essay:
1) Narrative hook
2) Introductory claim
3) Context and Background
4) Evidence
5) Analysis
6) Implications
7) Concluding claim

Your introductory claim should be formulated after you have done your research. This may be contrary to what you have heard before - that you should make a claim first and then find evidence to back your claim. Indeed, the scientific method is based on this practice - that you first come up with a hypothesis, then you put it to testing, analyze your experiments and the data, and then decide if you have proven your hypothesis to be correct or not.

Your hypothesis seems to come first; however, how did you come up with your hypothesis? From reading previous experiments and conclusions, and from previous observations. As everywhere else in this text, you are not coming to anything as a blank slate. So even in the scientific method, of proving a hypothesis, you do research first in order to come up with your theory.

The reason I am driving this point home is because many students will see a prompt, like in the ACT exam, where you are given a very short background information, then three perspectives. You choose a perspective and then set out to prove it. This is a very bad idea. Your job in these types of essays is to take your assumptions, your opinion, and prove that you are correct without doing any research. The formula is to make your claim, find three pieces of evidence that back your claim, find a counterargument which you then refute, then conclude that you are right, everyone else is wrong, you are a genius and everyone else a moron.

Uh, yeah, that's really deep thinking.

So, when I talk about writing an argument paper, please try to forget that the standardized tests made you work in this way.

So, the steps for conducting your research are as follows:

1) Find a topic and look at your assumptions.

2) Write a narrative about your experiences related to the topic. How did you arrive at your assumptions?

3) Question those assumptions. What are the other perspectives?

4) Do research about the topic - not just sources that back you up, but as many different sources with different conclusions about their research. Note: if the topic is an "open and shut case" and there really is only one conclusion, it isn't controversial and thus does not need to be written about. "Is there gravity?" - Yes.

5) After a thorough review of the literature (sources), write up your own literature review. What are all the voices that you can find? At least within reason, obviously this could go on and on with millions of hits on internet searches or library searches, so perhaps you will be limited to 3 or 5 or 10 or 20 sources, depending on whether you are taking lower division, upper division, or graduate level coursework.

6) After you do your literature review, then come up with a claim. This may be very different than your original assumptions. It should be, at the very least, more complicated than your assumptions. This is why argument synthesis is so important, as you did last chapter.

7) Gather your evidence and analyze it. What was revealed through your literature review that makes you believe that your claim is correct? Note here that you will have to spend a lot of time deciding what in your literature review actually is relevant to your particular claim and which is not. In other words, you need to be sure that your claim is focused enough to write within

your page limit. If your claim is too broad, your paper will lack focus.

8) Now, you can state the implications of your evidence. Now that you've looked further into the evidence, are you still sure that your claim is solid?

9) Restate why your evidence backs up your claim.

## Practice 8-3: Reading like a Writer

*Read Argument essays in the appendix. In groups, choose one essay to analyze together. Read it rhetorically. How has the author used the tools of rhetoric to convince you of their claim? Be able to dissect their essay in terms of organization. What is their claim? What is the context and background? What is their evidence? What is their analysis? What is their concluding claim? Did they use a narrative hook to pull you in?*

## Major Essay Task: Argument Paper

Now, it is time to write an essay wherein you take a stance on an issue. If you follow the guidelines above, you should be able to find an issue, work though the complications through gathering data, and then decide if your assumptions were correct or if they needed adjusting. Now, write the paper arguing for the position that seems, to you, to be the correct one given the data. This may not be your initial position! Make sure that your evidence is presented with concrete examples from your readings. Use all the tools you have learned through this text to present your evidence - summary and quotes. Use P.I.E. paragraphs and quote sandwiches. Use logos, ethos, and pathos in your argument. Appeal to your reader through who you are and your own experiences, through emotion and a desire for empathy, and through logic and reasoning. To do this properly, you need to choose an issue that resonates with you, that you have a personal investment in. However, this is sticky ground, as I urge you, again, to not hang on to your preconceived notions! Be sure that you are using the facts you learned to craft your argument rather than finding data that only backs up your initial assumptions. Dare to change! Dare to learn!

## Works Cited

Greenstone, Jerry. "The History of Bloodletting." BCMJ, vol. 52 , No. 1 , January February 2010, pp 12-14

Miller, Richard E. And Jurecic Ann. *Habits of the Creative Mind.* New York: Bedford St. Martins, 2016. Print.

Rapp, Christof, "Aristotle's Rhetoric", *The Stanford Encyclopedia of Philosophy* (Spring 2010 Edition), Edward N. Zalta (ed.), URL = <https://plato.stanford.edu/archives/spr2010/entries/aristotle-rhetoric/>.

# CHAPTER NINE

## *Writing About Literature*

Writing about literature, aka your "English class," is one of those things that most people either love or hate. What is 'close reading' and why is it important? What is the point of reading a story to figure out what the author intended? What is the point of fiction anyway? Aren't people who are obsessed with fiction actually just escapists living in a fantasy land with their heads in their books, ignoring the life around them?

As Graff and Birkenstein state in their text *They Say / I Say*, books have this strange place in society. They are revered as being a symbol of intellectualism. There's this book snobbery in the air - if you read you have 'cultural capital'; you can sit in the cafe with your Kindle or even an actual paperback or hardcover of Thomas Pynchon or Lydia Minatoya and feel superior to the sad sap watching YouTube videos. Yet books have also become more passé, as outdated as cassette tapes or LPs in an age of Spotify. Is there a point to the sustained reading of a novel at this point in time? After all, once upon a time, novels didn't even exist. Why should we hang onto this outdated mode of storytelling? There are so many films and television series, often adaptations of books, on Amazon and Netflix and Hulu that it would take a lifetime and then some to watch them all. So, who has the time to sit down and read a book, a singular story, that could take 10, even 20 hours or more to finish?

Insanity.

Move on people. Books are dead.

Okay, you know I don't feel this way. At all. And it's more than just a feeling, I've actually got some data that says we need to continue to read novels and longer non-fiction works. It's good for our brains. In *The Shallows*, Nicholas Carr states that "I'm not thinking the way I used to think. I feel it most strongly when I'm reading. I used to find it easy to immerse myself in a book or a lengthy article. My mind would get caught up in the twists of the narrative or the turns of the argument, and I'd spend hours strolling through long stretches of prose. That's rarely the case anymore. Now my concentration starts to drift after a page or two. I get fidgety, lose the thread, begin looking for something else to do. I feel like I'm always dragging my wayward brain back to the text. The deep reading that used to come naturally has become a struggle" (5-6).

## Practice 9-1: Attention Please!

*What do you think Carr claims is the cause of this change in his thinking? Do you have the same experience? Do you find it difficult to sustain attention reading long works? Are you one of those people who claim, or even boast, to "never read?"*

*Read the excerpt from Carr's book titled "Hal and Me." It's easily located on the internet. First, summarize the article. What*

*is Carr's argument? What is his evidence? Then, respond to the
article from your own experience and/or further internet
research. Do you agree with Carr? Why or why not?*

No text can be a complete picture, so when we read, we
we use our imaginations to fill in the blanks. Remember
my mention of Wolfgang Iser and those 'gaps' in the text
that we fill in with our 'schema?' Well, fiction, being also a
narrative, obviously allows us to do the same thing.

But if there are already so many interesting real stories
to tell, what is the value of making up stories? Why are we
compelled to read and write stories that are untrue? The
definition of fiction is that it is a story that is 'made up,'
that didn't actually happen. So why would anyone want to
spend time reading what are essentially lies?

There's perhaps two ways to define truth. One is facts.
Facts that happened are true. Things that are made up,
that didn't actually happen, are not true. However, when
you read a story, or watch a film, why do they seem true?
You know as you are reading or viewing them that
everything was made up, so why do they seem true
anyway? Perhaps because they tell us something about
ourselves that we cannot get from simple facts. Facts only
become meaningful through analysis, through translation,
through narrative. Think about it. Where does meaning
come from? This sort of reminds me of the old riddle, "if
a tree falls in a forest and there's no one to hear it, does it
make a sound?" Well, you could say "it depends on how
you define sound. If you define sound as the movement of
air molecules in a wave in response to the action of the
tree hitting the ground, then yes it does. If you define
sound as the reception of these waves that are then

converted by the brain into a perception of sound, than no."

But let's go further than that. What if there were no humans, in fact, what if there were no ears anywhere on earth? Does the tree make a sound? If no one could perceive those waves, if we didn't know they existed, we couldn't label them as sound, so no sound is produced. Just pressure waves.

The point is that meaning is created in the mind. We take facts and make meaning out of them in our minds. Sound isn't sound until the pressure vibrations are translated by our brains into what we call sounds. So what if we ran simulations of possible scenarios and then saw how we reacted to them? Pilots do that in order to learn how to fly before they actually get in a real aircraft and take it up into the sky. We run simulations on our computers to figure out all sorts of things - to make predictions. If we get data in a place that won't actually endanger our lives, then we can perhaps have some information to use when the real thing comes along.

We learn how to deal with future events, or just to understand alternate realities or beliefs or situations that we do not have direct access to.

Novels are essentially simulations.

Does this mean we are all ready for the zombie apocalypse because we watched *The Walking Dead*? Well, that's where symbolism comes in, which is a lot of fun, as you'll see below in my essay about Frank Baum's *The Wizard of Oz* and American Populism.

So, now we are going to take a look at some of the conventions that are expected when you write about literature. No, this doesn't mean going back to formula. It means using what we've already built on and applying it to this discipline.

When you write about literature, you will want to concentrate on your direct reading of the text itself. What does it mean to you? As throughout this book, start first with your experience. If you are responding to a specific prompt, then write about how the characters, action, and themes in the book relate to the prompt from your own perspective. This is very important. As I've mentioned before, what you really need to show in college level writing is your thinking. Before you go and look up what others have said about the novel, or poem, or short story, write down what you think. Use specific examples from the piece of literature under analysis. Use quotes to illustrate your points. Before you take on your own literary analysis, you will read a few essays to get an idea what I mean.

After you have thought about and written your response to the reading, then you can go to secondary sources to see what other interpretations there are of the work. Do they agree with you? Do they disagree with you? What have literary scholars found in the work that you found surprising? Of course, as with any paper, be sure that you stay focused. It is easy to go on tangents when you discover something surprising.

When analyzing art, film, literature, or any media, you always start with the primary source: the piece of work under scrutiny. Secondary sources are academic analyses of the work. Notice that usually this is not the same as a review of the work. In college, it is not your goal to review works in terms of quality, especially in terms of "I liked" or "I didn't like." Liking is very subjective and doesn't go very far. In the end, it doesn't matter if you liked a work or not, what matters is if the work accomplished what it set out to do. Did it make you think? Did it make you see the world in a new way?

I cannot reiterate this enough. Do not review literature, art, film, or music for a college essay unless specifically asked to do so. Instead, look at how the work communicates something about our shared cultures, values, psychology, politics, ideologies, etc. How is it a test simulation for our real world?

So, again, before you use any secondary sources, you should read, and re-read, the piece of literature and make some notes about the reading.

This is known as annotation.

## Annotating Primary Sources

When you first read a primary source, the actual piece of literature be it short story, poem, or novel, you ought to read it for enjoyment. Kick back, relax, and let the story wash over you. Then, reflect on your reading. Free-write any ideas that came to mind. What did you think of while you read it? In other words, what schema did it activate? Did it make you think of social issues? Did it make you think of political issues? Psychological and personal issues?

Next, you'll want to think about the theme of the story or poem. Think rhetorically. As I stated earlier, we enjoy stories because they tell us about ourselves. So, why did the author write this story? What does it tell you about their view of the world, and importantly, what does it tell you about your view of the world? How you read and analyze the themes and symbolism have as much to do with your experience of both reading the story and the experiences you had before you read the story. Again, that is those gaps in the text you fill in with your experiences. It is your interpretation.

Then, go back through the story or poem and read it critically. Are your thoughts and insights justified? Can you find quotes that back up your initial thoughts? Annotate the work as you go through it the second time. Underline important ideas. Make notes in the margin. Ask questions. Interact with the text. Go beyond your initial observations and thoughts - you may stumble across startling realizations.

When you annotate a work, you are actively reading it. You are interacting with it. Instead of lying back and passively taking it in, you are upright, pen in hand, underlining, writing notes, writing questions, as you read.

For some assignments, this will be the end. Sometimes all that you'll need to do is show your own interpretation of the work and not go to secondary sources. This is called explication.

Here's an example of an explication I did of the first section of T.S. Eliot's poem "Wasteland." First, I'll give you this part of the poem, followed by the essay. Then we will regroup and talk about how I approached the essay through close reading. Note that I did use the introduction to the poem in Greenblatt's text to help explicate it. The word 'explicate' comes from the Latin 'explicare,' to reveal. When we explicate a text, we reveal what might at first be hidden from plain view. We look for themes and symbolism.

## The Waste Land

By T.S. Eliot
*FOR EZRA POUND*
IL MIGLIOR FABBRO

*I. The Burial of the Dead*

April is the cruelest month, breeding
Lilacs out of the dead land, mixing
Memory and desire, stirring
Dull roots with spring rain.
Winter kept us warm, covering
Earth in forgetful snow, feeding
A little life with dried tubers.
Summer surprised us, coming over the Starnbergersee
With a shower of rain; we stopped in the colonnade,
And went on in sunlight, into the Hofgarten,
And drank coffee, and talked for an hour.
Bin gar keine Russin, stamm' aus Litauen, echt deutsch.
And when we were children, staying at the arch-duke's,
My cousin's, he took me out on a sled,
And I was frightened. He said, Marie,
Marie, hold on tight. And down we went.
In the mountains, there you feel free.
I read, much of the night, and go south in the winter.

What are the roots that clutch, what branches grow

Out of this stony rubbish? Son of man,
You cannot say, or guess, for you know only
A heap of broken images, where the sun beats,
And the dead tree gives no shelter, the cricket no relief,
And the dry stone no sound of water. Only
There is shadow under this red rock,
(Come in under the shadow of this red rock),
And I will show you something different from either
Your shadow at morning striding behind you
Or your shadow at evening rising to meet you;
I will show you fear in a handful of dust.

> *Frisch weht der Wind*
> *Der Heimat zu*
> *Mein Irisch Kind,*
> *Wo weilest du?*

"You gave me hyacinths first a year ago;
"They called me the hyacinth girl."
—Yet when we came back, late, from the Hyacinth
garden,
Your arms full, and your hair wet, I could not
Speak, and my eyes failed, I was neither
Living nor dead, and I knew nothing,
Looking into the heart of light, the silence.
*Oed' und leer das Meer.*

  Madame Sosostris, famous clairvoyante,
Had a bad cold, nevertheless
Is known to be the wisest woman in Europe,
With a wicked pack of cards. Here, said she,

Is your card, the drowned Phoenician Sailor,
(Those are pearls that were his eyes. Look!)
Here is Belladonna, the Lady of the Rocks,
The lady of situations.
Here is the man with three staves, and here the Wheel,
And here is the one-eyed merchant, and this card,
Which is blank, is something he carries on his back,
Which I am forbidden to see. I do not find
The Hanged Man. Fear death by water.
I see crowds of people, walking round in a ring.
Thank you. If you see dear Mrs. Equitone,
Tell her I bring the horoscope myself:
One must be so careful these days.

  Unreal City,
Under the brown fog of a winter dawn,
A crowd flowed over London Bridge, so many,
I had not thought death had undone so many.
Sighs, short and infrequent, were exhaled,
And each man fixed his eyes before his feet.
Flowed up the hill and down King William Street,
To where Saint Mary Woolnoth kept the hours
With a dead sound on the final stroke of nine.
There I saw one I knew, and stopped him, crying:
"Stetson!
"You who were with me in the ships at Mylae!
"That corpse you planted last year in your garden,
"Has it begun to sprout? Will it bloom this year?
"Or has the sudden frost disturbed its bed?

"Oh keep the Dog far hence, that's friend to men,
"Or with his nails he'll dig it up again!
"You! hypocrite lecteur!—mon semblable,—mon frère!"

## Practice 9-2: The Waste Land

*Before you move on to read the explication, spend 10 minutes writing your own notes about the poem. Can you make sense of it? Take it one line at a time. What can you figure out? What is Eliot saying here? What are the images he is giving us? The best way to figure out a poem, in fact, the fun in reading poetry, I think, is digging into it, in explicating the poem and watching it reveal its inner truth. So, do your best and see what you come up with. Write it down. Then read my explication of it below. You will be asked to compare your thoughts about the poem with the explication and see what you learned about reading poetry, about this poem, and indeed, what you discovered that perhaps I missed. The beauty of literature, especially poetry, is that there can be many different ways to interpret it. This doesn't mean that all interpretations are valid - they have to be backed up by evidence from the text itself. This is how you 'prove' your point when analyzing literature - by using direct quotes from the work itself and then talking about what they mean to you.*

## Man Without God or Nature:
## An Explication of T.S. Eliot's "The Wasteland,"
## Section 1: The Burial of the Dead
## By David Foulds

T.S. Eliot wrote "The Wasteland" in 1922. After the atrocities of World War I, it seemed more and more likely that Nietzsche was right: "Gott ist tott," God is dead. In a world that could create such a devastating spectacle, one where the value of human life seemed negligible and power was wielded by the few with so little regard to the many, one is left wondering how there could be a God in such a place. In this new godless universe, life lacks meaning. If there is nothing after this life, then what exactly is the point of life? Couple this with the move from an agricultural livelihood to dehumanizing factory work in the cities, the world humans have created does indeed begin to feel like a "wasteland." In the poem, considered by many to be *the* most important piece of modern literature, Eliot coalesces this feeling of anxiety and futility into a somewhat confusing but ultimately satisfying whole. A common theme throughout the poem is that of the futility of rebirth as a concept. Nature renews itself year after year, but this is just false hope for us, because without God, there is no rebirth, no renewal. There is just struggle and decay. Without God, nature is the boss. It goes on doing what it does regardless of our meaningless and tedious activity. Long after we are gone, the natural world will still be here.

Eliot opens the poem writing, "April is the cruelest month" (1). The reader immediately can sense that something strange is afoot. April is a rather delightful month. It is the beginning of spring; flowers are blooming, days are getting longer and warmer, birds are chirping. What could possibly make it cruel? But this is exactly what makes it cruel: the promise of rebirth and new hope, hope that does not come to fruition. April thus holds false promises and will not be able to deliver on those promises. The next line expands on this theme: "breeding / Lilacs out of the dead land" (1-2). Indeed, the flowers bloom from the dead of winter. He continues, "mixing / Memory and desire" (2-3). This desire is the desire for new life, new beginnings, but our memory of the war tells us that there is no hope. How will this time be different? Next, he writes, "stirring / Dull roots with spring rain" (3-4) further expanding on the springtime metaphor.

He continues with "Winter kept us warm" (5). Again we have what appears to be an ironic statement: winter is cold and dark, how can it keep one warm? But this warmth is not in temperature, but in protecting us from springtime desire and hope, for in the winter the snow covered up our memories of the past, it "cover(ed) / Earth in forgetful snow, feeding / A little life with dried tubers" (5-7) Note here that structurally, Eliot ends most of these lines with the action verb, "breeding," "mixing," "stirring," "covering," "feeding." This gives the rhyming repetition of the "ing" sound at the end of each line and emphasizes the action of nature on the world. Thus, we are at the hands of nature, it is acting *on* us, out of our control.

This concept is further elucidated in the next line, where he writes, "Summer surprised us" (8). Summer always comes at the same time each year. It is highly predictable, so how can one be surprised by summer? This again reinforces the helplessness of man over the forces of nature, and indeed tells the reader that man is now apart from nature, that he does not understand it. He is out of the rhythms of it. The line continues, "coming over the Starnbergersee / With a shower of rain" (8-9). The footnote in The Norton Anthology of English Literature states that this is a lake where King Ludwig II of Bavaria drowned in 1886. Ludwig was a huge fan of Wagner, as was Eliot himself, as his opera *Tristan and Isolde* is a recurring element in the poem. Eliot is here talking about rain and mentions the lake where this King drowned himself. The element, water, thus took the life of the king, a symbol of the old world and the peak of man's social hierarchy. Again, nature claims authority over man, and man is depressed and perhaps corrupt.

Eliot now brings in the narrator and his party, stating that "*we* stopped in the colonnade, / And went on in sunlight, into the Hofgarten, / And drank coffee, and talked for an hour" (9-11) (italics mine). Eliot has moved from the large natural world, down to the movements and idyll conversation of a few individuals. This rapid contrast provides a scale for the human inhabitants: they are quite small and inconsequential. This is then further clarified when his cousin takes him on a sled. Here is a child on the side of a mountain and is "frightened" (15). He is told to "hold on tight" (16) and they sled down the mountain. The persona then notes "In the mountains, there you feel free" (17). He here reflects that the natural world, which is out of our control and is frightening, is also real and true, it sets you free. This will contrast to the "Unreal City" of line 60.

Eliot returns to images of nature in the next stanza, with "What are the roots that clutch, what branches grow / Out of this stony rubbish?" (19-20). Nature again dominates over man, and will be here long after we are gone. One can imagine the roots pushing their way through the ruins of a city, the stony rubbish of a decayed civilization. The next few lines refer to Ecclesiastes XII: "Son of man, / You cannot say, or guess, for you know only / A heap of broken images, where the sun beats, / And the dead tree gives no shelter, the cricket no relief" (20-23). The "son of man" is Ezekiel, being addressed by God. Man knows only a "heap of broken images," referring to man's very limited way of knowing the world. Memory exists as such for us, fragmented memories strewn together haphazardly as we search for some kind of narrative, some meaning to our lives. The tree in Ecclesiastes is an almond tree which flourishes, but here the tree is dead and cannot provide shelter. In other words, God has gone from the garden and left the tree to die, so modern man has no shelter from him.

Eliot next refers to Isaiah 32, in which rulers would rule with justice and provide shelter from the wind, but here the rock is "red" (25, 26) and the shelter it provides is from the sun, not the wind. He writes, "Only / There is shadow under this red rock, / (Come in under the shadow of this red rock), / And I will show you something different from either / Your shadow at morning striding behind you / Or your shadow at evening rising to meet you" (24-29). The rock is not a protection from the elements, but from the sun, the giver of life. And the red rock itself has connotations of hell, so this might be the devil beckoning from under the rock, which is also deduced from the parenthetical "(Come in under the shadow...)" of line 26. It is as if the devil is hiding under there, his spindly evil fingers quietly seducing you to come in to the land of shadow. The loss of sunlight means a loss of direction, the shadow of the morning, the past, can no longer be seen, nor can the shadow of the evening, the future. It is man cut off from nature. Instead, he offers "fear in a handful of dust" (30), the dust having connotations of decay and entropy. Moreover, this whole section refers to old age and death via the reference to Isaiah 32. Death without God is meaningless. We fear becoming just a "handful of dust."

The next four lines are in German and are from Wagner's *Tristan und Isolde* I, versus 5-8. This keys back to the earlier reference to King Ludwig, and is a recurring motif throughout the poem. He also brings in Wagner on line 43, also in German, which reads "Waste and empty is the sea." The first entry is about youthful love lost, and the next is from when Tristan is dying and waiting for Isolde. Between these two entries, he writes, "'You gave me hyacinths first a year ago; / 'They called me the hyacinth girl.' / --Yet when you came back, late, from the Hyacinth garden, / Your arms full, and your hair wet, I could not / Speak, and my eyes failed. I was neither / living nor dead, and I knew nothing, / Looking into the heart of light, the silence" (35-40). Hyacinth was a man killed accidentally by Apollo and from his body this flower grew, thus they again represent rebirth from death. A woman here is brought an armful of hyacinths which were collected perhaps with difficulty in the rain ("your hair wet"), but the woman "could not speak" and her "eyes failed." This brings us back to the opening of the poem, where "April is the cruelest month": again the rebirth, the hope of renewal lacks meaning because of the death of the individual without God. She looks "into the heart of light" but there is nothing there but "silence." The sea is empty.

Eliot next takes us to an Egyptian fortune-teller named "Madame Sosostris" (43) who is "the wisest woman in Europe" (45). She does a Tarot reading and pulls "the drowned Phoenician Sailor" who has "pearls in his eyes" (47-48), the "Belladonna" (49), "the man with three staves" (51), "the Wheel" (51) and the "one-eyed merchant" (52). Tarot cards are used to tell a man's future. Eliot then has her draw a blank card, "which [he is] forbidden to see" (54). At this point in our civilization, we cannot see what is ahead. The fortune teller is the wisest because she knows that there is no future to tell. There is no heaven. Eliot also writes that he did "not find the

Hanged Man," which is actually not of death but of rebirth, again reiterating this theme.

Eliot begins the next stanza with just two words on line 60: "Unreal City." In this stanza, he often equates London with Dante's Hell. The fog is "brown" (61), the crowd which flows over the London Bridge is like the dead being ferried across the river Styx: "A crowd flowed over London Bridge, so many, / I had not thought death had undone so many" (62-63). Eliot himself notes that this scene refers to Inferno III, 55-57 and that the next line, "Sighs, short and infrequent, were exhaled" (64) refers to Inferno IV, 25-27, where the spirits stuck in Limbo let out sighs, as they will never be accepted into the kingdom of heaven. So, here we have very strong imagery of the world as a wasteland, as a hell with no meaning and no God. Everyone in London just stares at their feet as the clock strikes nine, the hour in which Jesus died. We are forever in Limbo with no way to get into Heaven.

The persona now sees a man he knew from a battle in World War I at the battle of Mylae and he asks, "'That corpse you planted last year in your garden, / 'Has it begun to sprout? Will it bloom this year? / 'Or has the sudden frost disturbed its bed?" (69-72). This brings us back to the earlier image of the Hyacinth growing out of the corpse and with the metaphor of winter keeping us warm by keeping the hope for rebirth at bay.

Eliot closes the section with the exclamation: "You! Hypocrite lecteur!—mon semblable—mon frère!" (76). This is from Charles Baudelaire's preface to *Fleurs du Mal* in which humans are "sunk in stupidity, sin and evil" (Greenblatt 2298) and is literally translated as "hypocrite reader!—my likeness—my brother!" Here Eliot is calling directly to the reader, calling him both his "brother," his "likeness" and also a "hypocrite," thus calling himself and everyone a hypocrite. To Eliot, we are all living a lie, a life in the shadow, a life of fragmented memories, a life of false hope and no happily ever after.

For Eliot, modern man is lost and disconnected from the natural world. We can no longer believe in heaven and life on earth is hell. The world we have created and continue to create is a wasteland, one where there is no hope for rebirth and renewal. And yet the poem is strangely hopeful. Nature continues to exist. Spring and Summer come to us year after year. Rebirth does happen. Perhaps if we reconnect with nature, if we are able to find God in nature, we will also be able to tap back into the cycle of rebirth and climb out of the wasteland.

## Works Cited:

Greenblatt, Steven (ed). *The Norton Anthology of English Literature 8th Edition, Volume 2*. New York: Norton, 2006. Print.

## Practice 9-3: Waste Land Part 2

*Now, compare your first impressions from practice 9-1 to my interpretation of the poem. What surprised you? What made sense? What was confusing? Now right through that confusion. Try to figure out what you can. I know poetry is not easy, so never fear, we will look at The Wizard of Oz next. Write some observations about the essay. How was it constructed? What was the thesis? What was the evidence? How was the evidence presented? Do you "buy" the argument I make?*

Now let's look at an essay that uses both primary and secondary sources. Here, the primary source is Frank Baum's *The Wizard of Oz*. Since most of you have probably seen the movie version, you'll already be somewhat familiar with the text. I urge you to read the original written text by Baum. It is much darker and absolutely fascinating.

## Intention or Reception?:
## Baum's Wizard of Oz as Political Parable
## By David Foulds

Although L. Frank Baum's *The Wonderful Wizard of Oz* was written in 1900, it wasn't until the spring of 1964 that a sociopolitical reading of the story came to the discussion of Baum's text. Henry M. Littlefield, then a High School teacher in New York, wrote a short essay that was published in the journal *American Quarterly* titled "The Wizard of Oz: Parable on Populism." In this essay, Littlefield argues that Baum's text can be used by educators to elucidate "to an astonishing degree the world of political reality which surrounded Baum in 1900" (48). His basic premise is that the "Silver Shoes" and "road of yellow brick" in the story represent the metals silver and gold, that the Wicked Witch of the East represents industrial capitalism, the Scarecrow is the average mid-west farmer, the Lion is William Jennings Bryan, Dorothy is "everyman," the Tin Woodman represents the dehumanization of labor, bleak Kansas represents the effects of "low prices, grasshoppers, and blizzards of…1886-87" and Oz is Washington DC (50-52). Thus, Littlefield argues, as Dorothy is delivered to safety through the power of the Silver Shoes, "everyman" will be delivered by the power of silver. This parallels the Populist platform of "free and unlimited coinage of silver" which would "inflate the money supply, thus making it easier for cash strapped farmers and small businessmen to borrow money and pay off debts" (Taylor 3). But did Baum actually have this parable in mind when he wrote the text?

Littlefield makes a compelling argument. At the time of writing, and in the story, Kansas was a "great gray prairie" which the "sun had plowed into a gray mass, with little cracks running through it" (Baum 13). Aunt Em, representative of the farm worker, is "thin and gaunt, and never smiled, now," and Uncle Henry "worked from morning till night and did not know what joy was" (14). Dorothy and Toto are whisked away by the Populist cyclone and their little house lands on the Wicked Witch of the East thus crushing the Eastern Industrial Complex. According to Quentin Taylor, Midwestern farmers often blamed their woes on the nefarious practices of Wall Street bankers, who have "enslaved" the "little people" (6). When Dorothy's house lands on the Witch, Dorothy frees the Munchkins from slavery and is given the Silver Shoes. Littlefield argues that this is the central Populist stance: give the farmers silver and they will be freed from "slavery" by the complex. He continues his discussion citing that the yellow brick road leads to the Emerald City (Washington) which is green (money) and run by a "humbug" who has no actual powers. The Scarecrow represents the farmer who is perceived as ignorant (no brains) but is actually very shrewd. The Tin Man is the dehumanized worker who has lost his heart in the mechanical jungle, and the roaring lion is Bryan himself, who is actually courageous though accused of being a coward.

Littlefield notes that "the relationships and analogies [he outlines] are admittedly theoretical, but...are far too consistent to be coincidental" (58). It is certainly difficult to believe that these connections were not the intention of the writer, as they do fit the political climate in which Baum was writing to a high degree. But other critics, such as Bradley A. Hansen, insist that Baum did not intend for these connections to be made. Instead, he says that historical research about Baum "undermines" (255) this proposition, that Baum "did not intend the book to be anything more than a delightful story" (Ibid). Did Baum write the text as a parable to the Populist movement, championing Bryan's push for "free silver," or was the book, as Baum himself claims, "written solely to please children of today"? (Baum 1).

Ranjit S. Dighe, Assistant Professor of Economics and State University of New York, points out that "Baum's great-grandson Roger...call[s] the Populist-parable interpretation 'insane'" (87), while historians tend to side with Littlefield. The fact is, "Baum left no hard evidence that he intended his story to have an allegorical meaning: no diary entry, no letter, not even an offhand remark to a friend" (Rockoff). It seems the argument that Baum consciously created the book with this trope in mind stems from a statement by Frank Josyln Baum, the author's oldest son, who wrote a biography of his father in 1961. In the book, he states that Baum "marched in torchlight parades in behalf of Bryan's candidacy." This seems to jibe with the pro-intention argument. If Baum was politically active in favor of Bryan, he was clearly mindful of the free silver debate, and when we turn to the text, there is ample evidence that this is so. However, Dighe notes that "his letters to family members and associates virtually never mention politics – the assertion that his father was a Democrat was likely mistaken" (88). In addition, for several years, Baum owned and edited a Republican newspaper and in the summer of 1896, he published a pro-McKinley poem in a Chicago newspaper (Parker). So perhaps Littlefield's analysis is correct in his assertion that Baum was writing a political parable, but was incorrect that it was pro-Populist. William R. Leach believes that the story "met – almost perfectly – the particular ethical and emotional needs of people living in a new urban industrial society," and that it "exalted the opulence and magic of the metropolis" (Parker). Certainly the people in the Emerald city do seem happy with their material, urban environment. Under this analysis, and with these new facts, it seems quite possible that Baum was not pro-Populist.

Thus, arguments about intentionality are inconclusive. Gretchen Ritter and others argue that intentionality is unimportant anyway. Instead, what is interesting is what each reader finds when closely analyzing the text. There is, of course, a whole field dedicated to this approach, called "New Criticism." According to Michael Delahoyde, "New Criticism emphasizes explication, or 'close reading' of 'the work itself.' It rejects old historicism's interest in biographical and sociological matters."

When writing a novel, an author brings his own experiences, his unique way of perceiving the world to his work. Some of what he writes may be intentional, some from his unconscious mind. The parables that Littlefield points out are very strong: they do exist. This may have been unconscious on Baum's part. But other readings are equally possible which may or may not have been intended. Littlefield's interpretation is only one of many possible interpretations; his analysis is one way of generating interest and stimulating a thoughtful discussion of both the text and the politics of the time. But that is the joy of New Criticism. Upon engaging directly with the text, each reader learns as much about their own perceptions about the world as those of the author.

While Littlefield's interpretation is interesting, it is limited. He concentrates on the colors of gold and silver because these colors fit his analysis. However, the road is not actually "gold," but is instead "yellow." Gold is mentioned several times in the text, but it is more often attributed to the West than the East, as is the color yellow. The Winkies live in a yellow castle, in the "Golden land of the West" (Baum 134), and the Golden Cap was created in the North. Yellow is the color of the West, the East is coded blue and the South red. What about these other colors? What do they signify in Littlefield's analysis? The only goldsmith mentioned in the book is a Winkie, and these are timid creatures who were easily enslaved by the Wicked Witch. It is a far stretch to imagine these creatures as representing powerful politicians who are in control of gold. Instead, I posit that this connection of "West" with "gold" is more likely associated with California's gold rush than with the powers of the East.

One might also take a socialist approach to the work. A strong theme of the book is that the "little guy" is the one that is needed to get anything done, and that true power comes from within. Dorothy, just a "little girl," is able to take down a witch because she is "good" on the inside. The Tin Woodman is found rusted in a field, and is only able to move again with the aid of Dorothy and the Scarecrow. The Scarecrow himself is only freed with the help of Dorothy. In other words, the creations of man only work with the help of man. Industry only runs with people manning the assembly line. A factory with no workers is useless. The lion makes an offhand comment that "it must be a very uncomfortable thing not to be alive" (72): machines lack life, lack a "heart" or "brains." The power comes from the workers, not the machine: the Woodman is already loving, the Scarecrow already wise, the lion already courageous. Dorothy herself gets no aid from Oz in her quest to return home. It is "good-ol' American ingenuity" that saves the day. The little people have the power, they just need to have faith in themselves.

These are just a couple of possible alternative ways of interpreting the text. There is also a strong current of slavery issues, Native American issues and feminist issues running through the tale. While a discussion of *The Wonderful Wizard of Oz* as a parable on Populism is a fascinating and informative way of analyzing the work, it is only one, and it exists independent of the writer's intention. It is certainly possible that Baum did consciously write the tale as a parable for, or against, the politics of Populism, but without further proof, it is impossible from the text itself to determine intention. Who knows where stories come from? Writers themselves often cannot say why they chose a certain color or setting or character. The fact that complete opposite analyses can come from reading the same text certainly says much more about the reader of the text than the writer.

## Works Cited:

Baum, L. Frank. *The Wonderful Wizard of Oz.* New York: Barnes and Noble, 2008. Print.

Delahoyde, Michael. "New Criticism." *Washington State University*, 2013. Web. 24 Sept 2013.

Dighe, Ranjit. "Oz, Populism, and Intent." *Essays in Economic and Business History.* (2002). Print.

Hansen, Bradley A. "The Fable of The Allegory: The Wizard of Oz in Economics." *The Journal of Economic Education* 33.3 (2002): 254-264. Print.

Littlefield, Henry M. 1964. "The Wizard of Oz: Parable on Populism." *American Quarterly* 16.1 (1964): 47-58. Print.

Parker, David B. "The Rise and Fall of the Wonderful Wizard of Oz as a Parable on Populism." *Journal of the Georgia Association of Historians* 15 (1994): 49-63. Print.

Rockoff, H. "The wizard of Oz as a monetary allegory." *Journal of Political Economy* 98.4 (1990): 739-60. Print.

Ritter, Gretchen. "Silver Slippers and a Golden Cap: L. Frank Baum's The Wonderful Wizard of Oz and Historical Memory in American Politics." *Journal of American Studies* 31. 2 (1997): 171-202. Print.

Taylor, Quentin. "Money and Politics in the Land of Oz." *News, Commentary and Analysis* (2005). Print.

## Practice 9-4: Analyze the Analysis

*Now, do a rhetorical analysis on my analysis of the book. If you haven't read The Wonderful Wizard of Oz, it would be smart to at least watch the film so you can get the most out of this exercise. While there are some significant differences between the book and the film, the movie should be sufficient. Since this is an activity rather than a major essay, it is okay to swap out the film for the book.*

*As before, I want you to break down the essay into its organizational parts. What is the thesis? What is the evidence? What are the counter arguments? What is the conclusion? Do I end up where I started? Do you see change in my opinion or my thought process as I work through the essay? Use quotes and paraphrasing from the essay to discuss how I made my argument and used evidence.*

## Major Essay Task: Literary Analysis

Now, it's your turn. Use what you've learned here to write about a short story, novel, or poem you chose to read or was chosen for you in your course. Follow the suggestions above. Read the text, think about it, write down ideas, re-read and annotate, come up with a thesis for your paper, find three secondary sources, read them and see how they help you better understand the work. Draft your essay and peer review. Your final essay should be 4-5 pages, MLA style.

## **Works Cited:**

Baum, Frank. *The Wizard of Oz.* New York: Penguin. 2008

Carr, Nicholas. *The Shallows: What the Internet is Doing to Our Brains.* New York: Norton, 2011. Print.

Graff, Gerald and Birkenstein, Cathy. *They Say/I Say: The Moves That Matter in Academic Writing.* Chicago: Norton. 2017. Print.

Iser, Wolfgang. *The Act of Reading.* John Hopkins Press, 1980. Print

# CHAPTER TEN

## *Writing About Visual Media*

Writing about visual media is really writing about visual semiotics. You may recall this word from an earlier chapter. According to Mediatexthack, an open text curated by Erika Pearson and Bernard Madill, and published by BCcampus, "Semiotics is the study of signs and their meaning in society. A sign is something which can stand for something else – in other words, a sign is anything that can convey meaning. So, words can be signs, drawings can be signs, photographs can be signs, even street signs can be signs. Modes of dress and style, the type of bag you have, or even where you live can also be considered signs, in that they convey meaning." We go around in the world, always 'reading' what we see, looking for meaning. In this definition, we can think of the whole world, really, as mediated signs, as everything we see is mediated through our senses, translated by us to mean something more than just what it is. This includes written words, as they are indeed not the thing itself, but instead point to the thing they are referring to. The word "tree" isn't a tree, but when I say or write "tree" you know what I'm talking about, and your brain brings up the image of a tree. Of course, we don't all think of the same tree, as I mentioned earlier when discussing our schema. How we translate any media into meaning has as much to do with our own experience of the world, in this case of particular trees, as does the word "tree" itself.

The fun in writing about semiotics, then, about this translation of signs to meaning, is thinking about what each sign connotes for us individually, socially, and culturally. Marketing is based on this concept. It is based on our need to associate signs with meaning. Let's explore this in the next practice.

## Practice 10-1: Reading Visual Rhetoric

*Google "Advertisements for beer" and filter your search so you only see images. Scan through the images and write down some things that occur to you as you do. What do the images have in common? You might start thinking about form first. What are some colors and shapes that are common? How are the ads composed? In other words, what is prominent in the picture? Then, look at the content. What is pictured in the ads? What common elements do you see? What type of people? What are they doing? What, overall, are we supposed to think from viewing these images beer will do for us? Pick one ad and really 'read' it closely. Describe what you see and what it is telling you to believe. Do you believe it?*

*Now Google "advertisements for lipstick" and repeat the above.*

*What are these advertisers really selling? What visual semiotics are they using?*

Yes, advertising often tries to link their product with a result that has nothing to do with the product itself. It is selling a lifestyle, or a social status, or just plain objectifying the female gender as purely sexual or the male gender as machismo. And, these are often seen as ideals. "If you buy this, you will be sexually attractive in the most generic, superficial way."

Perhaps you've already done some of this critical analysis of rhetoric used in marketing during your high school years. If so, it never hurts to be reminded that we need to think critically of what is being pushed upon us practically 24/7. You hold in your hand a sort-of brainwashing device. Every bit of content that you click was put there to convince you of something. Think about it. Why does anyone take the time to put anything on the internet? In an era where we are spending countless hours staring at media, we need more than ever to be awake, thinking critically, and not just passively receiving information. What are you being told about what it is to be American, Latinx, Japanese, young, smart, strong, sexy etc? How much of what you believe to be true is just a product of repeated exposure to these visual semiotics? We can just get so used to the noise of these messages, being repeated over and over, almost like a strange form of torture, that we just, without even realizing it, start to accept them as 'truth.' But they aren't truth at all. The goal of advertising is to sell you something by making you believe that if you give them money in exchange for their product or service, you will become rich, sexy, interesting, funny, etc.

The media, as you are fully aware, often perpetuates racial stereotypes. In my American Cinema/American Culture course, the first film we watch is Paul Haggis' *Crash*. While it won an Oscar for best picture in 2005, the film is not without controversy. Whether Crash opens up a conversation about race or merely perpetuates racial stereotypes is, to some, up to interpretation." For example, two African-American men, Peter (Lorenz Tate) and Anthony (Chris "Ludacris" Bridges) are walking in Beverly Hills. Anthony is complaining to Peter about the lack of service they got in a restaurant because of their skin color. He takes issue with the fact that they didn't get coffee. However, as Peter points out, "[they] didn't ask for coffee." Here, Peter is refuting Anthony's insistence that he was discriminated against since his argument lacks evidence. They didn't get served coffee not because they are black, but because they didn't order any. Anthony insists that they got bad service because white people think that black people don't tip. Peter again points out the flaw in Anthony's argument because the fact is that he did not leave a tip. Anthony retorts "With that service?"

This exchange brings to light a much larger issue regarding race and oppression. Arguably, Anthony fulfilled the very stereotypes that he is railing against, as Peter repeatedly points out. However, Anthony's rebuttals as to why he acted the way he did are equally valid. He felt the waitress discriminated against them, so he didn't tip, and we are left to assume that the waitress was likely angry when she received no tip, thus confirming the stereotype that African American men don't tip.

As Anthony and Peter continue up the street, a rich white couple, Jean Cabot (Sandra Bullock) and her husband Rick (Brandon Frasier), approach the two men, Jean then pulls Rick closer to him, as if afraid. Anthony points this out and wonders why she is afraid of two well-dressed young guys who look like college students. He says that if anyone should be afraid, it should be them. They are in a "neighborhood filled with white racists hopped up on caffeine." This points to the all too common incidence of African-America males being attacked by white police officers under the assumption that they are "thugs" with no evidence at all. The audience assumes, at this point, that the film will allow us to think about these assumptions and find out that they are not true: Anthony and Peter are good guys, and the rich white couple is wrong to be scared of them just because of their skin color.

But when Peter asks, "then why aren't we afraid?" Anthony responds, "Maybe because we have guns," and pulls a handgun out of his jacket. They proceed to carjack the Cabot's Lincoln Navigator, thus actually, in the end, perpetuating the very stereotype that it seemed Haggis was trying to dispel.

## Practice 10-2: Crash

*In a 2015 article in Variety magazine, director Paul Haggis talks about his approach to the film:*

*"On 'Crash,' what I decided to do early on was present stereotypes for the first 30 minutes," he said. "And then reinforce those stereotypes. And make you feel uncomfortable, then representing it to make you feel very comfortable because I say, 'Shh, we're in the dark. It's fine, you can think these things. You can laugh at these people. We all know Hispanics park their cars on a lawn, and we all know that Asians can't drive in the dark. I know you're a big liberal, but it's OK, nobody's going to see you laugh.' As soon as I made you feel comfortable, I could very slowly start turning you around in the seat so I left you spinning as you walked out of the movie theater. That was the intent."*

*What is problematic about what he says here? What are his assumptions about the world we live in? About people?*

## Practice 10-3: Minorities in the Media

*Think of how minorities are presented in the media. Think of the stereotypes we see. What occupations do particular minorities seem to always occupy? Who are typically portrayed as criminals? As the mafia or mob? As cooks or maids? As educated or not educated? As violent or non-violent? As friendly or mean? As overly sexualized or as asexual?*

*Now, Google "Margaret Cho talks about race" and "Margaret Cho - Shame." Write about what Cho says in her stand-up comedy routine. Respond to things she says that jump out at you. Analyze them. What does her comedy make you feel? Think? She plays a lot with "Asian" stereotypes in her comedy. Is she perpetuating or dismantling these stereotypes?*

## Writing about Film

Writing about film is much like writing about literature. This should be no surprise since both are, usually, narratives. What might be surprising is that both are referred to as "texts." You read a film just as you read a movie. Film theorists state that film has its own 'language,' a language of images. When you read, you create images in your mind. When you watch a film, those images are part of the text that you receive, and it is still up to you to interpret what you see and hear. Film, since it is image and sound, uses tools that convey meaning through these senses rather than just through words. This might seem obvious, but many people overlook how film is able to convey multiple layers of meaning through the senses, as we saw above. It isn't just what the characters say and do, it is also where the scene is set, how the light is created, what is in each shot (the mise-en-scene), how the camera is placed and how it moves, the depth of field (how much is in focus, what is blurry), the soundtrack, the sound effects, the editing, the color. All of these elements work together to convey meaning. Reading a film, then, means coming to understand how to read cinematic images and a basic understanding of film language.

Hollywood filmmaking, in particular, is all about masking the filmmaking process. This 'classical' style foregrounds character and story, so that we fall through into the world created by the filmmakers and forget that it is a created piece of art. Continuity editing, as it is called, is designed to hide the edits so that we feel like we are just there in the space of the film. Editors cut when characters or vehicles are moving in order to hide these edits from the viewer. When you are watching a film, are you conscious of when it cuts from one angle to the next? Not usually. Film both mimics our reality and creates a new one in ways that we are so used to that we don't even notice.

Learning about cinematic language allows you to do a formal analysis of a film: to see the signs, the semiotics, used not only by what we see but by how it is presented. Film, being the Bowerbird of the arts, collects from just about every other artistic discipline in its creation. Music, theatre, literature, poetry, photography, painting, graphic design... It also can be read through many different lenses since it is essentially about "us." We can study films socially, culturally, psychologically, politically... This is what makes film analysis so much fun.

Many think of film as mere entertainment. It is just an "escape from reality." Well, perhaps. But what does it mean to be entertained? Sure, there is an element of pleasure. But what else? Is horror pleasurable? Some say yes, some scream no! Sometimes it's funny, but why do we laugh? What do we laugh at? Sometimes it is devastatingly sad, and other times uplifting. Often, at its best, it is a combination of these things. Is this just entertainment?

Let's complicate the word "entertain." David Thorburn, Professor of Film at MIT, says that the word "entertain" not only means to "provide someone with amusement, enjoyment" but also "give attention to, or consideration to an idea, feeling, or suggestion." That changes things a bit. Now, when someone says that studying film in college is a waste of time because film is "just entertainment," you can complicate their assumptions.

In Richard Barsam and David Monahan's excellent textbook *Looking at Movies*, they urge film viewers to differentiate between implicit and explicit meaning. They state, "we should try to be alert to the cultural values, shared ideals, and other ideas that lie just below the surface of the movie we are looking at. Being more alert to these things will make us sensitive to, and appreciative of, the many layers of meaning that any single movie contains" (11).

Layers of meaning.

This is what Thorburn refers to as "the multiplicity principle" of film. Because we are hit through so many senses at once, and because film has a tradition that comes from literature there are many things happening in any given frame of film that can be read. A film's meaning is different than its plot. When someone asks you what a film was "about," you probably typically respond with the plot. This is the explicit meaning - the surface level reading of the film. Many students, when they first write about film or literature, write at this level. They recapitulate the plot. This happened, and then this, and then this.

Film analysis is different. It is looking at the implicit meaning of the film. It is looking at what it is really "about." If you've seen Jason Reitman's film *Juno* (2007), written by Diablo Cody, you might say that it is, as Barsam and Monahan state, "about a rebellious but smart sixteen-year-old girl who gets pregnant and resolves to tackle the problem head on. At first, she decides to get an abortion, but after she backs off that choice, she gets the idea to find a couple to adopt the kid after it's born. She spends the rest of the movie dealing with the implications of that choice" (12). Okay, that's technically what the film is "about," but why this story? Why do we connect to it? What does it tell us about ourselves? Is there an underlying message? Why do you think Diablo Cody wrote this particular script? Why did you see the film? Why was the film meaningful to you?

It is clearly more than entertainment in the usual sense. We also must "entertain" ideas about our social world and about our own lives. What is it that Juno is going through that is so powerful for us? There are so many things here to talk about. The pressure of growing up and having to make adult decisions (a bildungsroman). The ethics of abortion. The complicated issues around adoption, from both the adoptive parents' point of view and the biological mother's and father's point of view. Teenage sexuality and why it is taboo (or not).

Juno bonds with Mark (Jason Bateman), the to-be adoptive father, over their shared love of music. It seems that Mark is not willing, or able, to let go of his youth and go through with the adoption, and even decides to leave his wife with the fantasy that his bond with Juno is romantic. We might even then take this film and use it to jump into a conversation about how American society idealizes and worships youth, and argue that Mark's obsession with not growing up is a reflection of the society we live in: that being old is somehow bad.

When we write about films, we want to look at them, really any of them, even your Hollywood Blockbuster, through these lenses rather than simply recapping what happened. Your writing, as always, is about showing your thinking. About joining the conversation and making new connections. In particular, analyzing film and other visual media is about taking what you see (and hear) and using that to start a deeper conversation about meaning.

Above, I talked mostly about the implicit meanings of the plot, of what happens in the film. But we can, as we did above with the advertisements, read a film by looking specifically at its visual semiotics. What we see on screen is carefully planned even though it is made to look spontaneous. As I mentioned above, Hollywood film form is all about hiding the fact that you are watching a movie. So, we may assume that even if there is a script, the actors acted and the camera was just pointed at them and captured their performance. While this is true of a minority of films, those considered cinema verite, most films are carefully crafted, shot by shot. The mise-en-scene (A French word meaning what you see on screen; including camera placement and lighting, but mostly refers to costume and props as well as set design), is well planned. And by this I don't mean they plan the shots to look cool, but they plan the shots to contribute to the implicit meaning of the film in the layers that Barsam talks about.

For example, Barsam discusses a shot of Vanessa (Jennifer Garner) and Mark painting the future baby's room. Vanessa is dressed in an old Alice in Chains t-shirt. This, of course, references the values and time of their youth in the 90s, and particularly of Mark's ongoing obsession with the music of his youth. However, the once revered t-shirt is now considered essentially a rag: she wears it as a throw away shirt, one that she can get paint all over, and in fact does. The shirt is covered in paint, no longer a sacred item. In fact, it has been painted over with the symbol of adulthood, being a parent, as the paint is used to transform a room into a nursery.

A few other notes about reading films. Pay attention to how films use light and shadow, particularly those of films called "film noir." These are high contrast, black and white films about the seedy underbelly of the crime world, set in the 1940s after World War II. After the war, it was hard to feel like one could really be safe anymore, and even the male fear of women taking over (as they had to move into the workforce when an unprecedented fraction of the male population were off fighting in WWII) is evidenced in these films through the character of the femme fatale. These are those films with the slatted light coming through the blinds. The murders in the dark alleyways. And the vamp or spider-woman, highly sexualized and waiting her next victim. The dark shadows represent fear, the unknown.

You can also analyze camera angles. Most often (though this is actually contextual), when a camera points up at someone, they appear to be powerful, and when it looks down on them, they appear weak and passive. Just google "low angle shot" and "high angle shot" and you will see what I mean. Camera positioning, then, can also contribute to how we feel about a character or situation, how we interpret the meaning of a film.

While this look at analyzing film has been necessarily brief, I hope it provides you with some insights into how to 'read' a film and analyze it. I hope it deepens your enjoyment of filmmaking and encourages you to want to take film classes or at least read more about film criticism.

Below is an essay written by one of my excellent film students, David Turner. Read it as a model text, thinking about how his thesis is argued through viewing the film critically. Note how he analyzed specific scenes and used secondary sources as further evidence and discussion of the ideas presented.


American Culture's Fascination with Vengeance:
From Platoon to Jason Bourne
By David Turner


Our nation has always promoted the virtues of liberty, justice, egalitarianism, and prosperity for all who call it home. We pride ourselves in these and other similar ideals because they provide a template that we can all agree upon as we go through life together. These four virtues act as our nation's nervous system, with their cords intertwined along our fibers to alert us if anyone is infringing upon them. Ideally, those who encroach on our virtues are dealt with in a just and timely manner. None of this is revolutionary; in fact, these guiding principles are in use in one form or another all over the world. As Americans, we may sway more toward liberty while other countries more toward egalitarianism, but both are still fundamental. The same can be said for justice and prosperity. One curiosity I have noted about my country is our fixation on revenge. I must say that the United States promotes it like an additional virtue which we are taught to adhere to at an early age, the same way we are taught patience or forgiveness.

I believe that this vengeance as a virtue mentality stems from our nation's history. We have faced numerous enemies and were one of the last nations in modern era to have blank spots on its' maps. We are also a nation of contradictions. Our constitution is one of the robust and elegant documents in existence, which outlines how a government is to run and how fundamental a separation of power is. In the same breath, we were one of the last nations to have federally protected slavery, a right which was so beloved that we fought a civil war over it. We are also one of the last nations to have to conquer less technologically advanced civilizations for territory during our expansion westward. All of this turmoil cultivated a mentality of justifying why we deserve what we have, and why the less fortunate we put in those positions do not deserve what we took from them. At the time we used manifest destiny and religion to convince ourselves that we were justified, and then later revenge if the first two options fell out of favor. In the twenty-first century revenge is the only narrative tactic we still have to justify our violent behavior as a nation.

I believe it is something that is passed along from generation to generation, especially among men. We are born with a chip on our shoulder. We are expected to defend ourselves which is admirable. We are expected to protect those we love which is commendable as well. But we are also expected to not let any disrespect toward us go unanswered. That is a massive chip on our shoulder which is placed there by our upbringing, which now involves more and more influence from the media and less from our families. Our role models are just as often action heroes as they are biological fathers. Our culture promotes the viewpoint that if you let someone disrespect you, they will only escalate their harassment. Even though our nation is very safe statistically, we are very guarded and suspicious. We encourage our children to act in ways that will protect them and many believe that revenge is a good defensive measure.

We have begun to confuse revenge for courage, and instead promote this attitude of ruthlessness. In Oliver Stone's *Platoon* the theme of vengeance and retribution come up in the second act of the movie and push the plot until the very end. One scene I would like to go into detail with is when PFC Chris Taylor (Charlie Sheen) and the rest of his platoon begin fanning through a village in search of military-aged males. For some context, prior to the platoon entering the village, they lost two men to an improvised explosive at a nearby enemy campsite. They also discovered that one of their men on sentry duty was killed and his body put on display while they were responding to the explosion.

This put the whole platoon on edge as they approach the village where PFC Taylor now found himself looking for fighting-aged men. He and another soldier, nicknamed Bunny, come upon an elderly woman and her overtly crippled son. It is clear that this man could not be responsible for attacking any American soldiers. PFC Taylor is so enraged from the deadly events earlier that he began to fire at the man's feet in order to make him jump. Bunny gets an immense amount of pleasure from this and is openly hostile to Taylor when Taylor relents, mocking him when he does not kill both people, and instead takes it upon himself to kill them. Oliver Stone captured the energy of vengeance very well. Unlike justice or egalitarianism, vengeance perpetuates itself. People derive pleasure from it.

Some research has been done in the field of psychology regarding revenge. One study out of the University of Kentucky showed results which suggested that, "to obtain the positive affect associated with retaliatory aggression, individuals may actively seek out provocation in their daily lives." Doctors Chester and DeWall devised multiple studies involving college aged students in which they would be tasked to play a rigged game and lose, not knowing it was rigged. They would then be allowed to seek vengeance, in some trivial way, against the person that wronged them and have their brain imaged as they did it. The acts of vengeance looked like sticking a voodoo doll with needles or blasting music into a pair of headphones they thought their opponents were wearing, even though no one actually was.

The results showed the reward centers of the brain lighting up as someone inflicted vengeance on their enemy even over something as trivial as a computer game. The implications are fascinating and frightening. Humans appear to get the same type of satisfaction from both successfully accomplishing something and exacting revenge. To our brains, both of those results are victories. This may be why there are so many works in literature and film on vengeance. Humans appear to be intuitively drawn to the idea of it. It is such a trope that I believe it could almost be its' very own rendition of Joseph Campbell's Monomyth, the Punisher's Monomyth perhaps. Quentin Tarantino has made his whole career on tough people seeking revenge. I may be going out on a limb, but I cannot think of a Western or contemporary action movie where the protagonist does not endure some type of wrong which compels them to take up arms against their enemy. This sequence of the character first abstaining from violence and then tolerating violence as a last resort allows us as the viewers to watch all sorts of carnage without fear of actually applauding for something terrifying. We get to insulate ourselves from the reality that we love violence, and we tend to pick sides before we even fully grasp why both sides are fighting. *Platoon* tried to shine a light on this, the ambiguity of violence and war. More and more, directors have attempted to show the grey areas of violent conflicts, whether they are in police-procedurals or war movies; the film industry is trying to be less tone-deaf. The one problem is that they still need a popular protagonist.

*The Bourne Identity* directed by Doug Liman attempts to circumvent this problem by building plausible deniability right into the antagonist's storyline. Jason Bourne (Matt Damon) is an elite assassin within a top-secret unit of the Central Intelligence Agency. It is alluded to throughout the movie that he was very proficient at his job and had a capacity for violence. We meet him following his mysterious arrival onboard a French fishing vessel, where he is suffering from an extreme form of amnesia. Even though we find out later that he is still very capable as an assassin, he no longer desires to live that way. Flashbacks in his memory further elaborate on his past, showing that at one point he kills a bound and hooded man whom he knew nothing about. Jason Bourne would be the villain in any other movie had it not been for the amnesia. This amnesia allows the viewer to pinpoint a time where they can concretely determine that this man changed. The character regains our trust as viewers since we have the fortune of knowing that his motivations are pure. The movie goes on to have some great shootouts, car chases, and fight sequences, but they all stem from this reluctant hero who must avenge his past.

Taylor's rampage and Bourne's quest overlap in that they felt they were forced to act that way. Additionally, the directors of these two films use vengeance as a way to entertain and teach us. As consumers of action movies, we prefer when they fit a certain trope so we can have our release without the guilt of enjoying something bad like people getting murdered. Therefore, smart writers and directors make everyone who dies a really bad guy and the guy killing them really reluctant to killing them like in *The Bourne Identity*.

As for filmmakers who are trying to tackle difficult topics, like Oliver Stone in response to *Green Berets* by John Wayne; vengeance portrayed as it was with PFC Taylor humanizes it. He shows us how slippery vengeance is, and how quickly it can divulge into something that desecrates whatever it touches. When we project our hatred onto the most accessible thing around us we become evil. I believe that Oliver Stone is trying to drive the point home that vengeance in itself is not evil, nor is hatred. There is simply a correct time, location, and dosage for every action. Had PFC Taylor's platoon wished to seek vengeance for their lost, they would have had the opportunity later on to fight real soldiers who were there to fight, not civilians stuck between armed groups.

## Works Cited

Chester, D. S., & DeWall, C. N. (2017). Combating the sting of rejection with the pleasure of revenge: A new look at how emotion shapes aggression. *Journal of Personality and Social Psychology, 112*(3), 413-430.

Platoon, Directed by Oliver Stone, MGM Pictures, 6 Feb, 1987.

The Bourne Identity, Directed by Doug Liman, Universal Studios, 14 June, 2002.

## Writing about Art

Previously, I've asked you to look at an early painting by Pablo Picasso and compare it to his much more famous "Les Demoiselles" (1907). Hopefully that activity opened up your mind to the possibilities of art beyond representation. Or, perhaps it further solidified your opinion that modern art is just plain bad. This is certainly an area of contention, which means it's a great place to think critically and write critically.

Yes, overall, painting from earlier periods is more representational. It looks more like things and people in the real world. Before photography, that was its purpose. There was simply no other way to make reproductions of things in the world. And humans, being endlessly fascinated with themselves, loved to see pictures of themselves. Of course, until practically the 1800s, the only people who could afford to have themselves painted, or indeed were considered being worthy of painting, were the nobles. And before that, mostly we saw paintings of Christ and his disciples, or of kings and Roman and

Greek Gods and Egyptian Pharaohs. Of course there were exceptions, but this was the main output and purpose of art through most of human history. But if we go all the way back to the caves of Chauvet and Lascaux, some 15-30,000 BCE, the first pictures we find are of man on the hunt.

## Practice 10-4: Picasso

*Compare Pablo Picasso's painting "Les Demoiselles" with the paintings in the caves of Chauvet and Lascaux (just Google these terms and you will find ample examples). What can you conclude about them? Is either art? Are both art? What is their function? Does art need to have a function?*

## Practice 10-5: Pollock

*Now, Google "Jackson Pollock - Lavender Mist."*

*What do you think? You can start with whether you like it or not. We all do that automatically. But then, think past that. Does art need you to "like" it? Why or why not? Since photography can represent our world more realistically, does painting still need to do the same? What is the purpose of a painting post-photography? Is it just outdated and should be a relic of the past? Again, what is the function of art?*

*Now Google "Jackson Pollock Documentary" on YouTube and take notes.*

*Now, find and read Jennifer Ouellette's article "Pollock's Fractals: That isn't just a lot of splattered paint on those canvases, it's good mathematics" in the November 2001 issue of Discover Magazine:*
*http://discovermagazine.com/2001/nov/featpollock*

*Now what do you think of Pollock's work? Are you convinced that it is worthy of study and tells us a lot about our world or do you think "a kid could do that"?*

*Now, find the trailer for the documentary film My Kid Could Paint That. Better yet, watch the film if you decide to write your essay on art.*

Can art be about thinking, about discourse, or does it have to be simply a display of aesthetic beauty? Does all art need to be beautiful?

I know, I've been asking a lot of questions but not providing a lot of answers in this section. That is by design. In art, there are no hard and fast rules. What we call art is indeed in the eye of the beholder. Some artists, such as Andy Warhol, have even dared us to believe that silk screened prints of a Campbell's soup can is art (1961-62), and Marcel Duchamp took a urinal, signed it "R. Mutt" and placed it in the museum (Fountain, 1917). Feel free to Google these images to see what I mean. I'm sure many of you will roll your eyes. That's okay.

Sort of.

As you can tell, these questions are leading. You can tell what my stance is. Modern and Post-modern art are especially fascinating to me because they make you think. Because you have to look past, and even are forced to look directly into, ideas of aesthetic beauty. There is a whole movement of art that is termed "conceptual," because understanding it, indeed enjoying it, is about wrestling with its meaning.

What was Duchamp saying when he placed a urinal in the museum? Ken Carboune, writer for Huff Post, asserts that "By presenting a "readymade" industrial object without artist intervention as a finished artwork,

Duchamp challenged viewers with the assertion that an idea can be as significant as an artist's handcrafted work. This premise has been challenged, applauded, revised, expanded and reinterpreted many times over, and 100 years later, *Fountain* still remains an important influence on art and contemporary culture." Further, he writes, "Much of contemporary design and advertising also employs the same Duchampian techniques, using spectacle, sex, and outrage, to command a buyer's attention. Think Calvin Klein, Benneton, and Equinox Gym. In today's frenzied consumer environment, where subtlety risks being ignored, these strategies, though sometimes scandalous, can be very effective."

But is it art??? Can I just take anything, plop it in a museum call it art?

No.

Art has to have a purpose. Contemporary art needs to be surprising, complicated, complex, and make you think.

In 2001, I was walking through the Guggenheim Museum in New York City. There was a special exhibit of local artists going on, and I wandered into one of the many rooms of the exhibit. All that was in the room was a stack of posters in the middle of the floor with pictures of people on them. Alongside the stack was a note that said "Free: Take One."

People were very excited to get a free piece of art, so people were grabbing them happily, smiling, saying, "cool." Most rolled up their new prize, smiling, tucked it under their arm, and continued moving through the museum.

I too was excited to get my free poster. So waited until there was space, moved in, and picked up the poster.

I looked at it for a minute. It was black and white pictures of people. Pretty interesting. But then it dawned on me.

These were all pictures of killers. Murderers.

As I looked around the room at all the people, happy with their posters of murderers tucked under their arms, I was overcome with sorrow.

This was the art piece. I was part of the art piece. We all were.

This represented how numb we have all become, how consumed we are with materialism, how violence is glorified in our society. It represented how we don't look past our desire to have things long enough to judge whether our having them is harmful or not. As I looked around, I began to shake. I could hardly hold back the tears.

What have we become?

That is the power of conceptual art.

I wish I could remember the name of the artist so you could see the piece. I've searched for it online for years and have not located it. But it left me forever changed.

## Practice 10-6: Chris Burden and Performance

*Rarely do you find art that is more surprising, or shocking, than Chris Burden's 1971 performance art piece titled "Shoot." Content warning: this is a difficult piece to watch or discuss, so if you feel like this assignment will be too difficult, you may skip it.*

*Look up, read, and watch the short documentary on the New York Times website titled "Shot in the Name of Art" by Eric Kutner:* *https://www.nytimes.com/2015/05/20/opinion/shot-in-the-name-of-art.html*

*Write a reply to the piece. This is a very shocking, disturbing piece of work. When I first read about it I could not get it out of my mind. If you dare, look up some of Chris Burden's other work. Is this art or is he just in bad need of treatment? Was there a purpose to this? What has the experience of this left you feeling, thinking?*

## Major Essay Task: Writing about Visual Media

A lot has been covered in this brief chapter on analyzing visual media. Your essay task for this chapter is to either:

1) Watch and analyze a film of your choosing. I strongly recommend *Crash* (Haggis, 2001) as above.

2) Analyze a modern or post-modern piece of art. This can be conceptual, abstract expressionist, impressionist, or performance art. You may compare it to more classical art (Baroque, Renaissance, Rococo, Romanticism, Neoclassicism etc.)

You must do a thorough direct analysis of your response to the primary source (the painting or film itself) and then find 3 secondary sources to help you understand the work. You do not need to necessarily have an argument here. Instead, as with our earlier writing in this text, you may use the essay to explore an idea, to think through and learn about the subject. You will likely have ideas, positions, arguments, or questions that come up. You may want to simply argue that "modern art is crap!" I urge you to be more complicated than that. In fact, if you do make that assumption, your research should be trying to disprove your assumption rather than prove it.

If you are writing about a film, watch it, take notes, think about what it told you about our society, or the particular culture or cultures portrayed. Think about how it asked you to think about your own life, your own decisions and assumptions. Look for specific, visual details that back up the main ideas in the film. Be sure to closely analyze at least 2-3 scenes as evidence. Look at how the mise-en-scene is constructed. What does it tell you about the characters? What does it tell you about the themes in the film?

## Works Cited

"My Kid Could Paint That," Director Amir Bar-Lev. Film. 2007.

Barsam, Richard and Monahan, Dave. *Looking At Movies*. New York: Norton, 2013. Print.

Burdon, Chris. "Shoot." Performance. 1971.

Crash. Directed by Paul Haggis. Lionsgate Films. 2004.

Davies, Penelope J.E. et al. *Janson's Basic History of Western Art*. New Jersey: Pearson, 2009. Print.

Duchamp, Marcel. "Fountain." 1917. Artwork.

"Juno," Directed by Jason Reitman. Fox Searchlight Pictures. 2007. Film.

Kutner, Eric. "Shot in the Name of Art." New York Times, May 20, 2015. Web.

Oullette, Jennifer. "Pollock's Fractals" Discover, November 2001. Web.

Picasso, Pablo. "Les Demoiselles d'Avignon." 1907. Painting.

Pearson, Erika and Madil, Bernard. "Semiotics." *Media Studies 101*. BCcampus, The University of British Columbia. Creative Commons License.

Pollock, Jackson. "Lavender Mist." 1950. Painting.
Ristau, Reece. "'Crash' Director Doesn't Think It Deserved Best Picture Oscar." *Variety*. August 11, 2015.

Warhol, Andy. "Campbell's Soup Cans." 1962. Silk Screen.

# CHAPTER ELEVEN
## *Science Writing*

Science!

It's no wonder that Bill Nye shouts that word with enthusiasm nearly every time he says it. Through the scientific method, we have voyaged all the way down to the bottom of the Marianas Trench - the deepest spot in the ocean at over 35,000 feet deep, and past the edge of the solar system - Voyager 1, as of this writing, is 11,700,000,000 miles from earth and still traveling at 38,000 miles per hour. We have seen down to the subatomic level, to half the size of a hydrogen atom, at Lawrence Berkeley Labs. When reentering the atmosphere, the manned Apollo 10 Command Module reached 24,791 miles per hour.

But more than feats of speed or distance, science has helped us better understand our world. Where once some people claimed that the Norse God Thor created thunder, we now know, as Richard Brill, a professor at Honolulu Community College, explains:

"Thunder is caused by lightning, which is essentially a stream of electrons flowing between or within clouds, or between a cloud and the ground. The air surrounding the electron stream is heated to as hot as 50,000 degrees Fahrenheit, which is three times hotter than the surface of the sun. As the superheated air cools it produces a resonating tube of partial vacuum surrounding the lightning's path. The nearby air rapidly expands and contracts. This causes the column to vibrate like a tubular drum head and produces a tremendous crack. As the vibrations gradually die out, the sound echoes and reverberates, generating the rumbling we call thunder. We can hear the thundering booms 10 miles or more distant from the lightning that caused it.

When the lightning is within sight, however, we see it first because the speed of sound in air is considerably slower than that of the electron flow. Thus, the sound behaves more like a shock wave than an ordinary sound wave. The shock wave follows the path of the electrons like a fist in a sock. The speed of sound is even more insignificant when compared to the speed of light. The light from the flash reaches us in a fraction of a second, whereas the sound lags along like a snail following an interplanetary rocket.

The audiovisual spectacle of thunder and lightning is a combination of the dynamics of the vibration of air molecules and their disturbance by electrical forces. It is an awesome show--and one that reminds all of us of the powers of nature and our own insignificance in relation to them."

People often think of science as simply the reporting of cold, hard facts by boring geeks who work in a laboratory. Science is all about logic, not about passion, they say. While the scientific method is certainly logic based, and scientists need to report their findings in as objective a manner as possible, behind all this objectivity are very passionate people. To do science well takes dedication and passion. You need to be committed to solving problems that can perhaps change the way we live. For all scientific endeavor is an endeavor to understand our world at a deeper level.

In the best-selling book *Homo Deus*, Yuval Noah Harari writes,

"As the source of meaning and authority relocated from the sky to human feelings, the nature of the entire cosmos changed. The exterior universe - hitherto teeming with gods, muses, fairies and ghouls - became empty space. The interior world - hitherto an insignificant enclave of crude passions - became deep and rich beyond measure.... In medieval Europe, the chief formula for knowledge was: Knowledge = Scriptures x Logic. If people wanted to know the answer to an important question, they would read scriptures and use their logic to understand the exact meaning of the text... The scientific revolution proposed a very different formula for knowledge: Knowledge = Empirical data x Mathematics. If we want to know the answer to some question, we need to gather relevant empirical data, and then use mathematical tools to analyze them.

However, along with the scientific revolution, people still had that burning question: "But what does it all mean?" Humanism, the rise of man as able to think for himself rather than look to scriptures, the argument that our moral compass is within us not located in our belief in or fear of a wrathful God, has created a new formula for knowledge: Knowledge = Experiences x Sensitivity.

Through this view, I can change as I gather more life experiences and am sensitive enough to know how to choose what works for me and what does not. Thus, if homosexual relationships make both parties feel good and it harms no one, then it is good. Stealing is bad not because a god has stated that it is, but because it causes someone to feel bad. We can now even decide if believing in God makes us feel good, and it hurts no one, then it is good. It is up to us, not a requirement."

All this amounts to one thing: humanism and the scientific revolution have changed how we see and interact with the world and each other. Scientists are human and are often seeking answers because finding these answers will change people's lives. Why is a scientist driven to seek a cure for cancer? Likely because they felt the emotional pain of losing someone to the disease and have now dedicated their lives to fighting it, hoping to keep others from feeling that same pain. This type of research is born from love and empathy.

But even if you aren't conducting research looking for the next great cure, many scientists are conducting 'pure research' that is simply trying to figure out the world we live in. They are fascinated by what we don't know, which is a lot more than what we do. As they move through the world, they are always asking the questions "why?" and "how?" Why do snakes have different coloration? How do birds navigate across vast oceans? Why does heart disease happen more in some families than others? The more you learn, the more you realize how little we understand about the universe and ourselves.

Even though our desire to conduct scientific experiments may be bred from passion, in order to be able to view the results and interpret the experiments objectively, we need to try to eliminate two of the three elements of rhetoric. In science, logos is supreme. If we were to allow subjectivity, argument, passion, desire, into our studies as scientists, we would automatically bring some question of our work's validity. "You cannot argue with facts," as the cliche goes. Perhaps one of the biggest challenges scientists face is knowing when the data disprove their hypothesis and conceding that their beliefs were incorrect.

But this is exactly why it is so powerful. Remember that even when we write an argument I urged you to take your assumptions, do research and put them under scrutiny, and then formulate your thesis based on evidence rather than just feeling? Remember how I said that this is its most powerful when you are transformed through the process rather than simply having the data back up what you already thought?

That's essentially the process of science.

While conducting original research and then writing it up is beyond the scope of this text, it is important for you to understand the process of scientific discovery in order to best read and write about it. In our argumentation chapter, we looked briefly at the scientific method, let's reiterate that briefly here.

According to Frank L.H. Wolf, at the University of Rochester: The scientific method has four steps:

1. Observation and description of a phenomenon or group of phenomena.

2. Formulation of a hypothesis to explain the phenomena.

3. Use of the hypothesis to predict the existence of other phenomena, or to predict quantitatively the results of new observations.

4. Performance of experimental tests of the predictions by several independent experimenters and properly performed experiments.

If the experiments bear out the hypothesis it may come to be regarded as a theory or law of nature (more on the concepts of hypothesis, model, theory and law below). If the experiments do not bear out the hypothesis, it must be rejected or modified. A key factor in the scientific method is the predictive power (the ability to get more out of the theory than you put in; see Barrow, 1991) of the hypothesis or theory, as tested by experiment. It is often said in science that theories can never be proved, only disproved. There is always the possibility that a new observation or a new experiment will conflict with a long-standing theory.

Okay, pretty clear. This will come in handy when we read scientific articles. Like any other form of non-fiction, non-narrative writing, we can begin by what we know and what we assume. We can 'read' the world and decide what we are curious about and what our assumptions are about it. Then, instead of conducting original research, we can read scientific articles that are published that give the details and analysis of experiments about the question we have, and then do the equivalent of an argument synthesis paper using these articles.

When we do this, we can gather the empirical data and craft an argument based on it. We can search the scientific literature for facts in order to come up with some solid ideas about how our world works or why a particular ecological issue must be addressed.

When we read magazines like Discover and Scientific American, that is just what these journalists are largely doing. They decide what questions are in the popular conversation then look up scientific journal articles through peer-reviewed, academic sources. They do a literature review, distilling the complicated language of the sciences to more digestible, understandable language for people who perhaps make their living outside of the scientific community.

If you aren't familiar with these magazines, you are in for a treat. Let's first look at one article together, then I will ask you to find an article of your own and summarize it.

When I look at the January 2019 issue of Scientific American, the following stories are on the front page: "Oceans Are Warming Faster Than Predicted," "New App Uses Sonar to Detect Opioid Overdoses," "The Biggest Issues for Wildlife and Endangered Species in 2019," "Erupting Black Hole Shows Intriguing Light Echoes," "Monogamy May Be Written In Our Genes," "How Trump's Wall Could Alter Our Biological Identity Forever," "There Is No Such Thing As Conscious Thought…"

I don't know about you, but these all seem utterly fascinating to me. A hard choice, but I think a particularly interesting article will be the one about Trump's proposed wall between the US and Mexico and how that would "alter our biological identity forever." Remember how Malcolm Gladwell liked to look at issues from unusual angles? Remember how we liked to combine political, social, economic, poetic, and scientific points of view of any topic so that it is a more integrated approach? Well, this article seems to take a well-discussed political topic and take a new spin on it. How will this decision affect the ecosystems the wall crosses? At least, that is my assumption of what the article will be about. Let's give it a read and see what we find.

Jennifer R.B. Miller, PhD, the author of the article, opens with this paragraph:

"It's no secret that the Trump administration is attacking science. From scrubbing the words "climate change" from federal agency websites to cutting public health programs in the Environmental Protection Agency to burying its own climate report involving more than 300 leading climate scientists, President Donald Trump and his appointees take well-established scientific facts and treat them like science fiction. One environmental attack is particularly appalling, but headlines have focused more on its political theatrics than on its catastrophic consequences for North American biodiversity: building the wall along the U.S.-Mexico border. As a scientist who understands the implications of this decision for wildlife, I am astounded and outraged that such a precious biological treasure is being sacrificed for political gain. And I am not alone."

This is a powerful introduction. Why is that? She provides us background that we all share about "the wall," and the Trump administration, but then says "headlines have focused more on its political theatrics than on its catastrophic consequences for North American biodiversity." It is also filled with passion. You can see here how Huffaker, as a science writer, is able to take the objective facts of scientific inquiry and use them to fuel her argument - to be passionate about a scientific issue, which crosses over into a moral issue. Indeed, as we will see as we walk through this article, how Huffaker blends those two revolutions, the scientific revolution and the humanist revolution, to create an impassioned work that is, at its heart, a rhetorical one.

If we want to do due diligence to this, we can look this up. According to the National Resource Defense Council, a council formed in 1970 of 500+ scientists, attorneys and law students, published an article in Nov. 2018 with the title "The White House Tried To Bury A Major Climate Report: It Backfired, Big Time" written by Jeff Turrentine, a regular contributor to The Slate, The Washington Post, and The New York Times book review. The same month, Coral Davenport wrote an article for The New York Times titled "Trump Administration's Strategy on Climate: Try to Bury its own Scientific Report." Similar stories were also reported in The Washington Post, Vox.com, The BBC, and The Guardian.

So, you see how already we have started the process of research through this single article that lead us to search for further evidence. We found it and could not find any evidence that refutes the fact that this is what he did. We may assume that what Miller states is true from her "ethos" as a PhD and senior scientist at Defenders of Wildlife, but it is always smart to question anyone's motivation when emotions come into play.

Back to the article at hand. Miller states that over 2500 scientists have agreed that building the wall would "cut through the habitats of over 1,500 wildlife species." These species each have carved out a niche in this extremely biodiverse habitat that often requires they traverse north and south to survive - in other words, if you build the wall, they will die.

She notes that they have data from the 600 miles of the border which is already walled. She argues, "This 600-mile stretch of wall is an unclimbable barricade for 346 nonflying animal species, not to mention flighted species like the endangered Quino checkerspot butterfly and the threatened and endangered ferruginous pygmy-owl that cannot fly high enough to surmount the wall. Without passage, animals cannot disperse to new populations to spread their genes, potentially leading to genetic inbreeding akin to the plight of the African cheetah. During natural seasonal flooding, the wall traps flood waters and kills wildlife and vegetation. During natural disasters like heat waves, when water or food on one side of the wall is not available, those species will be left to perish, unable to access resources on the other side." The implications of this are that if Trump is allowed to build his 1,953 more miles of wall, the effects would be even far more disastrous.

In conclusion, she states, "In one generation, humans will have successfully disintegrated an extraordinary biodiversity web that evolved over millions of years." Then she declares that we can stop this if we stop the building of the wall: essentially a call to action.

As you can see, popular science articles can indeed be articles of argumentation. The writer may begin with a message they want to get out, use scientific data to back them up, and then analyze that data and extrapolate it to the new situation. Here, she used the data they already have from the 600 miles of wall to argue that 1,953 miles of wall would be a biological disaster of greater proportions. She uses facts about ecology, evolution and biodiversity to strengthen her claims.

## Practice 11-1: Popular Science

*Look up Discover and Scientific American magazines. Find and read one article that is the most interesting to you. Summarize the article for your readers in about 3-4 paragraphs.*

*1) First, before you read the article, look at the title and free-write for 5 minutes what you know, or think you know, about the topic. What are your assumptions? What do you think it will be about and what conclusions do you think will be drawn?*

*2) Then, after you read it, what was the central question on the table? Is the author trying to make an argument? Is the article a "call to action" as Miller's was above?*

*3) What evidence and experimental data was used to find out the answer or prove their point?*

*4) What assertions are presented that might need further research? Research those facts and see what you find.*

*5) What were the conclusions? What actions are you compelled to take? How has reading article changed you? Or was it not convincing?*

But not all scientific articles, even in popular science magazines, are in the mode of argumentation. Some are, as I stated above, essentially literature reviews which get us excited and inform us about what is going on in the scientific community. These writers essentially translate the complicated writing of scientific papers that requires specialized knowledge in the field to fully understand into language we can. They basically move from one discourse community to another, from PhDs in biology, physics, chemistry, and biology, to those of us who have a lighter knowledge of these subjects yet are interested in knowing about the latest scientific work.

In that same issue of Scientific American (January, 2019), the leading story is "Erupting Black Holes Shows Intriguing Light Echoes" by Clara Moskowitz. In this article, Mozkowitz is translating the work of Erin Kara, an astronomer at the University of Maryland. Moskowitz includes a hyperlink to the original paper in her article. To see what she has done, go ahead and find this article, or one like it that you are able to access, and find the original article it is referencing.

Here's the opening of Moskowitz' article in Scientific American:

'We tend to think black holes gobble up all the matter around them—but they can actually spew out as much as they suck in. And sometimes they seem to go downright crazy.

Astronomers recently spotted one black hole, nearly 10,000 light-years from Earth, belching out an enormous explosion of x-ray light. Measurements of this tantrum have given scientists one of the clearest pictures yet of what happens when black holes erupt with energy. "One of our big questions is how do we go from this process of material flowing into the black hole to this process of flowing out?" says astronomer Erin Kara of the University of Maryland, College Park, lead author of a paper in *Nature*. "We know this is happening but we don't understand how it works in detail." Kara presented the discovery Wednesday at the American Astronomical Society's annual meeting in Seattle.'

This is a fairly clear summary of what Kara found and the question she was up against: they found a black hole that was "belching out an enormous explosion of x-ray light," so they want to find out how black holes, which normally suck light in, switch to spewing it out.

If you go into a scientific discipline, or when you just take your GE courses in science for your degree, you will learn more about conducting original research. That is beyond the scope or purpose of this text. Instead, I'd just like you to get used to some of the methods, thinking, and approaches to scientific writing so that you are prepared when you enter those courses. But more than that, I hope to spark a bit of interest, despite your declared major, to want to follow scientific discoveries through magazines like Scientific American and Discover.

A note about theories versus laws. According to the Understanding Science project at UC Berkeley, some scientific ideas are blown off as being "just a theory." The issue here is that there are really two uses of the term "theory." In the article, the author writes that "in common usage, the word theory means just a hunch, but in science, a theory is a powerful explanation for a broad set of observations. To be accepted by the scientific community, a theory must be strongly supported by many different lines of evidence. So biological evolution is a theory (it is well-supported, widely accepted, and powerful explanation for the diversity of life on earth), but it is not "just" a theory.

In your entry level science courses, you may be asked to do library research on a topic, and then possibly present that topic to the class. Below, I have included a paper I wrote for a course on Ecology. Having grown up in the Bay Area, I have always wondered about the SF Bay, so I decided to find out about the ecosystem of the bay. Through my research (again, that's library research not original, field or lab research) I found out some pretty amazing and fascinating facts about the bay. Note: your paper need not be nearly as long or as in-depth as this one. You can use 5 sources and cover less about your topic since the goal here is to understand how to write about scientific topics rather than actually learn in-depth factual knowledge about a topic.

## SAN FRANCISCO BAY: AN ESTUARINE ECOSYSTEM
## INTRODUCTION
### By David Foulds

The San Francisco Bay is an estuarine environment. Because estuaries are located where fresh water and ocean water meet, they receive a lot of sediment and nutrients from the watershed that feeds the rivers. This allows for a great abundance of life, and these are often some of the more biologically productive areas, although typically not very biodiverse. Estuaries have a primary production of about 1250 g/sq. m/year, which is more than twice that of lakes and streams, and about 10 times as much as the open ocean (Ricklefs, 2001).

The San Francisco Bay Area is considered to have a "Mediterranean" climate, which is marked by the existence of wet winters and dry summers. However, the seasons are much more extreme than the typical Mediterranean clime. There are 5 months per year that have virtually no rainfall, and the winter climate, although not extremely cold, is colder than most "Mediterranean" climes and the days are short (Goals Project, 2000).

### Location

The San Francisco Bay is located in the middle of the California coast, receiving a large upwelling of water from the Pacific, thus creating a greater than average production of life off the coast of California. The offshore sea animals often use the Bay as a nursing or rearing ground for their young.

Located at 38' latitude and 122' longitude in Northern California, the San Francisco Bay and Delta Estuary is the West Coast's largest estuary. In fact, it is the largest estuary on the West Coast of North and South America. It is approximately 1600 square miles and drains more than 40 percent of California and southern Oregon. It is home to more than a million shorebirds, and is a major stop on the Pacific flyway. The San Francisco Bay itself is about 400 square miles and has an average depth of only 14 feet! The deepest point in the bay is under the Golden Gate Bridge, where the depth plunges to about 360 feet. (Estuary Project, 2001).

The Bay is actually comprised of several sub-bays: the Suisun Bay, San Pablo Bay, Central Bay, and South Bay. Water enters the bay primarily from the Delta, which is formed at the junction of the Sacramento and San Joaquin Rivers. These rivers collect over 40% of the water from the Northern California watershed. Most of this water is from the Sierra Nevada and Cascade mountain ranges. However, of the amount of water that drains towards the Bay, only about 60% reaches it. The rest of the water is diverted in the Central Valley for use in farming and other municipal uses (Bay Institute, 2001).

The San Francisco Bay meets the requirements for several species of fish; the primary ones being the Chinook Salmon, Striped Bass, Northern Anchovy, Pacific Herring, and Halibut, as well as being a fruitful stop-over for many birds on the Pacific Flyway, such as the Mallard, Tule Goose, and Canvasback.

## Formation of the Bay

There are many ways that an estuary may form. Drowned river valley estuaries are formed from the rising of the sea level, as occurred in the last ice age, about 18,000 years ago. Bar-built estuaries are created by the accumulation of sediments at the mouths of rivers. Tectonic estuaries are formed due to movement of tectonic plates.

The Pacific coast is on an active margin (the East Coast is on a passive margin), where a great amount of subduction of the pacific plate occurs, causing high cliffs on the coast and deep valleys offshore. The San Francisco Bay was created when the (now) Bay Area land sank due to Pacific tectonic plate subduction into the mantle. It is a tectonic estuary (Castro, 2003). But there was more to the formation of this estuary than mere sinking, it may also be a drowned valley (S.F. Bay Model Visitor Center, 2001).

There was a large lake in the Central Valley of California called the Concoran Lake. When a volcanic eruption in the Bishop area of the Central Valley occurred about 760,000 years ago, tons of ash and volcanic ejecta was thrown into this lake. Then, around 560,000 years ago, through tectonic movements, the Bay Area continued to sink and the south end of the Concoran lake was pushed up. The water rose, and eventually spilled over the mountains into the valley, forming the Carquinez Straight.

At this time the future bay was a beautiful valley, and the Straight fed the valley with flowing rivers. About 435,000 years ago, Mount Lassen erupted, throwing sediment into the valley. This is known as Rockland Ash, and can still be seen on the cliffs of Fort Funston. As the ice melted from the last ice age, the water filled the sunken valley through the Golden Gate, forming the Bay that we know of today (Martin, 1999).

## Hydrology

The main sources for freshwater into the San Francisco Bay are the San Joaquin and Sacramento Rivers. The Delta is formed where these rivers meet with many other rivers from the Sierra Nevada and Coastal Range. The Delta has 57 islands and 1,100 miles of levees. It is a main source of water for agriculture and home use in Northern California. From the Delta, the fresh water meets at Suisun Bay, forming Suisun Marsh, which is the largest wetland area in the Western United States.

## Temperature

Bay water temperatures range from 8 degrees Celsius in the winter to around 22 degrees Celsius in the summer. While this is not a large variation, it does mean that the plants and animals of the bay need to be able to survive and thrive in this temperature variation. Those that cannot sustain life within this temperature variance and are mobile will move to sustain an environmental temperature that is most suited for their physiological needs.

## Tides

On the California coast, there are mixed, semidiurnal tides. This means that there are two high tides and two low tides per day, each of different strengths. Tides are caused by the gravitational pull of the moon and the sun on the water of our planet (Castro, 2003).

Since estuaries are mostly protected from the direct action of tidal waves, they are typically not affected by the erosion and impact that the tides have on the coast. However, since the San Francisco Bay has a small entry space to the Pacific Ocean (the Golden Gate), tidal changes can be larger then is typical of those on the beaches directly on the Pacific.

Since the tides must flow through a small inlet, the tides swell to a larger size due to the bottleneck effect. This is known as the tidal prism and equals about ¼ the total amount of Bay water volume. The energy effect of the tides is felt the greatest at this bottleneck (at the Golden Gate) and then distributes throughout the bay. The areas farthest from the pacific feel the effect the least. (SFSU, 2001)

## Salinity

The hydrology of the estuarine environment is one of the most complex on the planet. Since there is an influx of fresh water from the watershed and an influx of salt water from the ocean, there is a large salt gradient within the estuarine environment. The animals and plants that live here have adapted to specific salt concentrations or migrate with the tides to attempt to maintain an environment that is suitable.

Because highly saline water is more dense than fresh water, the water that comes from the delta tends to float on top of the salty ocean water coming from the Pacific. The ocean water is typically around 34 ppt where the freshwater is around 0 ppt. (SFSU, 2002) For example, the salinity of Suisun Bay is about 7 ppt, whereas the Central Bay averages around 30 ppt, and the South Bay can reach 35 ppt (Goals Project, 2000). The more fresh water there is in an area of the bay, the lower the salinity. In addition, since saltwater is more dense, it sinks, creating a salt wedge. This means that the water at the top of the water column is less saline than that at the bottom. This salt wedge moves back and forth with the tides, creating a situation where animals and plants that are in fixed positions are subject to a wide variance in salinity daily. In San Francisco, where the tides are mixed semidiurnal, this means that the salinity changes drastically four times daily (Castro, 2003).

## Substrate and Sediment

Most estuaries substrate, or benthic layer (bottom) is primarily soft mud. This is due to the large amount of muddy particles that settle out of the river flow as the river slows at the mouth. This mud is typically a combination of silt and clay. These particles also remain suspended in the water column, allowing less light to penetrate and reducing water clarity (Castro, 2003). This reduces the amount of photosynthesis that can occur, thus reducing the amount of photosynthetic organisms that can live here.

There are two main types of sediment: inorganic silts and clays, and organic sediment. The inorganic silts are usually brought in from the watershed that feeds the bay or from the tides of the ocean, and the organic sediment is created by the plants and animals that inhabit the bay itself (SF Bay Environment, 2000).

There are about 200,00 acres of shallow subtidal and tidal flats in the bay area. These areas are marked by their relation to the tides. Subtidal flats are between mean lower low water (MLLW) to about 18 feet below MLLW. Tidal flats are between the mean tidal level (MTL) to about 2.5 feet below MLLW. The tidal flats are mostly composed of clay, silt, sand, shell fragments and organic debris. The S.F. Bay subtidal areas have a high concentration of suspended sediments, ranging from 70 to 97% clay. Total suspended solids (TSS) in the Suisun and San Pablo Bays range from 50mg/ml in the summer to 200mg/ml in the winter. Human activities also effect the clarity of the bay. These include dredging and propeller wash (Goals Project, 2000).

## Communities

There are many plant and animal communities that comprise the San Francisco Bay. Following is a sample of some of the key organisms.

Eelgrass (*Zostera marina*), is the only seagrass found in the San Francisco Bay. It is found primarily in the intertidal areas, and is an excellent breeding ground for fish. It anchors the soil by its extensive roots, slows current flow with its leaves, and provides shelter for many bay fish and other organisms, particularly during spawning season. *Z. marina* leaves are typically 1.5 to 12mm wide and can grow up to 15 meters in length. Growth of eelgrass is limited by light availability, an thus only grows in shallow areas or tidal flats. It requires between 3-5 hours of irradiance-saturated photosynthesis (Hsat) per day to thrive, however, it can survive up to a month of light limitation by living off of its reduced carbon reserves. In addition, epiphytes (young plants) of the eelgrass provide up to 22% of the primary production in the bay. *Z. marina* has a noxious sulfated phenolic compound within it that inhibits bacterial degredation and animal grazing. Birds, such as the California Least Tern (*Sterna albifrons browni*) often use the eelgrass as a source of food, eating the juvenile and small fishes that are found amongst its roots, particularly in the area from Oakland International Airport and Alameda Naval Air Station (Goals Project, 2000).

Some macroalgae (seaweed) thrive in the bay, although considerably less than the microalgae. *Gracilaia sjoestedtii*, *Enteromorpha spp.* and *Ulva spp.* are found in the mid-intertidal to shallow subtidal zone. These seaweeds are often attached to rocks and organic detritus, primarily shells in muddy areas of the bay. *Ulva* is more commonly seen in the summer and spring, and is virtually absent during the winter. (Goals Project, 2000).

The Franciscan Brine Shrimp (*Artemia fanciscana Kellogg*) are a member of the order Anostraca. They thrive at temperatures from 21-31 degrees Celsius. They are most likely found in saline areas. They feed on phytoplankon and blue-green algae. Populations are highest in salt ponds adjacent to the San Francisco Bay, at saline concentrations of 70-200 ppt.

The Oppossum Shrimp (*Neomysis mercedis*) is a key player in the food web of the San Francisco Bay. Young shrimp consume phytoplankton and rotifers, where the adults also feed on copepods, particularly *Eurytemora affinis*. Opposum Shrimp are an important food source for juvenile Striped Bass, Longfin smelt and Spittale. They thrive in 2 to 6 ppt salinity areas and so are found mainly in Suisun Bay and the western Delta.

Dungeness Crab (*Cancer magister*) are an important commercial and recreational outlet for the bay. They reproduce in nearshore coastal waters from March to May. They use the eelgrass a nursery, particularly in the northern parts of the bay. The larvae are planktivores (primary consumers), while the juveniles and adults are higher order consumers. They are consumed by Chinook Salmon, other Dungeness crab (cannibalism), and various other fish of the bay. They usually consume bivalves (clams), crustaceans, and small fishes.

Other invertebrates common to the bay include the reticulate water boatman (*Trichocorixa reticulata Guerin*), Tiger Beatles (*Cincindela senilis senilis*), and various mosquitos (from the Summer Salt Marsh (*Aedes dorsalis*) to the Winter Marsh (*Culiseta inornata*) (Goals Project, 2000).

Bat Rays (*Myliobaus californica*) are also present in the bay. These are members of the family Myliobatidae (eagle rays). They reproduce during the summer and are primarily bottom feeders, consuming benthic and epibenthic inverebrates.

The Leopard Shark (*Triakis semifasciata*) is the most common shark in the bay waters. It is usually found around piers and jetties. It consumes ghost shrimp, rock crabs, arrow goby, shiner perch, and many other fish. They are primarily a marine species but venture into the bay for pupping and rearing of young sharks.

The Pacific Herring (*Clupea pallasi*) has a high commercial, recreational, and ecological value, mostly for it's eggs. These eggs also hold a great value for other fish (Sturgeon), ducks (surf scooter), and rock crabs. The Adults are consumed by halibut, sea lions and seals. Herring prefer to hide out in *Z. marina* or macroalgae such as *Gracilaira sp*. They are found in areas of low sediment and salinity ranges from 8 to 22 ppt. They also thrive in temperatures from 5.5 to 8.7 degrees Celsius.

Northern Anchovy (*Engraulis mordax*) is the most abundant fish in the bay. Their numbers peak in the spring, during coastal upwelling. The larvae consume dinoflagellates and zooplankton, while the adults feed on larger phytoplankon and zooplankton. They are found throughout the bay, but a large number congregates downstream of the Carquinez Straight. Their key predators are California halibut, Chinook salmon, yellowtail, Leopard shark, harbor seal, sea lions, brown pelicans, sooty headwaters, and *cormarant spp*. They compete with Sardine, Jacksmelt and Topsmelt.

The Chinook Salmon (*Oncorhychnus tshawyscha*), is andromous: it spends most of its life in the saline environment of the ocean, and returns to the freshwater to spawn. The Chinook is also semelparous. This means that it dies after it spawns. They typically live about 3 to 6 years. They are usually only found in the bay proper on their way to their spawning grounds upstream in the San Joaquin or Sacramento rivers (or tributaries). The Chinook is actually the least abundant of the west coast Salmon species, and winter run races are nearly extinct.

Striped Bass (Marone sazatalis) found its way to the estuary in 1879, and are most likely found congregating in the San Pablo and Suisun Bays in autumn, while they go upstream and spawn between May and early June. The timing of their spawning depends on salinity and temperature of the water. They prefer salinities less than 1 ppt and are thus found near the Delta, where the freshwater dominates.

There are many other fish commonly found in the bay. The Sacramento Slittail (*Pogonichthys macrolepidous*), Steelhead (*Onchorhynchus mykiss irideus*), the smelts: Delta Smelt (*Hypomesus transpacificus*), Longfin Smelt (*Spirinchus thaleichthys*), Jacksmelt (*Atherinopsis californiensis*) and Topsmelt (*Atherinops affinis*), California Halibut (*Paralichthys californicus*), Bay Goby (*Lepidogbius lepidus*) and many others are key to the bay ecosystem (Goals Project, 2000).

The Harbor Seal (*Phoca vitulina richardsi*) is the only permanent mammalian resident of the San Francisco Bay. These animals prey on many fish, particularly Goby, Sculpin, and Jacksmelt. They have been seen as far upstream as the Sacramento River, but usually inhabit the Central Bay. They are most commonly seen out of water at Yerba Buena Island, Angel Island, and several places in the South Bay and near the Golden Gate. They most commonly pup (rear their young) at Castro Rocks, Newark Slough, and Mowry Slough (primarily in the South Bay). They feed in the deeper waters, usually the Golden Gate to Treasure Island or around Yerba Buena Island.

Another pinniped (seal), the California Sea Lion (*Zalophus californicus*) can sometimes be observed within the Bay. Although not a primary resident, they can be found at Angel Island, Pier 39, and Seal Rock, particularly during the winter herring run (December through February).

The North Amercican River Otter (*Lutra canadensis*) ranges in size from 900mm to 1300mm. River otters are towards the top of the food chain, and eat a wide variety of prey, however, crayfish are their primary food item, which are found in the freshwaters of the upper estuary, and birds and fish were also preyed upon by the otter. They are usually found in freshwater habitats, as well as brackish and salt marshes. The river otter is one of the sentinel species in monitoring freshwater pollution (Goals Project, 2000).

Birds are particularly dependent on the San Francisco Bay ecosystem. As mentioned previously, nearly half of the birds on the Pacific Flyway make a stop at the Bay, particularly from March through April. It is especially important for the diving ducks such as the Mallard and the Canvasback.

The Canvasback (*Aythya valisineria*) is a diving duck that comes from the upper Mississippi and Great Lakes, as well as the Gulf Coast and Atlantic during its flyway. Of all its Pacific wintering grounds, the San Francisco Bay is it's largest one, centering on the North Bay (38-59%) and the Suisun and South Bay (up to 17%). Very few winter in the Central Bay (less than 1%). They are benthivores, preferring to feed on the bottom of the bay, obviously in shallow waters. Canvasbacks dine primarily on plants (80%) and on animals (20%).

The most common wintering puddle duck is the Northern Pintail (*Anas acuta*). Again, they are most commonly found in the Suisun Marsh, but their arrival has digressed about 90% in the last few decades. However, their populations are on an upswing (1.8 million in 1991 to the current 5.1 million estimated).

The Mallard (*Anas platyrhynchos*) are most often found in the Suisun Bay and generally around the whole bay. Mallards are the primary bird found in both Suisun Bay and the South Bay wetlands. They mostly migrate to the bay from two key flyways: the Mississippi Flyway (from the east), and the Pacific Flyway (from the west).

The Tule Goose (*Anser albifrons gambelli*) winters in the Suisun wetlands. They leave Alaska around mid August. They arrive in the bay in early fall, and concentrate on the Suisun Marsh, feeding on alkali bulrush ponds. They roost in upland grass-pickleweed.

The Ruddy Duck (*Ozyura jamaicensis*), the Western Snow Plover (*Chardrius alexandrinus*), the Western Sandpiper (*Calidris mauri*), the Long Billed Dowitcher (*Limnodromus scolopaceus*) and the Red Knot (*Calidris canutus*), while not within the scope of this report are equally essential to the Bay ecosystem, as well as many other bird species (Goals Project, 2000).

## Trends and Future

Estuaries have a high rate of primary production due to the large amount of nutrients brought in by the tide and from the watershed. In addition, the large amount of nitrogen and carbon fixation adds to the nutrient broth that is the estuary. The surplus detritus from the estuary is cycled into other ecosytems by a process called outwelling (Castro, 2003).

However, only 60% of the freshwater that should feed the San Francisco Bay actually reaches it. This is due to the large number of dams and levees in Central California that divert the water for agricultural and other needs of the human population. This has a negative effect on the estuary itself, reducing valuable nutrients and water that the estuary ecosystem depends on to thrive. Where there used to be a large number of Chinook Salmon making a run up the San Joaquin in all seasons, currently there only remains a Fall run (Bay.org, 2001).

Over the last 45 years, there has been many new water diversion projects that take water away from the estuary. There are the Madera and Friant-Kern Canals, the Central Valley Pump Canal (CVP, which has diverted so much water that literally no fresh water pumps from the Sierras to the San Joaquin), and the State Water Project (SWP). Salts accumulate as rock weathers, and while the CVP and SWP extract pure water from the system, the salinity in the San Joaquin River increases tremendously as a bi-product at a rate of about 1,600,000 tons per year. Obviously, this increase in salt concentration makes it very difficult for the plants to absorb the water they need (Bay.org, 2001).

Eelgrass in the bay is also on the decline. Compared to Humboldt Bay and Tomales Bay (two other large estuaries on the west coast), eelgrass is nearly wiped out due to pollution, temperature and salinity issues. In addition, an exotic plant, Asian seagrass (*Zostera japonica*), that was probably brought to the bay on the hull of a ship, threatens the continuation of eelgrass in the bay (Goals Project, 2000). The eelgrass re-plantation attempts have not been as successful as one would have hoped, mostly due to poor planning and replantation problems due to lack of physiological knowledge of *Z. marina* (Goals Project, 2000).

Loss of more than 90% of the wetlands in the San Francisco Bay Area in the last 150 years has greatly affected the migrating waterfowl as well. There are many projects in place to attempt to reestablish and rehabilitate the Bay wetlands, particularly the tidal marshes, which are key feeding grounds for the migrating birds. In fact, the S.F. Bay has been identified as one of the 34 waterfowl habitat areas of major concern (Goals Project, 2000).

There are also many other issues concerning San Francisco Bay pollution that have been addressed in the past and continue to be addressed. Pollution from the Central Valley's farms and industries deposit at least 65 pollutants into the estuary each year, which add up to 5,000 to 40,000 metric tons of pollutants from industry, commerce, transportation, agricultural uses. These chemicals include molinate carbofuran and methyl parathion. Urban runoff from storm drains in the public sector contribute large amounts of pollution in the form of oils, tires, combustion byproducts, garden chemicals and batteries.

The bay has shrunk in size by about a third since the gold rush. In 1850, there were 310 sq. miles of salt marshes. Today there are only 48 sq. miles of undiked marshes (SF Bay Environment, 2000). In order for this ecosystem to continue to thrive, a decrease in the amount of pollutants and an increase in the amount of water actually reaching the estuary must increase.

Many people, plants and animals depend on the estuary, and by attending to these issues and many others we have a hope of continued enjoyment and use of our beautiful San Francisco Bay.

## Works Cited

Bay.org. About the Bay.
http://www.bay.org/about_the_bay/

Castro, Peter. 2003. Marine Biology, fourth edition. New York: McGraw-Hill Company.

Friesen, Larry Jon. 2001. Biology 122 Ecology.
http://www.saturdaze.net/eco/

Goals Project, 2000. Baylands Ecosystem Species and Community Profiles: Life histories and environmental requirements of key plants, fish and wildlife. Prepared by the San Francisco Bay Regional Water Quality Control Board, Oakland, Calif.

Grove, Karen, 2001. Estuaries and San Francisco Bay Home Page.
http://squall.sfsu.edu/courses/geol103/labs/estuaries/estuaries.home.html

Martin, Glen.1999. Bay Today, Gone Tomorrow.
http://www.sfgate.com/cgi-bin/article.cgi?f=/chronicle/archive/1999/

Mono Lake Committee, 2000. Sierra District State Parks-Information Zone.
http://ceres.ca.gov/sierradsp/mono/

Ricklefs, R. E. 2000. The Economy of nature, fifth edition. New York: W.H. Freeman and Company.

San Francisco Bay Environment, 2001.
http://response.restoration.noaa.gov/cpr/watershed/s
anfrancisco/

San Francisco Bay Model Center. San Francisco Bay and
Delta Estuary.
http://www.spn.usace.army7.mil/bmvc/sfbay/

San Francisco Estuary Project, 2001. The San Francisco
Bay-Delta Estuary.
http://www.abag.ca.gov/bayarea/sfep/reports/fact/sf
estuary/

Wetmaap.org, 2000. Mono Lake Background.
Http://wetmaap.org/Mono_Lake/Supplement/ml_b
ackground/

## Major Essay Task: Science Writing

For your essay for this chapter, you can write about
either a scientific topic under debate or a literature review
about a topic you are curious about. An argumentation
paper, like the article about biodiversity and the border
wall, is essentially a call to action about a particular issue.

If you do this, more than likely it will be about an
environmental issue, as these are the most widely
contested (mostly because they involve investing funds in
something that doesn't have a financial payback, and
indeed acknowledging environmental issues can be
directly in the way of financial gains for particular
companies).

A literature review will be more like the essay above,
where I wanted to find and gather information about a
particular topic and present that topic to the reader.
Whatever you are fascinated with and want to learn more
about, now is your chance for a deep dive into science.

## Works Cited

Carr, Nicholas. *The Shallows: What the Internet is Doing to Our Brains*. New York: Norton, 2011. Print.

Davenport, Coral. "Trump Administration's Strategy on Climate: Try to Bury its own Scientific Report." New York Times, Nov. 25, 2018. Accessed January 12, 2019.

Harrari, Yuval Noah. *Homo Deus: A Brief History of Tomorrow*. New York: Perennial, 2017. Print.

Johnson, Steven. *Everything Bad Is Good For You*. New York: Riverhead, 2006. Print.

Miller, Jennifer R. B. "How Trump's Wall Could Alter Our Biological Identity Forever." *Scientific American*, January 2, 2019. Web.

Moskowitz, Clara. "Erupting Black Hole Shows Intriguing Light Echoes." *Scientific American,* January 11, 2019. Web.

"Science at Multiple Levels" University of California Museum of Paleontology. January 2019.

Turrentine, Jeff. "The White House Tried To Bury A Major Climate Report: It Backfired, Big Time" *NRDC.org*. November 30, 2018. Web.

"What Causes Thunder." *Scientific American*, 2019. https://www.scientificamerican.com/article/what-causes-thunder/

Wolf, Frank L.H. "Appendix E: Introduction to The Scientific Method" *University of Rochester*. http://teacher.nsrl.rochester.edu/phy_labs/appendixe/appendixe.html

# CHAPTER TWELVE
## *Business and Economics Writing*

In *A Guide to Writing in Economics*, Paul Dudenhefer confirms the central premise of this entire textbook, that "writing is thinking." He cites economist Deirdre McCloskey, who, in her work *Economical Writing* that "Economically speaking, the production function for thinking cannot be written as the sum of two sub functions, one producing 'results' and the other 'writing them up.' The function is not separable. You do not learn the details of an argument until writing it in detail" (McCloskey in Dudenhefer 8).

As in most other discipline-based writing, there are several approaches to writing in economics. You may be asked to do a literature review, argue a position, or synthesize an argument. You should pick a topic that is particularly interesting to you, of course, and note that like the other disciplines, economics does not work in a vacuum. Like how we may take on highly politicized topics like global warming or the building of the wall on the Mexican / American border from a scientific point of view, we can look at these issues from an economic point of view.

Not only would we need to address the cost of building such a structure, but the economic impact on both countries due to its presence. While the subject is mostly controversial because of human rights issues, it is also, as may have been surprising, an ecological issue. Doing an economic analysis of the issue is yet another way to discuss this proposed project and come to some decisions as to whether or not it makes solid economic sense.

If you wish to take this particular topic on (if it is still a topic on the table at the time you read this) in your essay, feel free to do so.

Dudenhefer points out some differences between economic and other arguments. He states that "economics use economic assumptions, concepts, and theories in order to understand the phenomenon in question" (26). Again, this is similar to our other disciplines but well stated here. Each discipline uses the underlying 'truths' that it operates under. These are theories that have been proven to always be in operation, and thus no longer have to be part of the inquiry process.

Again, while going into detail about economic theories is beyond the scope of this text, we can look at a few and use them as lenses to understand an issue from an economics point of view.

According to Donald Marron, director of the Urban-Brookings Tax Policy Center and professor of macroeconomics at Georgetown, the top 25 theories to understand in economics are:

1.   Supply and Demand (Invisible Hand)
2.   Classical Economics
3.   Keynesian Economics

4. Neoclassical Synthesis (Keynesian for near-term macro; Classical for micro and long-term macro)
5. Neo-Malthusian (Resource Scarcity)
6. Marxism
7. Laissez Faire Capitalism
8. Market Socialism
9. Monetarism
10. Solow Model (growth comes from capital, labor, and technology)
11. New Growth Theory (Romer & endogenous growth)
12. Institutions and Growth (rule of law, property rights, etc.)
13. Efficient Markets Hypothesis
14. Permanent Income / Life Cycle Hypothesis
15. Rational Expectations
16. Rational Choice Theory
17. Something Behavioral (e.g., Prospect Theory)
18. Adverse Selection and the Lemons Problem
19. Moral Hazard
20. Tragedy of the Commons
21. Property Rights as a solution to the Tragedy of the Commons
22. Game Theory (e.g., Prisoner's Dilemma)
23. Comparative Advantage
24. New Trade Theory
25. The Trilemma (exchange rates, capital flows, and monetary policy)

For your essay, you are welcome and encouraged to research one or more of these theories in order to understand economic thinking. You might begin your research by learning about a few of these theories and then think about issues that they would help you understand.

Here, let's dissect a few of them and see how they can be used to think through an issue. Perhaps we should start by learning what economists mean by "classical economics."

## Classical Economics

According to the Encyclopedia Britannica: "Many of the fundamental concepts and principles of classical economics were set forth in Smith's *An Inquiry into the Nature and Causes of the Wealth of Nations* (1776). Strongly opposed to the mercantilist theory and policy that had prevailed in Britain since the 16th century, Smith argued that free competition and free trade, neither hampered nor coddled by government, would best promote a nation's economic growth. As he saw it, the entire community benefits most when each of its members follows his or her own self-interest. In a free-enterprise system, individuals make a profit by producing goods that other people are willing to buy. By the same token, individuals spend money for goods that they want or need most. Smith demonstrated how the apparent chaos of competitive buying and selling is transmuted into an orderly system of economic cooperation that can meet individuals' needs and increase their wealth. He also observed that this cooperative system occurs through the process of individual choice as opposed to central direction."

## Supply and Demand (Invisible Hand)

According to Israel M. Kirtzer, Emeritus professor of Economics at New York University, the basic law of supply and demand is as follows: "at any given moment a price that is "too high" will leave disappointed would-be sellers with unsold goods, while a price that is "too low" will leave disappointed would-be buyers without the goods they wish to buy. There exists a "right" price, at which all those who wish to buy can find sellers willing to sell and all those who wish to sell can find buyers willing to buy. This "right" price is therefore often called the market-clearing price... Supply-and-demand theory revolves around the proposition that a free, competitive market does in fact successfully generate a powerful tendency toward the market-clearing price. This proposition is often seen as the most important implication of (and premise for) Adam Smith's famed invisible hand. Without any conscious managing control, a market spontaneously generates a tendency toward the dovetailing of independently made decisions of buyers and sellers to ensure that each of their decisions fits with the decisions made by the other market participants."

This seems to make a fair amount of logical sense. When there is a high demand but low supply, the market is driven up by an "invisible hand," since sellers can get higher prices for an in-demand product. If there is excess of a product and the people aren't that interested in purchasing it, the price must go down in order to make sales. Just think about the price of new cars, new phones, new computers. When they first come out, they are quite expensive: demand is high. They offer what the older models do not. Thus, the older models' prices immediately go down - less people want to buy them, so in order to sell them, they have to be a better "deal."

## Laissez-Faire Capitalism

According to Chegg.com, a private tutoring company, "Laissez-faire capitalism is a belief that unregulated capitalism will create the greatest benefit for all. Proponents of such a system believe that government interference, including tariffs or social safety nets, ultimately causes more harm than good by promoting or protecting inefficiency. In extreme forms, the philosophy has been used as a reason not to intervene in humanitarian crises, such as the Irish famines (1846–49), despite evidence that many "natural" catastrophes are the result of government actions or lop-sided concentrations of wealth and resources. Adam Smith's belief in the "invisible hand" that balances economic systems is sometimes cited as evidence of his support for laissez-faire policies, though his call for government to intervene to prevent monopolies shows he was not an absolutist."

Interesting that this theory references "the invisible hand" theory of Adam Smith, as we saw above. The term "Laissez-Faire" is actually French for "hands free." This is an approach wherein the government is supposed to let the market run itself - no interference.

So, now let's find an article that uses Laissez-Faire Capitalism as a model. Matthew Chrisler, a student at the University of California at Riverside, has written an argument synthesis paper about laissez-Faire economics. Since I do not have the rights to this paper, it is not included in this volume, but is readily available online.

251

## Practice 12-1: Reader Response

*Outline the argument synthesis that Chrisler has made above. What are the two opposing positions? What does each side argue? What is their evidence? What is Chrisler's conclusion?*

## Practice 12-2: Research

*Take a look at the Finance and Economics page of an issue of The Economist. Find an article, read it and summarize it. What was the article about? What drew you to it? What surprised you as you read it? What did it make you need to know more about? What economics theories were used, or could be used, to understand it?*

## Major Essay Task: Business and Economics Writing

Look up a few of the economic theories above. Be sure to be able to explain them in your own words. Think of any issue that you discussed in class, have talked about with friends or family, or have even previously written about. Now, take an economic point of view. Be the economist. What are the economical factors involved in the issue? How does taking these factors into account help you understand the issue? Does it help you make a decision?

## Works Cited

Chrisler, Matthew. "Are Laissez-Faire Policies to Blame?" *Sticks and Stones*, New York: Bedford St. Martins, 2016. Print.

"Classical Economics." Brittanica.com

Dudenhefer, Paul. *A Guide to Writing in Economics.* Dec. 2009. Web.

Kirzner, Israel M. "The Law of Supply and Demand." Foundation for Economic Education. January 1, 2000.

Marron, Donald. "The 50 Most Important Economic Theories." *Seeking Alpha.* April 17, 2009. Web.

# CHAPTER THIRTEEN

## *Going for a Mind Walk*

Okay, movie time! Grab the popcorn and get comfy.

But first, be warned. This is not an action-adventure movie. You will hopefully be entertained, but it will be a different sort of entertainment than you are probably used to.

This film is called *Mindwalk* and it is based on the book *The Turning Point* by Fritjof Capra. The film consists of a long conversation between a poet, a politician, and a scientist. I know, you are chomping at the bit to get started. Bear with me.

This movie, if you let it, can change your whole view of the universe. Of reality.

Or it can feel bewinderingly dull and about 3 pompous adults wandering around an island and gabbing endlessly about things you could give a damn about.

I can't promise which camp you'll fall into. But shoot for the former. If you end up in the latter, at least you tried.

Is there a point to watching this film in an English class? That's something I want you to figure out after you view it.

Don't look down until after you've viewed the film. Spoilers!

## Practice 13-1: Free-write

*Watch Mindwalk, directed by Bernt Capra and starring Liv Ullman, Sam Waterston, and John Hurd. Then reflect on why the heck you just watched this film in an English class. You may, if you wish, include your personal feelings about it. Go ahead and vent if you think it was a waste of time. But then go past that. Try to do your own 'mind walk.' Try to think about the ideas presented in the film. What did each character contribute to our understanding of it? How can different perspectives, different 'lenses' help us understand and complicate a topic of debate? Think about all this talk of interconnections. You will next do some group work....*

## Practice 13-2: Your own Mindwalk

*Get into groups of 3. Choose who will be the poet, who the politician, and who the scientist. Pick a topic (these can be rather broad, it is about finding connections and digging deeper). Suggestions are: poverty, crime, waste management, global warming, gun control, racism, sexism, deforestation, animal rights... You get the idea. Pick a topic, then each member of the team looks up related works that look at this issue through their discipline. The poet would, of course, find poetry (or any art really), the politician would look at the political debate about the topic, and the scientist would look up objective facts that can be used to further understand the issue. In other words, as art, arguably, tends toward connecting to us through the personal, the poet/artist finds stories and poems and images that bring a personal/emotional connection to the issue. The politician is supposed to have the interests of the people at heart, so they would look at the issue from a social level, but also look at how these issues could be blocked because of special interest groups as Jack Edwards does in the film. The scientist will look at the science (this can include psychology as well as the 'hard' sciences of physics, chemistry, biology, engineering etc), but also look at the moral ramifications of the science as Sonia Hoffman does in the film.*

I recommend creating a group Wiki if your school has the capability to do so through an online platform. Then, you will present your findings as a discussion to the class. Don't just go one by one and talk about what you found, but instead engage in a conversation from each point of view while the rest of the class listens in. Other groups are encouraged to find connections between the different issues as they do in the film. This should be a lively, almost disorganized discussion, each group contributing to a deeper understanding of the connection between each discipline's approach to their given issue and between the issues themselves.

## Major Essay Task

*Writing Goal: The goal of your individual essay is to synthesize what you have found as a group and then write your response to your findings. Your essay will present the topic in a way that explains how looking at the topic from different perspectives adds, complicates, and deepens your understanding of it. You may, and should, include your own perspective as the 'glue' to hold your essay together. In other words, talk us through your journey of the topic through each 'lens' (poet, scientist, politician). What becomes the new question that you want to answer as you read about and talk to your group-mates?*

For example, if your group researched child abuse, the 'poet' in your group might have found Susan Slattery's poem titled "Child Abuse." You could then open your essay by quoting the opening verse of Slattery's poem:

My name is Sarah
i am but three
my eyes are swollen
i cannot see
i must be stupid
i must be bad
what else could have made
my daddy so mad

Before you go further, you should probably first talk about how the poem affected you. Reflect on the words and connect them to your own experiences or beliefs about the topic. You would analyze the poem, likely noting how Slattery has stated a sad truth about many cases of child abuse: that the child believes that they somehow deserved the abuse because 'Daddy' is supposed to be essentially all-knowing, so the poor child grows up thinking there is something wrong with them. You would cite the specifics lines "I must be stupid / I must be bad / what else could have made / my daddy so mad." Maybe even then research the poet and find out why they wrote the poem.

Next, you could look at the scientists' perspective, in this case probably largely taking on the role of a psychologist, and use articles which study the psychology behind this phenomenon. In other words, you don't simply stay on the surface of the topic, but find what interests you from each perspective and use that to go deeper, to answer questions as they arise. The 'scientist' in your group may have found an article in Psychology

Today by Beverly Engel, LMFT, titled "Healing the Shame of Childhood Abuse Through Self Compassion." Here, Engel writes, "If you were a victim of childhood abuse or neglect, you know about shame. You have likely been plagued by it all your life without identifying it as shame. You may feel shame because you blame yourself for the abuse itself ("My father wouldn't have hit me if I had minded him"), or because you felt such humiliation at having been abused ("I feel like such a wimp for not defending myself")." You would summarize what the article said, and even find more articles that perhaps go even deeper into one or two aspects of the topic. You could look into psychological or even biological studies on guilt or shame to deepen your understanding.

You would then connect how the scientific observations help you understand the lines of the poem, and indeed how you now have a deeper understanding of the shame related to child abuse. Note that while you started with a large topic "Child Abuse," you found a trail and followed it, thus narrowing down your topic through what interested you the most.

But what would be the political issues related to this topic? The political aspect of this might involve laws about child abuse – when to report it, who to report it to, and so on. The politician might have found the California Department of Education's website titled "Child Abuse Identification and Reporting Guidelines." They may look at the laws about when a child should be removed from a home because of suspected abuse, but then the poet might complicate the law by questioning how the child would perceive this and how it might be interpreted by the child as further evidence that it was somehow their fault. This could again then go back to the scientist, and you can research what the removal of a child from their parents does at different life stages.

This essay will thus feel fairly loose and open ended. You likely won't have a clear and logical solution. You likely won't have an answer or even just an argument. Instead, use the three perspectives to complicate, analyze, question, and explore the topic, allowing your curiosity to drive how you use the research and what specific aspects of the topic you end up writing about.

## Works Cited

Engel, Beverly. "Healing the Shame of Childhood Abuse Through Self Compassion." *Psychology Today*. Jan 15, 2015. Accessed Nov. 25, 2018. Web.

Slattery, Susan. "Child Abuse." *PoemHunter.com* January 12, 2006. Accessed Nov. 25, 2018.

Zarenda, Nancy. "Child Abuse Education and Reporting Guidelines." California Department of Education. August 7, 2017. Accessed Nov. 25, 2018. Web.

# CHAPTER FOURTEEN
## *Wrapping it Up*

As I stated from the outset, the purpose of this text was largely to write-to-think. You've seen as you've progressed through the readings and writing prompts how writing and research are the processes that we use to figure out what we want to say. They are processes that help us better understand our world. They are processes, not products, and yet a product is the end goal. As such, you also learned that by going through the process of writing, interacting, researching, summarizing, quoting, discussing, arguing, synthesizing, that reading and writing are essential elements to learning. Students state that they learn more by writing about a subject than they do from memorizing facts. It's true, our working memory is quite small. How many facts have you memorized throughout your school career that are forever lost to you? The majority probably. But does this mean that there's no reason to memorize facts? No. Some stick with you. Even though I haven't had an anatomy class in 15 years, I still know the heart inside and out. Of course, when I think about it, I also wrote about heart anatomy. I thought about it in relation to function.

That is key to learning. Function. What is the function of all this work through college? Why go through so many different disciplines? Why GE requirements? Why not just learn a marketable skill and then go work?

Because I want more for you than to just be a good employee. I want more for you than to just make a decent income and be able to buy a house and a car and raise kids if that's what you want to do. I want more for you than to just do all the things you are told will make you happy. I want you to be critical, to think about what matters to you. To be able to look at your assumptions and turn them upside down, to be able to be critical not only of the world but of yourself and your place in it.

Going back to David Foster Wallace's "This is Water," hopefully the parable that Wallace opens his speech with has a deeper meaning to you now. Here's a reminder:

"There are these two young fish swimming along, and they happen to meet an older fish swimming the other way, who nods at them and says, "Morning, boys, how's the water?" And the two young fish swim on for a bit, and then eventually one of them looks over at the other and goes, "What the hell is water?"

If at this moment you're worried that I plan to present myself here as the wise old fish explaining what water is to you younger fish, please don't be. I am not the wise old fish. The immediate point of the fish story is that the most obvious, ubiquitous, important realities are often the ones that are the hardest to see and talk about."

I hope you now have a deeper understanding of this parable: "the most obvious, ubiquitous, important realities are often the ones that are hardest to see and talk about."

This is questioning your assumptions, for assumptions are just that, taken as 'given.' As obvious facts that "everyone knows."

Question these. Question the 'givens.' This is how we look critically at our worlds. This is how we use writing, thinking, to make change. This is how we open our eyes and actually see what is around us.

Good luck to you in your college careers and beyond. As Roberto Benigni says, even in the face of some of the most awful circumstances, "life is beautiful." It is indeed.

## Works Cited

Wallace, David Foster. "This is Water." Kenyan College Speech. 2005.
"Life is Beautiful," directed by Roberto Benigni. Miramax Films. 1998.

Appendix: Student Essays

Autobiography Esays

# May He Rest in Peace
By Monica Flores Huerte

On May 12th, 2014, I woke up at 2am out of nowhere. It wasn't just a regular kind of waking up. It was that kind where you abruptly find yourself sitting up, crumbling your blanket sheets in your hands, and you're suddenly breathing very quickly. I thought nothing much of it. I probably had a bad dream that I simply couldn't remember. I went back to sleep innocently unaware that a bad dream was just starting and it would continue even when I was awake. At that same time and day, in the Mission District of San Francisco, specifically on 21st and Valencia Street - which was a block or two away from my grandparents' tiny apartment, a bullet pierced through the silent night as well as through my uncle's flesh. My uncle had committed suicide.

If I'm correct, they say there's 5 stages of grief: denial, anger, bargaining, sadness, and acceptance.

## STAGE 1: DENIAL

I couldn't believe them. I couldn't believe that my uncle would be capable of pulling a trigger that he placed directly on his forehead. Even when I stood there watching the investigators struggling for two days to scrub away the blood that stained the concrete, I couldn't believe it. Even when we drove in silence to the police station to collect his things and identify his pale and cold body, I couldn't believe it. Even when we went to sign the death certificate, got his grave spot, and set the funeral dates, I couldn't believe it. I just *couldn't* believe it. I could've sworn he was still here.. I had just talked to him not that long ago. There was no explanation for everything except that this was some cruel joke or a bad dream and I just needed to wake up.

*"Wake up Monica. Come on, wake up."*

## STAGE 2: ANGER

I sat in a pool of tears. I had headaches every day. I wasn't eating. I wasn't sleeping. I have never felt this way before. How dare he. How dare he leave us all broken hearted without any explanations. No explanations whatsoever. How dare he leave my grandma drowning in her own tears because she had to bury her youngest son. How dare he leave his son fatherless. How dare he leave us so soon. How dare he not allow us to see the great future he had ahead of him. We would never attend his wedding, go to his graduation, celebrate any birthdays with him anymore, and so much more. He wouldn't see *me* grow up anymore either. I would want him to be at *my* wedding, meet *my* kids, go to *my* graduations, celebrate *my* birthdays with him, and so much more. He swore he would stay by my side forever and now he's no longer here. He broke his promises and lied to all of us. He made us think that he was okay when he wasn't.

## STAGE 3: BARGAINING

I kept thinking "what if." What if I said I love you more? What if I visited him more? What if I called or texted more? What if I was older and smarter at the time, and I could've actually sat down with him, had a deep conversation with him because I simply asked him, "How is everything?" or "How are you feeling?" What if he left angry at us or sad because we didn't support him like a true family was supposed to? I prayed to God if I could at least say bye and see him just *one* more time. God answered my prayers, not how I wished, but he made it happen. Because then the funeral happened.

## STAGE 4: SADNESS

I had spent most of my time collecting and transporting the roses we received. There was so many. They seemed to be sent from every house in El Salvador, Washington D.C., and San Francisco. I don't know how I carried so many roses around considering they were *so* heavy and I was so fragile at the time. I was exhausted and drained mentally, emotionally, and physically. But I managed. I remember the roses had such an intoxicating smell. It was too much. They sickened me more than I already was. However, I still always chose to be in the room with all of them then be in a crowded hall,s haking hands and hearing "I'm so sorry" a thousand times. I found "I'm sorry" to be so ironic. How can they be sorry? They didn't pull that trigger. But I understood it perfectly because I was sorry as well. I had failed him. In that room, I continued to write. My love for writing blossomed some more and became my solution/therapy/cure to some extent. It was the only way I could express myself and let some words actually come out. I wrote him letters and updated him on how things were. I wrote him poems. To this day, I still do. In fact,I leave them on his grave or rip them up to see where the wind takes those little shreds in hopes that the words I could never tell him anymore get to him. I'll end up printing a copy of this speech and visit him. Anyways, I wrote and wrote. I let the tears mix with my ink. And soon followed by my blood since a rose I held onto so tightly had pricked me a bit too much. It dawned on me that this was it. I couldn't hide forever. I had to go and say goodbye. I walked slowly out with my flower still in hand. I kept walking with my messy stack of papers. I walked all the way to the podium where the pastor had just stood. The papers almost fell out of my hands with so much trembling. I didn't have to talk, but I felt like I needed to. I looked at everyone in the room and let the words spill out as best as I could. My dad and uncle held on to me for the physical support. I refuse to let my sobbing and shaking stop me. I looked into the casket and slowly walked over. Alone. I placed the rose with him. I said goodbye. He was a Flores. A flower. To me, he was like that cut rose. Beautiful to all of us but dying in the inside.

## STAGE 5: ACCEPTANCE

Days turned to weeks which turned into months which

then became years. I have accepted my uncle's death. I cry here and there of course but I'm okay. I can't do anything about it anymore. He's gone and I can't go back in time. If I could, I would. However, I can't. His death has taught and molded me into the person I am today. As you read this, know that whatever you're going through, you're going to be okay. Don't forget that there's so many people that love and care about you, your feelings are always valid, you're important and you're an actual blessing to this world. Most importantly, our lives can be taken at any second so hug your family and friends as tight as possible and say "I love you" more whether it's to yourself or to others.

# Don't Think Twice
## by Anise J. Netterville

It was a Friday night and that meant that plots was going up. This Friday plot was a mansion party that had been highly anticipated. I ended up getting picked up by Messiah, a tall, skinny, gay girl who always wore a pony tail; and her friends who were all a few years older than me. They picked me up in this big brown Tahoe; it was dirty on the inside but they were all so welcoming to me. On the way to the party we always had a pre turn up: smoking, drinking, and just listening to music to get our energy up. When we arrived there was a shuttle bus that had to take you there and back, but there was only one. Therefore, we had to wait a long time for it to get us because the streets were packed with kids trying to go to the party. When the shuttle pulled up, all of the kids looked like ants running to the van. The line was so long. There was an older lady and man who got out of the van.

"If you got any form of drinks or weapons you can't bring that to the party. Weed is fine." The lady said.

We were hot because we had to get out of the long line just to put the stuff back in the car. Since we now had to wait for the shuttle to come again we decided to drink as much as possible. As we were waiting, I saw my homegirls Kaylie and Matae. We were just talking about random stuff and catching up, when I noticed a red headed girl behind them talking to some mexican dude.

"Who is that?" I said asking Kaylie
Kaylie smiled and responded, "That's the homegirl, Leslei."

Kaylie then introduced us. She was red headed, little,

and had a sexy style to her. I was very attracted to her, so of course I began to flirt a little with her trying to make myself familiar to her. We talked a little longer then the girls ended up walking away.

"She is bad as hell," I said

"On god she is," Messiah responded.

Finally, the shuttle pulled up and we were the first ones in line this time. When we arrived to the house, it was definitely not a mansion, but instead sat at the top of a hill with an extended driveway. The house also had many lights on the premises, making it look as if it was Christmas time. As I walked in there was a lot of people and the vibe seemed good. We went to the kitchen and I started to roll up. When I was done we went outside and started smoking as more of the homies started to pull up. They all noticed the red headed girl and we made a bet on who can get her number first. The party was solid; I was pretty faded so I don't remember much of it. I ended up having to pee, so I went looking for a bathroom, but I found the redhead girl instead.

"You look good tonight." I said
She blushed and said, "Thank you, you don't look bad yourself."
"Aye you should follow me on instagram." I said
"I already follow you, but you don't follow me back, boujee." She responded.
I laughed "Oh okay bet unfollow and follow me again so I notice you."
"Okay." she said.
I then walked away and went into the bathroom. I was so excited because I basically just won the bet. I ended up just dancing the rest of the party and had a real good

time. It took awhile to get back to the car because, like I said, there was only one shuttle that took you back to where all the cars were parked. When I got home I instantly followed her back and to me I felt as if the night was a success.

It was two weeks before my highschool graduation and today was one of those rare days where it seemed as if the sky was about to fall on top of you. As I reside in the desert where its scorching hot ninety- five percent of the time and the sun literally feels like it's your worst enemy. Today was a Wednesday, which meant it was a late start at my school (instruction beginning two hours later) allowing me to have extra time to sleep in and condone in other affairs unrelated to school, smoking or selling marijuana. But, this day I had gotten an unexpected DM on Instagram from that same red headed female I had met a few weeks before at the mansion party. I didn't even remember her name. All I remember is her bright red hair and that she had this sexy yet dangerous demeanor to her that was very attractive.

This mystery girl hit me up saying all kinds of crazy stuff like, "Hey daddy," "you should come see me tonight."

Now, the reason these texts were so left field was because my friend told me that this girl already had a man and was posting about them engaging in sexual acts. I automatically became suspicious but was also intrigued because at the time I assumed maybe she was that type of girl to mess around with whoever no matter her circumstances. As the conversation between us escalated, she suggested that I pull up on her tonight to sell her some weed and have some "fun". I honestly didn't know how to feel or what to say, but I knew was that I was eager to tell my friend, Messiah, to discuss what had just happened.

When I got to school, I ended up having to wait till nutrition, after second period, to be able to make the call. The conversation went just how I expected. She expressed to me her own theory, suggesting that I need to be careful with this girl as she already had a reputation of dealing with sketchy people and being involved with scams. Also, reiterating the fact that she already had a boy she was posting and how this whole thing could be a setup.

Throughout the whole day I went pondering whether I should trust this or not. Coming to the conclusion that maybe she was just popping it and wasn't trying to be on no sneaky stuff. Messiah was just a few years older than me and has a med card, so I would always ask her to pick up weed for me because dispensary weed is usually better than weed from a plug. Just like any other time, I asked she said yeah, but I had to wait for her to get off work at seven.

As I was waiting for it to be seven, the girl had hit me up proposing that she wanted to pick up nine grams of weed, but instead of her coming to me she wanted me to go to her in San Bernardino. Now, if you don't know San Bernardino is known for it to be the king of sketchiness, dirty, and emvalmous for people getting set up and robbed sometimes even killed. I promptly got this gut feeling telling me that something was wrong. I have been in some scary situations but nothing to the degree of getting robbed, so I was beginning to have doubts with this whole thing.

Around the same time Messiah texted me saying that she is on her way and to get ready. I decided that I would wait to respond to the mystery girl for her opinion. As soon as I got into the car words started pouring out of my mouth. Talking so fast that I was surprised she was able to make sense of it. At the end of my spill of words she seemed very convinced that this mystery girl was up to no good and it was in my best interest to keep my distance; pointing out the inconsistency within her story. I argued against her claim that she could be telling the truth and there is no way I could pass up making this much money. As my passion for making quick money was more of an obsession at this point and I was willing to do anything. We both concluded that if things actually worked out, that I should not go by myself. After a few hours passed it was around 7:30 pm and the sun was starting to go down. The rain was still persistent gradually getting harder as the night went on. I am terrified of driving in the rain let alone the rain and the dark.

"I just got home, you can come around thirty minutes." She texted out of nowhere.

"How much weed did you want," I replied, as I was still on the fence if I was going to go or not.

Two seconds later she responded, "Nine grams and I will slide you twenty dollars for gas, but I only have a hundred dollar bills so I'm gonna need change."

Not thinking anything of the fact that she only has large bills, but that it only makes sense for her to just slide me a hundred dollars because I never have cash on me. I replied, "Just slide me one hundred dollars."

She persisted, " No I will give you twenty dollars in gas so I'm going to need ninety dollars back."

I felt kind of on edge about all of this just because I couldn't understand why she wanted to give me an extra ten dollars when I wasn't even tripping. The idea of me making a hundred and ten dollars clouded my judgement, convincing myself nothing was wrong. I wasn't a hundred percent sure whether to go or not, so I called up Messiah but she wasn't answering. And that's when I made one of the worst decisions of my life, I went. Being driven by the sticker price yet neglecting the danger that may lie ahead. I frantically began gathering my stuff. I grabbed my backpack from my room stuffing it with my air pods, weed, and wallet, proceeding to leave out the front door. The first place I went was Walgreens. It had the nearest atm and I had to get ninety dollars change.

As I was pulling the money she texted me saying, "Do you have a friend with you?...my little sister is trying to come."
 To be honest at this point I was super turnt up about this whole plot, so all I was thinking was I'm about to make some money, smoke for free, and possibly get some play. I replied saying, " Nah I don't." Laughing it off knowing I lowkey wished Messiah answered.

I pulled out a hundred in cash, then left to San Bernardino. The whole time driving I had this gut feeling that something wasn't right, giving me anxiety. I even got off the freeway twice and debated if I should go back. She would periodically text asking me how far I was almost as if she was in a rush. As I got eight minutes away she sent me another address for me to go to claiming that she was going to her dad's house now, which was only a few minutes closer.

I arrived to the location, but I was scared that I had to pull over a little before the house. My heart had to be beating about a thousand times harder than it should be, I was shaken. I instantly called this girl I was dealing with at the time, Britney, and told her that I made it as she knew I was coming before. She told me that she loved me and to be safe. I was so anxious that I kept telling her that I love her. Looking down the street it just looked super sketchy. As I approached the house there were these two boys standing across the street, one seemed to be Black the other Mexican. I made a U-turn and pulled up. I made sure to park in a direction that was clear for a getaway, my doors were locked, and I kept my car on and in drive. I was mentally preparing for the worse.

I texted the girl, "I'm outside."

She said, " I will be right out. I'm putting on makeup."

I was a little confused because what do you need makeup for? A few minutes passed then she texted me saying, "Get out of the car and walk up to the gate. My dad wants to meet you."

I became very attentive to my surroundings. I told her ,"I'm not getting out of the car. You guys can come outside."

She kept trying to persuade me to get out of the car. While, I'm wondering what took her so long to come out and why does she want me to come outside that's weird. I don't know why I stayed as long as I did. It was obvious something was going on. I took off my Apple Watch and hid it in my car along with my wallet just to be on the safe side.

 I have been waiting outside for 10 minutes on this girl to come I even texted her, " You better not be trying to set me up."

She then told me, "To move my car up a little bit." Completely ignoring what I said.

Looking back at it now, I know the only reason why she told me that was so that they could identify me. Those same boys standing across the street when I pulled up ended up coming to my passenger side window and got my attention. So me being scared I just barely cracked my window and turned on the light in my car.

The black guy said, "Hey are you here for Leslie?"

It took me a few seconds to realize that the mystery girl name was Leslie." Yeah." I replied.

"Her dad sent us over here to check you out and make sure you was alright, we are her cousins." The black kid replied.
I thought to myself how in the hell they can be cousins this dude is black.

I replied, "What's the deal bro."

He responded, "Can I get in the car bro and talk it's cold out here?"

This man is crazy, "Nah bro," I said.

He went on to ask me a series of questions, "Do you bang? What's your name? Where are you from?"

His questions made me wonder why are you asking me all this. I told him I didn't bang and lied about the rest.

"I'm trying to pick up and Leslie would give you the money for it." he said.

I said, " Do you got money bro." I'm not just giving out weed that just isn't a smart business plan.

He kept asking me throughout our conversation if he could get into the car. He even took it so far and stepped back and raising his hands saying, "Look bro I'm not on no sneaky stuff I just

just want to get some weed."

I felt kind of relaxed when he did that, making my first big mistake. I decided to reach and the back to get my backpack, but before I reached back I put my car in park, *noise car unlocking*. Honestly I wasn't even aware of my car having this feature of it unlocking when I put it into park, so I didn't pay it any attention. I reached to the back to grab the weed from my backpack and as I was coming back within an instant the black boy sprang into my car instantly pointing a gun in my face. I have been to parties and it got shot up but they weren't aiming for me, so it's a completely different feeling when you know you're the target. My heart sank to my feet and I was in so much shock because you only believe things like this happen in movies or stories just like this one.

I raised my hands up and started to say," I don't got nothing" on repeat. At the same time the Mexican kid opened my back door and tried to take my backpack. I turned around and said," Why are you gonna take my backpack there is nothing in there but school work." He just looked at me and closed the door and at that point I knew I had the advantage. I knew in my heart that if he wanted to shoot me that he would have done it by now. He was just as scared holding the gun as I was staring at it. I was no longer focusing on my fear in the moment, but on ways I could get myself out of this situation.

I began to scan my car for things that can help. My first instinct was to try and lift my phone in an effort to call the cops, but before I could push any buttons he realized and attempted to snatch my phone out hand. I pulled back on it maintaining possession of it. I'm not gone let no one rob me. You're going to have to shoot me or something. Within that moment I saw a small opening and went for it, throwing the capsule of weed I had in one hand at him and within a split second reached for my gear stick and put it into drive. As I began to smash on the accelerator he jumped out of the car and started shooting at my car. Ahead of me all I saw were people running frantically in the street. I never skirted off that fast from a scene in my life. I was swerving through the neighborhood while trying to pull up the GPS. When I got out of the neighborhood I pull over at a gas station in an effort to relax.

After I got a breather I went home and reflected where I went wrong from start to finish. I noticed that the black boy seemed familia. Later discovering that he had hit me up two weeks prior trying to get me in San Bernardino for the same reasons. Also, that the black boy was the mystery girls boyfriend, the same guy she was posting. When I learned this information it freaked me out because it made me feel as if they've been watching me.

That was the craziest day of my life, it gave me nightmares for weeks. Making me more nervous every time I get around a large group of people. I'm constantly looking over my shoulder and analyzing who could be potential predators. Ultimately, affecting the way in which I view certain things and the way I move. I started to devalue the "flashy" lifestyle. Altering my approach when I get dressed. I try to draw less attention to myself, regulate the types of clothes I wear and not wear a lot of jewelry. I began questioning a lot about myself and wanted to learn more about my purpose in life. Coming to the conclusion that all I want is to be successful and happy.

## My Community
## By Luis Delgado

I grew up in a Mexican dominant community and was known as the ghetto part of town. When you drive into the community I live in you will see a lot of marijuana dispensaries, liquor stores, and graffiti from local gangs. However, growing up I didn't really know I lived in a ghetto because it never felt like a hood. It was home. I could walk down to the local market and buy my bag of chips and green tea Arizona, and make it back home safely without ever feeling scared or in danger.

I went to a k-8 school which means it was an elementary school, and middle school all in one. My eighth grade year I participated in a leadership class and was really involved in the school and community. At the time in the leadership class we were planning on an event called What If Week. Our goal was to find a way to help students come closer together by asking what if questions; such as, "What If Kids Didn't do Drugs". We had the event on campus and a lot of important people from the school district had come out to support and see what What If Week was all about. I ended up making a really good first impression to the leadership director of the high school I was going to go to, and she had asked my principal about me. She wanted me to interview for a leadership position for the ASB class at the high school I was going to go to. I decided to apply and I got two interviews. A week later I got a call from the school saying I was the ASB freshman class president. I didn't know what I got myself into because I never heard of ASB.

The high school I went to was white dominant, and was in the rich part of town. The kids from my community were known as the ghetto kids and we were always looked down upon. On the very first day of school there was a rally and the principals introduced me as the freshman president to the entire student body. Many of the students didn't know who I was, and were surprised that a kid from the ghetto was the freshman president. I dealt with a lot of people being really rude and unkind to me because of where I came from, but it only made me stronger. I learned to prove people wrong about my community and would talk greatly about it in the leadership class. After talking more to the principals of my high school they started to get more involved and assist our community with tutoring, and start donations for food and clothes drives.

Being apart of ASB made me want to show people in my community that they shouldn't feel ashamed of where we come from. Embracing your culture and where you come from is a beautiful thing. Along the way I dealt with a lot of pressure from my homies from my neighborhood because they didn't like that I was cool with the white kids on campus. They said I was one of them and not one of them. It really hurt that my life long friends at the time didn't like the idea of me being involved in ASB.

Once I got to my sophomore year I started hanging out with my homies again from my neighborhood, but was starting to lose myself and not really take my leadership position seriously. The principal who got me the interviews saw me hanging around the wrong crowd, and one day she called me out of class to talk to me. I went to her office and right when I walked in she asked me why I was hanging out with the "cholos" on campus. I told her that those were my childhood friends and that I wanted to help them out and be a good influence to them. She then told me to stand on top of her chair that was in her office; I was really confused but I got on anyways. She said, "Luis grab my hand and try to pull me up." I couldn't do it. Then she pulled me down from the chair and said, "do you see how easy it is for someone to pull you down, and how hard it is to pull someone up.

Ever since I started realizing that I needed to start taking school seriously again, and giving back to my community in a positive way. I started tutoring and coaching at the middle school I went to and ended up working hard to get into a 4-year university. The homies I kicked it with eventually got transferred to a continuation school or dropped out. It was really hard to see the friends I grew up with in the streets up to no good, but my pops warned me since I was a kid that my friends would take their own paths in life. Sadly, he was right.

Unfortunately, one of my homies that was in the group that I stopped hanging out with recently got shot and passed away. He ended up being a gang member, and was really involved in the streets. When I stayed home over summer I saw Oscar on my grandma's street. I pulled over and we talked about how easy it was when were kids. He told me he was proud of me and that he knew I was going to make it out the hood. Sadly, that was my last time seeing Oscar. He had a such big heart, and loved to joke around. I wish the principal told my friend what she had told me and maybe things for him could've been different for him. Rest in peace Oscar I love you bro and I will use your story to get these kids off the streets.

## The Hike
## By Ella Spandorf

I remember gazing out of the window looking at a tiny town at the base of Yosemite, with old wood houses and probably a population of three. It was about 2 o'clock and we were 3 hours into our 4 hour drive from our home in Oakland.

"I told you we were gonna be late," I muttered.

"Yeah well, we left late. I think we'll still get there in time though; we can talk to the ranger about it."

I really didn't know what I was expecting to happen. Every time my dad and I do something together, it's always super fun and we both have a great time, but we are always extremely late. That day we were on our way to Yosemite in his little black Ford Escape, packed full of our backpacks and empty McDonalds bags, our favorite road trip snack. It was one of the hottest days of the year, and a week before I started 7th grade. We were planning on backpacking through Tuolumne Meadows in Yosemite and meeting my brother that night at a lake that he was already at.

But of course on the way there, we had to stop at a grain store and pick up chicken feed, we thought wouldn't have enough time on the way back. And we had to pick up a struggling biker on the verge of heat stroke, and bring him back to the town in the opposite direction of our destination, which together set us back for about an hour.

I remember my dad explaining how dangerous it could be to hike at night, especially if we didn't know the trails, "It's super easy to lose the trail, especially on rocky terrain, and a lot of animals are nocturnal, which can be really dangerous."

The last thing I wanted to do was encounter an animal. Just the thought of seeing an animal in the dark chilled me to my bones.

And all I remember saying is "it'll be fine if we walk fast enough, we'll get there just in time to see the sunset on the lake." Even though I knew little thirteen year old me didn't know anything about this trail and I wasn't accepting how un-believably late we were. Especially since it was about a ten mile hike to the lake with a 25 pound pack.

After talking to the ranger at the Tuolumne Meadows visitor center, and seeing his concerning looks we started to weigh our options. He was tall and skinny, with thick, dark eyebrows and reminded me of my boring science teacher. I didn't listen to much of what he was saying, instead I sat down looking at the map and the trail we were about to go on. There was some elevation and a big valley, with multiple little lakes on the way. We decided to just go, and accept it if we end up having to hike in the dark. We've already driven this far, and it seemed silly to not go now.

The first bit of hiking is always hardest in my opinion. You're not used to wearing a pack, so you really feel the weight. The elevation is pretty tough too, but we weren't going to get any-where if you take breaks every few miles, so we just push through. One mile in we pass the first little lake, Dog Lake, and I enjoyed the subtle smell of trees and the constant babbling of rock against water, I was finally in my happy place and never wanted to leave.

At one point we climbed up so much elevation that I got a bloody nose, and when we stopped to tend to it I noticed how dark it had gotten. The sun hadn't quite set, but our shadows were long and we could see the sun go right below the tree line. We had probably about 4 miles left. I could see the valley below the monstrous hill we just climbed and when we get down again it was mostly all downhill from there.

In the middle of eating his Clif bar my dad turned to me and said, "We gotta hurry, we should at least be to the valley before it gets super dark, the trail is easier after that."

We hurried down the hill, tree after tree, and finally got to the valley. The long stalks of grass seemed to cut through the cool, crisp air. It was almost completely dark, we didn't waste any time, and continued on through the trail.

When we got to the end of the valley and back into the trees, we stopped to get our headlamps out of our packs. Eagerly searching through, trying not to mess up all the clothes, food and random gear I was carrying. I felt a sinking pit in my stomach and remember seeing it on the counter at home, and forgetting to grab it.

"Shoot, I think I forgot mine."

"You're lucky I brought an extra flashlight," And my dad handed me this little flashlight, probably the size of a sharpie.

And we went off, in the pitch black forest, illuminated by the lights we were carrying. I was behind my dad, too scared to go first, as I could just imagine myself falling off a cliff or tripping on a disorderly root. We were focused on getting to our destination, we didn't talk and we didn't stop.

I occasionally heard a rustling in the trees next to me or get it in my head that a bear is right behind me about to grab me. But I never looked back, never looked at the rustling, I was too scared that I would see something and not be able to move forward, or I would lose my dad and be alone in the dark.

After what felt like the longest hike of my life we saw the reflection of water from our flashlights. And realized we were at the first lake of the three Young Lakes. My brother was at the third one, but we decided to just make camp here and meet him at the third one in the morning.

While trying to get closer to the lake, we suddenly heard a loud sound, about ten feet away from us. This time we both shone our flashlights towards the sounds and see two big, round yellow eyes. We both instantly knew it's probably a bear. My first instinct was to run. But I know enough about bears to know not to run, so I slowly walk away. My dad on the other hand stood there, shining his light at it until he realized I've started to leave and came with me.

"Never just walk away from me in dangerous situations like that," he frantically exclaimed.

But my heart was racing and I couldn't seem to think straight and at this point, I was so exhausted and hungry that all I wanted to do is just sit down and finally relax. We walked about 20 minutes around the lake in the opposite direction from the eyes and set up camp.

Even though we both were thinking in our heads how stupid it would be to make hot dogs right now, right next to a bear, we still did. With a full stomach and a realization of 'oh my god what just happened' going through my mind, I laid down and hoped to sleep it away.

# Mountain Getaway by Janvi Kumar

To see the sun come up in the mountains is just one of the most beautiful sights to ever witness. But it didn't quell the anxiety rising in me. I felt strangely out of place, like my body and mind were separate, my body in the car and my mind where the sun is.

I was wide awake, even if it was 6:30 am and I have been up since 4. I felt warm in my friend's sedan surrounded by their presence. On one side of me was Lena, who was peering outside the car window, and on the other side was Kathy, whose eyes were drooping in exhaustion. Lena's dad and his girlfriend were in the front, talking quietly.

"How you kids holding up?" Lena's dad asked.

"Good," we replied, not really in the mood to talk and to just sit in the silence.

"We're about a half an hour away," Lena's dad said, turning his attention to the road in front of me.

"Sir," I asked, "Do you have spare goggles for me to wear?"

Lena's dad tensed, "I thought you had them already?"

"I don't."

"And poles? We didn't rent those out either."

"No, I don't have those either."

Lena let out a snicker.

He sighed, and I could suddenly tell that he was trying to hold back his anger. "We'll buy them for you there," he said.

"How are you finding 3rd Grade, Janvi?" the Girlfriend asked, trying to dispel the awkwardness of the car. I could imagine her doe like eyes wide in feigned curiosity, fixed on the road ahead.

"It's fine," I mumbled, wishing I was like Kathy and not awake having this conversation right now.

It was amazing that I even managed to be on this trip. My over-protective parents frowned at the thought of their 9-year-old child going off on a ski trip without them. It took a lot of convincing with finally the point of, well it's not like you guys can take me on a Blue Slope, better my first time be with a family of renowned skiers.

They muttered in Hindi for a while, before saying yes.

I looked out the window and spotted the infamous frozen waterfall, jagged icicles ready to pierce the ground. We were 10 minutes out.

I was so excited that I could go skiing with one of my best friends but soon that excitement turned into nervousness of I'm going on a Blue for the first time when I've been only doing Greens.

That nervousness turned into panic as I saw Lena's dad's face at 5 am, purple bruises under his eyes in the shape of cresents, worry lines pronounced on his forehead, and a frown taking a permanent place on his face. I could clearly see he was not happy with me coming along. I knew nothing I could do to quell his irritation; he never was okay with his daughter being friends with an Indian girl.

The sedan pulled over to the frost-covered parking lot, and I listened to the satisfying crunch of the tires on the snow.

The Girlfriend helped me into my ski boots and skis while Lena's dad went to go get my goggles and poles. Kathy was putting on her helmet, with stray hair peeking out.

We headed toward the line leading us to the chairlift, me awkwardly getting used to my poles by using them to pull me forward while Lena and Kathy slid gracefully. They had fun teasing me, 'skiing' circles around me, trying to get me to lose my balance more then once.

"Knock it off both of you," the Girlfriend ordered, then turned to me, "you okay sweetie," her voice dripped in honey.

"Yes ma'am," I grunted, staring at Lena and Kathy as both pouted.

The two 9-year-olds soon got over it as they started to chatter eagerly, but I found myself not saying anything. Despite the cold, I broke out in a sweat.

Lena's dad pulled me aside. "Kathy and Lena will sit together on the chairlift," he murmured. "I'll help you on the chairlift and off."

I nodded, not trusting myself to speak.

We shifted forward in the line. "How long have you've been skiing?" Lena's dad asked.

I eyed the skiers in front of us, there were two left. "Only 3 months."

One skier left. Lena's dad smirked, a bushy eyebrow raised, "Not long at all then."

There were no skiers left, we were next in line. "Not really."

I looked up, the mountain seemed to loom more ominously than ever. "Ready?" Lena's dad asked.

I placed my poles in one hand and stretched my other arm out, ready to grab the railing of the chair for support; I looked over my shoulder and saw the chair coming in the corner of my eye.

"Yes."

Simultaneously we sat, and I felt the ground disappear under my feet.

Throughout my first round down, Lena's dad taught me how to ski down with the "french fry" technique and using poles. After that first trip, Kathy, Lena, and I spent the whole day skiing down the blue slopes. It was exhilarating, flying down the mountain at high speed, the fleeing of the skies momentarily touching the ground in a slick icy feeling. Seeing the white landscape blur around me; the path ahead was the only thing in focus. I was bobbing and weaving through other skiers and I was racing the snowboarders as if we were in a contest.
Soon, I felt like a pro skier.

Finally we were all waiting on line to go up the ski lift. I looked up at the sky, "I think this is our last one," I observed, looking at how dark it was getting. Lena nodded, "Yeah it's best we finish after this one."

While on the chair lift, on the way to the top we saw Lena's dad in the middle. Lena and Kathy shouted excitedly gaining his attention while I waved shyly.

He shouted out something.

"Did he just asked us to meet him there?" Lena asked.

"Yeah he did, I heard it," Kathy breathed, twisting her body to look back at Lena's dad.

"He was at the black slope though wasn't he?" I asked nervously. No matter how much I have improved in one day I knew that I couldn't handle that slope at all.

Lena shrugged, "I guess we have to, it shouldn't be too hard."

"It will be hard for me!"

"We'll help you, don't worry," Lena soothed me before turning to Kathy.

Lena and Kathy excitedly chatted while I stewed in my anxiety. We got off the chair and went toward the slope. The sun was setting faster than I thought, and I realized we had about 20 minutes before the sun will disappear.

Instead of going to the right, we went to the left. My jaw dropped, "The slope just ends!" Instead of any slope all we could see in front of us is the ground disappearing and a steep cliff.

Kathy shook her head, "Did we miss it?"

"Do you see any other slopes?" Lena snapped, "No, this is it."

To our astonishment, a skier appeared right beside us. He gave us a curious look, then just skied off the cliff.

My mouth felt dry, "Yeah that's a black slope all right." I started freaking out. We couldn't go back to the chair lift unless we hiked up the mountain but it was so steep. The only way to go down was go over the cliff. I could just imagine it, gravity taking over and I would just fall down the mountain like a rag doll.

"What do we do!" my voice came out in a shrill squeak. I would've felt embarrassed but I was too deep in my anxiety.

"God I'd probably break my knees if I fell down." I thought in my head.

Lena skied to the side and looked over a guarded off barrier where there was a hill. She peered over."If we skied over this we can make it back to the blue slope," she said thoughtfully.

"Do you not see it blocked off," I hissed.

Kathy was already pulling up the red rope. "It's just powdered snow, we'll be fine."

Lena nodded, "Watch Kathy, it will be easy." Kathy was already standing on the other side of the rope. She pushed off with her poles and skied down the powdered snow as easy as if it was hard packed snow.

"Great job Kathy," Lena called. She turned to me, "I'll go next and you'll follow," she ordered.

Lena turned and skied down the hill. I watched as she and Kathy high-fived. Lena then yelled at me, "Just follow our ski marks."

I looked down dubiously, the hill went about 50 feet before dropping into the blue slope. I took a deep breath and pushed off with my skis.

Going down was frightening; I just kept my eye on the ski tracks and for a split second I thought I could actually do it. But about three quarters of the way down I lost my balance, I fell to my side and winced as I felt the frost hit my cheek. My fall knocked my skis off of my boots.

"Just walk the way back." Lena yelled.

I grabbed my skis and started marching up the hill. It was about a twenty-foot walk but with each step I felt myself sinking and sinking into the snow. With a startled scream, I felt the snow give out and it sank up to my waist.

I froze, panic seizing my limbs. Immersed in snow, the dying light of the setting sun was slowly vanishing; every thought of Himilayan climbers suffocating, submerged head to toe in snow, popped up in mind.

I sat back on my butt, tilted my head towards the pale pink sky, wailed, "I can't do it!" and started crying.

Lena and Kathy exchanged looks then just stared at me. I could see Kathy's gloved fist clenched. "It's only a little bit ahead." she said, looking annoyed.

I sniffled, "Ok." I trudged up the hill, finally making it to where my friends were.

"Ok, just put your skies on and we can go now," Lena sighed.
I dropped my skies on the ground and tried to step in them. My brow furrowed when I couldn't get them on.

"What's the hold up," Kathy asked impatiently.

"It's not going on," I said, voice going shrill again. The sun had almost vanished at this point.

Lena kneeled down and looked at my boots. She grimaced, "Ice has set in the boots." She started to chip at it with her pole, "Kathy, come help me with this."

I stood there awkwardly, feeling more useless as ever, as they chipped at the ice. Finally we got the ice off and the skies were on. We skied down with only a minor mishap in the woods. The Girlfriend was waiting for us at the bottom. "What happened to you guys!" she gushed.

"We got lost," I muttered. Her eyebrow raised and she turned to Lena. "Your dad was worried sick!"

Lena looked pained. "It took us a while to get back."

Lena's dad bounded toward us, his arms spread wide, "What happened," he asked, repeating the Girlfriend's question.

"Why did you ask us to meet you at the black slope?" Kathy demanded. Lena's dad frowned.

"I did not!" he remained silent for a few moments, stroking his bushy beard. "I said I'll meet you there," he declared, looking at us. "As in, at the bottom."

We all stood there agape. I closed my eyes, feeling exhaustion seeping into my bones. All that stress for a miscommunication? "Well no matter, let's go," the Girlfriend shooed us into the car. As we left, everyone was silent, all muddled in our own turmoil.

"Janvi," Lena murmerd. "Let's do this again."
I nodded, knowing she was lying. And she was, we never did.

College Life Essays

# Strategies of a Successful Student
## By Jaylene Acosta

From Kindergarten all the way to a senior in high school I had the same 8a.m. to 3p.m. school schedule. I would get home around 3:30p.m. eat a light meal then work on my homework until I was finally done. However, my first year of college erased that schedule and forced me to create a more flexible schedule. My second semester was when I found the flow and was finally feeling like I was a college student. I was surprised by how many changes that occur once you get out of high school. For example on x days my first class started at 9a.m. while on y days my first class started at 11a.m. Then I had that one day where my only class was during the afternoon. Being a college student felt so hectic until I had a comfortable schedule. For most days I would eat an early lunch and then do my homework until my next class started. Every Wednesday I would meet with my Java tutor and every other Tuesday I would meet with my calc tutor. When I finished my spring semester I thought I had college all figured out.

This fall semester is even more hectic than the last one because I'm working out three to four times a week and going to Bible study twice a week. Half of the time I'm not getting home until after the sun sets. I'm trying to not cheat myself academically or physically. But recently I noticed I would make excuses to go to the gym instead of starting on my homework. It feels as if I became even better at procrastination after the summer break. This semester I feel very overwhelmed and behind on all my classes. If other students feel this way then how can we change this feeling of hopelessness? How do I go back to giving my all on assignments? Are there easier ways to adjust when each semester has a very different schedule? How do other people adjust to a college schedule?

I started off by doing a simple google search about time management for students and kept getting generic articles that just talked about quick tips. I could tell from the short articles that they were not going to work out for everyone such as keeping a journal. Then I remembered that our school has an online library and the results had thorough articles. I started reading one called the "Crux of Time Management for Students" by Felix Blast. In his article he first talks about how crucial it is in the beginning of the academic quarter to set up personal productivity goals. Blast even starts his article talking about how he takes a class period with his new students talking about how to effectively prioritize. Then he moves on to talk about how critical it is to cultivate productive habits. He says that every time you complete or even start something written on your schedule you are essentially competing with yourself to be the best version of yourself. From the first half of his article I realized that I am not together during the first few weeks of the semester. I tell myself that I will eventually pull myself together but that mentality is self-sabotage. Setting aside time from your busy schedule to go over what worked for you or times during the day that you need to change and improve are things I never thought were important. I now realize that if you don't reflect on past experiences and failures then ultimately you can't move on and be a better student.

In the second part of his article, Blast focuses on health and says the essentials are exercise, meditation and sleep. He says that you can look up on youtube 30 minutes of moderate-intensity workouts and that staying consistent is the most important part. Blast's look into research has also shown that there is an association between meditation and lower stress levels. Lastly, since most people sleep in 90 minute cycles and need an average of 7 hours, Blast suggests that students plan their bedtime accordingly so that they wake up at the end of the cycle. Time management for students is not just fitting in studying time because no one is just a student. These are all factors that affect every person's health and students need to be more aware of what's happening to their body every time they do an overnighter or skip eating multiple meals. Since nobody knows how to manage everything on their own we seek others' advice and opinions so that we don't feel alone. That's why it is called the student body, because we need to rely on each other as a community.

Then I was interested in how physical health in particular benefits college students. Since Blast only briefly talked about exercise in his article, I wanted to find a full fledged article describing why people should incorporate exercise in their weekly routine. Natalie San Luis describes in her study paper, "Exercise Key To Better Moods, Less Stress For College Students," how physical activity can improve mental health. In a nutshell, the article is about how a study was conducted in the form of a survey for students about "the relationship between exercise, stress, mental health, and socializing in students at a four-year college." What was most interesting about the research was that "they found that students who were more social and exercised three or more times per week reported somewhat better moods and less stress than students who exercised with similar frequency but were less social." Even though this semester has been the most crazy, I have finally made friends with people I have had class with last semester and others that are in the same or similar major. Personally, I do think social interaction helps with mental health and stress because again you don't feel like you are tackling college alone. Mental health is also important because it can affect your motivation to do well academically. Overall, it's very intriguing to see that exercise, stress, mental health and socialization are connected and play an important role in college student's life.

I wanted to hear my friend and personal trainer, Robbie Guerrero's experience on how he managed working out, training other people and being a student all at the same time. Robbie graduated from SFSU last semester while living in the dorms and working at the Mashouf Wellness Center (MWC) as a personal trainer. During our training time last semester he said he had a lot of papers to finish before he graduated. His way of getting them done was forcing himself to write at least a sentence a day on each of his papers. So I thought he would be a great candidate to interview since he was so involved in the community. When I first asked him if he wanted to be interviewed he talked about how Google docs helped him through college but I wanted to delve deeper into how he survived SFSU.

I first asked him how he incorporated the responsibilities of being a trainer at the into his schedule when the MWC first opened up. Robbie told me that when the MWC first opened up he had 3 classes between 9am to 10pm on Tuesdays that were all 3 hour classes. So on the days where he wasn't on campus all day he would make himself available to train/teach students at the MWC. Additionally, I asked Robbie how his schedule changed after the MWC opened up. He said, "the major thing that changed from my prior schedule was that I was able to make it as packed or as free as I wanted. It all depended on how much time I wanted to dedicate to training people." After he answered these questions it made me realize that ultimately I'm in control of my situation. My physical health goals and school goals are a good guide on how to base my schedule but they can't hold my mental health hostage.

The next set of questions came from wondering how to not cheat myself physically and slack off academically. I asked Robbie, "When there were times when a lot of deadlines were coming up (midterms/finals/projects), how did you keep up with your gym routine and training? Did you ever have to sacrifice working out in order to keep up with school deadlines?" What worked for Robbie was to schedule out times to finish essays or presentations. He said sometimes it would be a half hour to finish a paragraph or slide, then other times up to 3 hours to completely finish up a project. As for training others, he said during finals he told his clients he couldn't come in. But he told me that since his clients were also students that they liked having a break from training to allow them to focus on their studies. The part that resonated most with me is when Robbie told me, "Since you have been going to the gym for so long even if you miss a week or two you will make it up in someway." After he told me this I felt better missing some days at the gyms. Instead of going to the gym in between my classes with long breaks, I went to the library to work on projects instead of using the gym to procrastinate.

Lastly, I wondered what other advice Robbie could give me since he spent the past four years at SF state and I am only a Sophomore. I asked him which semester was the hardest for him and why. He answered, "My hardest semester had to be my junior year spring semester. I was able to get all the classes I needed to graduate. I also had 18 units. Work was never an issue, it was simply my preference of actually trying to learn." There will probably be other classes that I take that I am not interested in taking but am forced to in order to graduate as well. However, if I really take his advice to heart then I will have a less stressful time since I will have a planned out schedule. Instead of doing things half-heartedly to finish them fast, I can take my time because I already have planned to spend that time focusing on a specific goal.

My action plan for the rest of this semester is to rearrange parts of my schedule. Instead of going to the gym Monday, Tuesday, Thursday and Friday I will only go Monday and Friday. I will spend my breaks between classes on Tuesday and Thursday to catch up on my homework by eating a quick lunch and staying in the library instead of Caesar Chavez. During this time I will not let Discord, the social media site I use, control my life. I won't play the minigames on there because I use them to procrastinate school work. For next semester I am planning on a lighter schedule. Since this semester taking calc 2 and physics 1 was too overwhelming I will take either calc 3 or physics 2 next semester. During the beginning of the new semester I am going to take Mr. Blast's advice and set aside at least an hour to schedule out my study times and rest times. Instead of going to the gym for more days I will go less and create more intense workouts so I feel fulfilled. For others I recommend having a friend to motivate you to go to the gym as well as trying to connect with other classmates in the beginning of the semester so that you have study groups. Ultimately, my goal is to have a mindset of pre action instead of reaction for college.

Bibliography:
Bast, Felix. "Crux of Time Management for Students. (Report)." Vol. 21, no. 1, 2016, p.    71., doi:10.1007/s12045-016-0296-6.

Luis, Natalie San. "Exercise Key To Better Moods, Less Stress For College Students: Study." *HuffPost*, HuffPost, 7 Dec. 2017,

# Sleepy in College
## By Nathalie Hernandez

I felt like I wasn't ready for this huge transition of living the college life, but after a few weeks of college, it didn't seem so bad. While signing up for classes, I thought that I would have no problem waking up for an 8am, since I was used to waking up early in high school. So not true, I struggle to wake up for my 8am class because I didn't get enough sleep the night before. Sometimes I can't sleep at night, or people in my building are being super loud, leading me to not sleep at all. Naps feel like heaven, but sometimes I regret taking one because I end up oversleeping. Sleeping for 30mins is the best thing because me feel so refreshed after, but sleeping for two hours makes me feel more tired, making it harder to fall asleep.

One night, I stayed up late doing homework, after I got ready for bed. Around 12am, our neighbors started to blast music and speak loudly, and everything could be heard through the thin walls. Soon after, there was laughter and yelling in the hallway, and someone riding their skateboard. Our R.A. told them to quiet it down, but the girls next to our room were still loud. Around 1am, my roommate came back to our room and walked in with her blasting music, while she was singing. She got ready for bed and pulled out her laptop with her brightness all the way up and snacks in her hand. Suddenly, she starts to laugh really loud and started a conversation with me about the thing she was laughing at, as I was about to fall asleep. I got scared and woke me up, making it more difficult to fall asleep because of the adrenaline I felt. We started to talked and I went on my phone for a bit to help me fall asleep again. I was interrupted again by a loud sound outside and I looked at the time only to realize it was 3am. I had a class at 8am, and I ended up taking a 2 hour nap when I got to my room after my morning class.

Once you start to get used to the feel of college and find your way around the school, sleep doesn't stay consistent. In reality sleep has a big impact on how you focus in class, do homework, and act throughout your day. John Tuttle, a student from Biola University, is a writer for the student life blog at Biola. One of the blogs focused on sleep; when you lack sleep and how to fix your sleep, based on his own tips and experts. Tuttle states that "Sleep deficit results from not getting enough sleep for several nights. Building up your sleep deficit results in a decrease in daytime function. It can affect your physical health by weakening your immune system." The longer you're awake, the harder your body is working to keep up with you. As the body and brain are overworked, your physical health is affected, making your immune system weak. A few weeks ago I felt sick; I had a headache and didn't feel like eating. I felt like this for a few days, and I told my mom about it and she asked if I was getting enough sleep. Realizing that I had about 6 hours of sleep the last few days, I knew that I needed to make sure I got enough sleep. My brain and body were trying to keep up with my lack of sleep and I started to feel the effects of sleep deficiency.

Sleeping less started to affect my academic life, I could barely stay awake in my class and couldn't keep up with the professor; my eyes wouldn't stay open. These professors have provided some data on the effects of not sleeping enough. Daniel Taylor and Adam Bramoweth, two professors from the University of North Texas worked together to study the psychology of sleep. Bramoweth and Taylor's main focus is "The college transition presents many challenges … , which can lead to irregular sleep schedules and sleep deprivation. Sleep deprivation in turn can cause driving accidents [4], depression [5], and worse academic performance [6]" (Pg. 610). Many professors know that one of the challenges that incoming freshmen face is the "irregular sleep schedules" because you're getting used to a new environment, people, and college life in general. Without getting sleep, your senses will start to become less aware, which can cause driving accidents, depression, and worse academic performance. All this can cause you to be negative in everything, which can lead to more physical and mental problems. In my morning class, we were going over poems about European immigrants and watching a video about Greek immigration. It was a very interesting topic to me, but the lack of sleep was catching up to me. I tried to sit up straight, but my eyes weren't focusing because I was so tired. In order to pay attention in my other classes I took a nap, but I was asleep for 2 hours. Sleeping too much made it hard to fall asleep later that night.

Many college students continue to lack sleep, while balancing a social life, school, and work. Melissa Hernandez, a 4th year university student from San Jose State University is majoring in child and adolescent development. Melissa is currently working, is a full time student, and is involved at her church. When I asked her how much sleep she gets on average, she said, "On average, I get 6 to 7 hours of sleep. It depends on what I have planned and how much homework I have to finish that day." Melissa goes to school twice a week, has work almost everyday of the week, and goes to church 4 to 5 times a week. Sleep is the last thing on her mind because she has to do homework and balance her social life. I asked her another question, what do you do when you don't get enough sleep? She replied, "I will take naps, but only on accident. I usually drink coffee when I'm super tired." Melissa usually never naps, only when her body and brain are too tired, she'll nap. Coffee is something she always gets at least once a day, to get through her busy day. Then I asked her, How do you feel when you lack sleep? Her response was, "When I lack sleep, I usually feel light headed and nauseous. Which tends to lead to headaches." I've seen her when she's sleep deprived, she also tends to not be in the best mood. Her body is trying to keep up with her, but can't because there's not enough energy left in her body. I also rely on coffee or naps to get me through the day because sometimes there is not enough time in the day to do everything. With homework, studying, and sleeping, I have to pick which one is most important that day. I will nap and stay up late or I drink coffee and go to sleep a little earlier.

Sleep is super important to all human beings, but when you constantly use your brain in school work and other things. For example, when sitting in a lecture, many students tend to fall asleep because of their lack of sleep they can miss important notes and information for their next assignment or test. It may not seem important because you can "catch up" on sleep during the weekend, which is not true. Make sure that you're getting enough sleep in order to avoid getting sick and sleep deprived. Once you get used to college, make sure you find a good routine to get to bed because sleep is essential. And learning about the benefits and the effects of sleep, it will be eye opening because you'll realize why it's hard to wake up and function in general.

For myself, I've been taking shorter naps, trying to sleep later, and drink less coffee. Although coffee is my most favorite things in the world and I usually drink coffee at least once a day. Since coffee carries a lot of caffeine, I've been trying to substitute it with water and tea with honey. These little changes are helping me fall asleep more naturally because it was of these changes I have been applying to my daily life. My roommate has also noticed that I've fixed my sleeping routine and am able to sleep better during the night. Sharing these tips and ideas as will be beneficial to other college students has they start to get use to the college life. Sleep deficiency is real and can cause problems for incoming college students, learning the effects of lack of sleep is important to know.

## Work Cited:

Taylor, Daniel J, and Adam D Bramoweth. "Patterns and Consequences of Inadequate Sleep in College Students: Substance Use and Motor Vehicle Accidents." *Journal of Adolescent Health*, vol. 46, no. 6, 2010, pp. 610–612. https://www-sciencedirect-com.jpllnet.sfsu.edu/science/article/pii/S1054139X09006788

Tuttle, John. "Not Sleeping? Gotta Fix That." *Student Life Blog - Biola University Blogs*, 5 Mar. 2017, https://www.biola.edu/blogs/studentlife/2017/not-sleeping-gotta-fix-that

Hernandez, Melissa. Personal Interview. 21 October 2019.

# Being Shy in College
## By Andy Li

Being shy sucks sometimes. I can go from being confident and the loudest person around my friends to being completely mute and timid around people I don't know. I was never shy as a kid though. Making friends was effortless in elementary school. Then middle school came. All my friends I've known for those six years went to different schools, but I was able to meet some of my closest friends in middle school. High school was a whole different story. For some reason, I just couldn't talk to anyone. Anytime someone came up to me, I would panic a little. I got scared of doing anything because of the fear of what others would think of me. This made me struggle throughout high school because I was too afraid to ask anyone for help. Not even from teachers.

As a shy person, I never questioned why I was shy or how I became shy. KidsHealth reveals that shyness is caused by genetics or life experiences in their article called *Shyness.* KidsHealth says that "About 20% of people have a genetic tendency to be naturally shy. But not everyone with a genetic tendency to be shy develops a shy temperament. Life experiences also play a role" (KidsHealth, 2016). They also explain that shyness can also be caused by having overly cautious or overprotective parents of shy kids. My family is an example of this. Even though I'm in college now, they like to be very cautious about a lot of things I do. When I do go somewhere by myself, they would give me a whole lecture of dos and don'ts. I usually end up telling them I'm old enough to take care of myself. Knowing the root cause of your shyness can help you change that part of your life so you can overcome shyness easier. In an article, *Overcoming Shyness at College,* Diana Rodriguez interviews Kaveh Zaminian, who is a clinical psychologist. Zaminian talks about the different ways that you can overcome your shyness. One way you can start to overcome your shyness is to "Start in small groups and work your way up" says Zaminian (Rodriguez, 2010). Start by joining a club you are interested in to help you make friends. Having something in common can help you bond with someone better.

Towards the end of my freshman year of high school, I started going to this church my sister invited me to. I hesitated a little and was reluctant to go because I would be going to a building filled with a bunch of strangers, which is pretty much the worst thing that could happen if you are shy. I ended up going anyways though and it ended up being one of the best decisions of my life. I met a lot of people and made a lot of new friends through church who I now hang out with every Sunday. I even became a program leader in my church's day camp where I take care of kids. Now, I'm not saying that suddenly I'm not shy anymore, because that's far from reality. But being to make so many new friends is one of the best feelings to have as a shy person. So, do try to find a group or a club that you can join. There are tons of clubs at SF State that will pique your interest. If you are like me and love video games, then joining the Gaming Gators would be a good start. There are also many clubs for specific majors if that is what you are looking for, like the Economic Students Association or the Accounting Students Association. Joining a club can become one of the most beneficial things that can happen to you in college.

Joining a club or group can be hard to do if you have the mindset that others are constantly judging you. I also had the same mindset throughout high school until recently. California College San Diego released an article, *"Overcoming Detrimental Shyness"*, where they also explain ways you can overcome shyness. We are told that you need to "Become self-aware, not self-conscious with the understanding that others aren't constantly judging" (CCSN, 2016). My communications teacher told us one thing that stuck with me. She told us that others are too busy worrying about themselves to be worrying about you. Every time I had a speech or presentation, I would keep telling this to myself repeatedly. Knowing that there are others like you worrying about themselves can help you feel relieved and calm you down whenever you feel anxious. I wish I had this mindset back in high school so I wouldn't have struggled so much.

Now that I'm in college, I kind of accepted that I am a shy person. Being shy is what makes me who I am. Megan Scott, who was a student at University of Wisconsin, recounts her experience of being a shy college student in her article, *7 Things I Learned From Being A Shy College Student*." At the end of the article, Scott tells us "As long as you are not letting shyness stand in the way of finding passions and achieving goals, then there is nothing to worry about" (Scott, 2017). If you really want to do something but your shyness is getting in the way of it, try to find an alternative instead of giving up. Even if you know for sure you won't be able to do it, then that's okay too. Not everyone will be able to overcome their shyness right away, it takes time.

During a retreat over the summer, I had a conversation with my older friends about being in college and the future. I was asked what I wanted to work towards in college, but I couldn't think of one. My friend then recommended me to study abroad. Study Abroad wasn't something that was on my mind at the time. Going to another country where I didn't know the language, the culture, and being alone there? That was a big no from me, but I started to think about it more. I started thinking of the benefits of studying abroad. Tuition wouldn't cost more, I could learn a new language, and experience a new culture. This may be a big step up for me from being a program leader in terms of challenging my shyness. But I'm not going to let that get in the way. Study abroad became the end goal I want to achieve in college, besides graduating of course.

Even though I accepted who I am, there are still many things I'm still afraid to do, such as initiating a conversation with a stranger. That's on my list of "Will have a heart attack if I tried", right next to skydiving and going on a Ferris wheel. Obviously, this isn't something I want to keep on my list forever. Even if I can't overcome shyness now, I will not let it stop me from achieving my goals and having the future I want.

## Works Cited

"Blog." *California College San Diego*, 17 July 2016, www. cc-sd.edu/blog/overcoming-    detrimental-shyness. Accessed 11 Nov. 2019.

Rodriguez, Diana. "Overcoming Shyness at College." *EverydayHealth.com*, 17 Mar. 2010, https://www.everydayhealth.com/college-health/overcoming-shyness-at-college.aspx. Accessed 11 Nov 2019.

Scott, Megan. "7 Things I Learned From Being A Shy College Student." *The Odyssey Online*, The Odyssey Online, 14 Nov. 2017, www.theodysseyonline.com/7-things-learned-being-shy-college-student. Accessed 11 Nov. 2019.

"Shyness (for Teens)." Edited by D'Arcy Lyness, *KidsHealth*, The Nemours Foundation, Oct. 2016, https://kidshealth.org/en/teens/shyness.html. Accessed 11 Nov. 2019.

# The Clock Is Ticking
## By Sophia Hernandez

All I can think of is doing homework or studying for the next test. Every day is a continuous cycle. In the morning I get up from my bed drowsy and unaware to the bathroom to wash my face and get ready. The cold water wakes me up and I'm ready to go to school. Once I get to school, I go through the day with all 5 of my classes. Every other day I have homework or have to study for tests and speeches. Taking some time for myself and managing my time well is just something I can't do. I have so much things to do when it comes to my work for school. Sometimes I spend hours of just doing work and forget to eat. I don't have to time to make myself food so I eat out which doesn't help with eating healthier. I want to work out and go to the gym but because I have to study or do homework I don't go. Spending time with my family is always restricted because I always have homework. How do I manage time in college? I know I should be taking the time but if I don't do it now I would have even more homework later on. Sometimes I feel like there's an endless amount of work that I can't escape. If I don't do it, I feel like I'm not being productive. The pressure of schoolwork and making time for yourself is exhausting. In the article "5 Ways to Maintain Balance Between Work, School, and Life", John McClung suggests to "Organize your work in a meaningful way based on when projects, papers, and other work events are due". McClung suggests by organizing and prioritizing the work we can excel in getting the work done faster. This can lead to students being able to have time left to relax and have free time. McClung also states that, "By procrastinating you are allowing your to-do list to grow and grow into an intimidating amount of work". In my opinion I think that this is true for me as a college student I tend to push off some work because of how much I have to do. Just the thought of me having to do it gives me a bad appetite and leads me to procrastinate and do nothing.

Since I tend to procrastinate I have trouble focusing on work and lose track of my time so Zoey Bullock in the article, "6 Ways to Master Time Management in College" states to "Identify your most common distractions and seek to eliminate or at least minimize their sources". Bullock suggests getting rid of distractions and time wasters. This quote is something that every student has to try because of we all get tempted by our phones and environment when studying or doing homework. When we are too distracted this leads to homework piling up and leaves you to do your homework all day. Bullock also suggests that "Ideally for every hour or two of school work, you should give yourself a 5-10 minute break". In my opinion I think that this is especially true for studying. When I study non-stop it can leave me mentally exhausted. Having the ability to take a short break can give me more energy to finish your work in a more efficient way.

When told that students don't take time for themselves outside of school my cousin Alexis who has been going to San Francisco State University and is in her junior year says that the most important factor that has helped her throughout her years here was to take time for herself. Alexis says, "Even if it's an hour or a 30 minute break just those minutes have helped me relax and get work done faster than if I hadn't". This is something that I think even if its short can have a big impact on performance when doing homework and also in a way can help make you finish faster and more efficiently. Leaving you more time for yourself.

When doing homework for school another aspect that can has an impact on procrastination is your emotional state on work. In the article "Why Wait? The Science Behind Procrastination" by Eric Jaffe says, "the best way to eliminate the need for short-term mood fixes is to find something positive or worthwhile about the task itself". When starting assignments there is a certain mentality that I have sometimes and I'm sure a handful of students have of "ugh I have to do this work" that makes us dread the thought of having to do homework. In my opinion I agree with Jaffe I think we all have to change our mentality and think about the positive outcome of finishing the work. Sirois says that, "You've got to dig a little deeper and find some personal meaning in that task". While thinking about it personally we can see the importance of the class and what values and knowledge we get from assignments that our professors give to us. Students can tie in assignments and associate them which can help with their career. Ultimately, we can remember why we are here in college and put it into our own perspective.

Staying motivated and keeping track of yourself is an important part of your college life. There is a lot of responsibility with making sure as students we also have time for not only ourselves but also create time with our loved ones. I think that by starting assignments with a positive attitude I can improve on procrastination. I do agree with all of the points that the authors were making and want to stop procrastination by planning ahead. By doing this I can help make time for myself and still have a balanced college life.

## Works Cited

McClung, John. March 9, 2015, "5 Ways to Maintain Balance Between Work, School, and Life". *Wayup.com.* https://www.wayup.com/guide/community/5-ways-to-maintain-balance-between-work-school-and-life/

Bullock, Zoey. "6 Ways to Master Time Management in College". Plexuss.com. https://plexuss.com/news/article/time-management-college-students

Jaffe, Eric. March 29, 2013, "Why Wait? The Science Behind Procrastination". psychologicalscience.org. https://www.psychologicalscience.org/observer/why-wait-the-science-behind-procrastination

Explain a Concept Essays

# BigPharma by Perry Perry

Many may have not heard of the term BigPharma. Well, Big-Pharma is a nickname given to the world's pharmaceutical industry. These are large pharmaceutical companies, especially when these are seen as having a powerful and bad influence, but here is the thing, I have some beef with them. When I was about 7, I was diagnosed with ADHD, but I don't think that's fair to me. At 7, all you want to do is play, run around, and maybe run around some more. Homework is not a priority, at least not to me. So, during an annual checkup, the doctor asked some specific questions about my behavior in class and at home. My mother, being very stubborn at the time, said I wasn't "the best." With a quick 75 question test, I was diagnosed with ADHD. Ever since 7, I have now taken Adderall every day and sometimes even twice a day. I absolutely hate it. I feel as if to be the true me society wants it is only possible on this drug. These BigPharma companies direct their schemes towards our future, the children. They have been marketing and promoting these drugs to the children so that they can have a hold on them for a lifetime. I won't be focusing on all the drugs that BigPharma specializes in that is directed towards kids, but I will be focusing on the Adderall/Ritalin problem, as well as the Xanax.

The advertising plans BigPharma has is almost impeccable, with so many forms of seeing these constant illnesses and then furthering it to "self-diagnosing" yourself, they truly have it laid out, like a directory at an amusement park. Anyways, one way that is given around $2.8 billion a year to by BigPharma is television ads. These ads are wide-ranging from Cartoon Network to PBS to Food Network. Anyone could be watching these programs. This is a bit of a side note because Adderall/Ritalin and Xanax are not allowed to advertise on television. The numbers, however, are staggering. Just the insane amount of how much these BigPharma companies shell out for ads have drastically grown from, "...1997 drug companies spent roughly $17.1 billion on marketing for prescription drugs… "(Quartz). You wouldn't believe how much that has grown. In almost 20 years, the number is roughly $26.9 billion. Not only has the number skyrocketed, but today it is still growing. Directing the focus to Adderall/Ritalin and Xanax, we have seen this trend of doctors being caught in the money. Now, don't get me wrong, not all doctors are bad, I have had some amazing ones for my medical experiences, but there are some that are in it for the money. You know that saying, "ask your doctor if this is right for you." Well, that can easily be a fraud. Remember the numbers from the television ads? Well just wait for this, "In 2012, the pharmaceutical industry spent $24 billion marketing its premium branded drugs to health-care professionals — eight times the amount it spent on advertising to consumers"(Groningen 2017). BigPharma is very smart in the aspect of going directly to your doctor to push out their medicine new or old. So when parents become concerned about their child's well being in school and home life, the doctor could easily be backed up by the pharmaceutical company supporting Adderall/Ritalin and Xanax. One last crazy thing BigPharma has stepped to is comic books. Companies have been pushing out comic books to elementary and middle schools throughout America that specialize in certain drugs. To further explain it is Rebecca Robbins, a writer for STAT, she writes that, "The books are produced by a company called Medikidz, which uses doctors to write and peer-review each edition. More than 3.5 million books have been distributed. Drug companies (as well as other organizations) often sponsor editions; the sponsor's logo sometimes appears on the back cover"(Robbins 2016). These comic books dive into ADHD and anxiety which are typically medicated with Adderall/Ritalin and Xanax. If you are in an online school, don't fret, there are digital versions that can be downloaded for your reading pleasure. Overall, these are just a few ways that BigPharma can target parents of "misbehaving" kids and kids themselves.

This advertising done by BigPharma is crazy enough right? Well, no they go the extra mile to overprescribe these drugs [Adderall/Ritalin and Xanax] to our youth. As I mentioned previously, a personal perspective Adderall/Ritalin seems to be prescribed to those kids who don't meet society's standards. Once again, these numbers do not stop increasing. In a Ritalin research done in 1990, "600,000 children were on stimulants" (Schwartz 2016).Another crazy thing is "...by 2013 3.5 million kids were then on stimulants" (Schwartz 2016). This is just based on the research behind Adderall and Ritalin. Heading over to Xanax, this is a heavy-hitting anxiety drug that has more recently been seen to be overprescribed in kids. Xanax has been on an incline ever since 1996 in kids. With these reports, we have seen an "Increase by two-thirds between 1996 and 2013, from 8 million to nearly 14 million"(Vestal 2018). A whole two-thirds, what an insane statistic. On a child, a heavy drug being taken is mostly never a good idea for those growing bodies. All of these have been seen in the news as well, from an article by Chi Chi Izundu, a writer for BBC News, he states that "...incidents involving the family name of the drug, benzodiazepine - and it said that in 2017 it had attended 240 call-outs for Xanax abuse by children aged between 11 and 18"(Izundu 2018). Kids are winding up in the hospital because of this. These kids and parents don't understand the harms of these drugs and truly what they can do to a growing adolescent.

One may now ask, "What truly happens in the long run once BigPharma gets you hooked off of Adderall/Ritalin and Xanax?" Now that there are millions of kids taking these extensive pills there are studies coming out more and more about how these cripple the youth. The side effects now shown for Adderall/Ritalin from the young age of 6 and above are: loss of appetite, vomiting, nervousness, and insomnia. That is just to list a few side effects. The long term effects consist of slowing down of growth development and much more. For Xanax, they have seen side effects such as slurred speech and unsteadiness. The long term effects may scare some, but they consist of loss of brain cells, difficulty in concentrating, the brain not knowing how to work properly when not on Xanax, and finally loss of control over thought process, emotion, memory, and consciousness. Not to mention on top of all the effects, the pills have not been tested on children. They say it is harder to hold studies on kids, which is understandable, but that's a tough sell if you trying to help your kid and hear all those effects and now you are basing it off of others' experience. A wild card.

Trust me, BigPharma isn't all bad. You might come to a point where medication is needed, and that is okay. There are things where you know what, BigPharma got it right, but some things are off. Medicine is an option once you do the research. Don't go out willy nilly self-diagnosing and especially for your kids or future kids. I don't want to sit here and yell at you for giving your kids or yourself these medicines because they are sometimes needed. All I ask is to research a bit more and let your kid run around and extra hour or two. Not everyone is the same. There are many alternatives to these medications as well if you'd like to not go down the BigPharma route, there are natural remedies as well. It is told that saffron helps the anxious and hyper body which would lead to less of the overprescription of Adderall/Ritalin and Xanax. Overall, you can let BigPharma run your world. You could also put some time in effort into yourself or kid and get into the root of a problem. Try other routes, be the best you. We need a lot of happy people in this world, so if you can put that effort into your kid or yourself, maybe we can see a better you. I am not here to run your life, but next time you head to your local doctor research, ask them, try some natural remedies, get second opinions, try it all! Please make your own decisions and let you be the best you! If you don't have to support those who advertise their medicines to kids and spend billions of dollars a year doing that then don't. Start yourself and your kids off for success.

## Works Cited

"BIG PHARMA: Definition in the Cambridge English Dictionary." BIG PHARMA | Definition
in the Cambridge English Dictionary,
dictionary.cambridge.org/us/dictionary/english/big-pharma.
Boorady, Roy. "The Side Effects of ADHD Medications." Child Mind Institute,
childmind.org/article/side-effects-of-adhd-medication/.
Groningen, Nicole Van. "Big Pharma Gives Your Doctor Gifts. Then Your Doctor Gives You Big
Pharma's Drugs." The Washington Post, WP Company, 13 June 2017,
www.washingtonpost.com/opinions/big-pharma-gives-your-doctor-gifts-then-your-doctor-gives-you-big-pharmas-drugs/2017/06/13/5bc0b550-5045-11e7-b064-828ba60fbb98_story.html.
Izundu, Chi Chi. "Xanax: Children as Young as 11 Taking Anxiety Drug." BBC News, BBC, 3
May 2018, www.bbc.com/news/health-43431453.
Lautieri, Amanda. "Long Term Effects of Adderall on Brain, Personality, and Body." American
Addiction Centers, americanaddictioncenters.org/adderall/long-term-

Connecting Global Warming and Humans
By Alexander Hernandez

Children today are being influenced to go green. Many elementary schools today always had these assemblies telling kids about the three Rs. Reduce, Reuse, Recycle. I, for one, had experienced this myself through. At the time, I didn't understand why we were supposed to do that. I just did what I was told. As the time went and gone and kept hearing the words global warming and climate change. I have learned the main reasons was to help the planet survive. And the purpose of that is that climate change is causing the world to heat up and shorting the habitable state of the Earth. Climate change has been debated for decades and still is now.

What do fossil fuels, deforestation, and carbon emission (CO2) have in common? They all have a factor in human activity. Ilissa Ocko from the Environmental Defense Fund (EDF) claims that more than 97% of scientists believe that humans are to blame for global warming. So, the majority of scientists agree, which gets you wondering what about the 3% of scientists and the data that had led to the conclusion of humans not being responsible for global warming. Research into 97% of scientist data. It comes from a petition called the Global Warming Petition Project. To qualify to sign this petition, you'll need to have, at minimum, a degree of Bachelor of Science or higher in appropriate scientific fields. The range of scientific fields is pretty diverse because it includes the areas of Atmosphere, Earth, environmental, computers, math, physics, aerospace, chemistry, medicine, general engineering, and science. Interesting to see the general side of engineering and science to have a category.

All of the other fields seem to have close related material than the general stuff. Since we have a large group of fields, there are going to be some fields that are not closely related to climate change. Let's take computer engineering, for example. This field has little to nothing to do with others like environmental engineering and geochemistry. You wouldn't go to a computer engineer for answers to climate change. You would want a person with the knowledge and expertise on that specific topic. Anyway, there will always be outliers, and it's no different here.

Taking a look into the skeptics of climate change. They have multiple reasons for their conclusion. Another reason is general hysteria from alarmist. This makes sense since we are bombarded with tons of stats that assume the end times. The website *Skeptical Science* provides even more reasons such as the climate had always been changing, see stats as unreliable, and countless more.

The denial of science plays a part in it as well. *Best Value School* stated, "Those who deny climate change exists refuse to look at that evidence. There are claims that any evidence that proves it exists is a type of fake science done by those who want to change public opinions". It seems the mindset of the deniers take the evidence and disregard because they believe that the scientist behind the research is pushing some agenda. No, doubt that being skeptical is good. Looking at stats shouldn't be your last stop, view the sources and the people behind it.

Fossil fuels are natural fuels formed by the remains of living organisms. There are four types of fossil fuels, which are petroleum, coal, natural gas, and Orimulsion. The primary energy consumption is, indeed, fossil fuels. The *U.S Energy Information Administration* claims that "In 2015, fossil fuels made up 81.5% of total U.S energy consumption". The problem with this is the fact that these fossil fuels produce carbon dioxide, which is a greenhouse gas. Carbon dioxide is the most prevalent greenhouse gas and is the leading cause of global warming. The amount of carbon dioxide emissions in 2018 rose by 3.4 percent, reported by *The Washington Post.* With all of this bad news, there are still hope, but humans need to change our action.

One of the ways to reverse these carbon emissions is to look for alternatives for energy consumptions. Renewable energy seems to be an alternative that people are willing to turn too. Renewable consists of wind, solar, biomass, geothermal, and hydropower. According to *Our World in Data,* modern renewable energy in 2016 increased 5 to 6-fold since the 1960s. Hydropower is the commonly used renewable energy. With the wide variety of renewable energy, the transition could be smooth, but why are we still using fossil fuels instead of renewable energy? Well, for one, it is more expensive to maintain it than to fossil fuels. It's more feasible for the economy to use more fossil fuels. Less green equals more green money.

Carbon dioxide is the most abundant form of greenhouse gases, and deforestation does not help this statistic get better. Deforestation contributes to global warming, as well. Since trees absorb carbon dioxide, we would have fewer trees to get rid of Carbon dioxide. According to the World Bank, we lost over 1000 football fields worth of forestry in the years of 1990-2015. The loss of trees is due to humans cutting down trees for resources and wildfires. However, fires can be caused naturally by lightning strikes. The trend of fires doesn't seem to stop. The recent Paradise and Amazon fires are signals for us.

The effects of global warming are pretty alarming. The most apparent effect is that the Earth's temperature is rising. Another result is that ice glaciers are melting, causing the sea level to rise. This is not only bad for us but animals too. Many creatures who live in Antarctica, north pole and general artic area will suffer and most likely die. Some other impacts given by NASA are more droughts, heatwaves, hurricanes will become stronger, precipitation patterns change, and the Arctic will be ice-free.

A common misconception about climate is that it's the same as weather. I've seen people who don't believe that climate change is not real because they are in an area that is snowy or cold. Climate is the long term whether the weather is short term changes.

From what I learn from this is the power of influence. People need to conduct their own research and find resources that are reliable and doesn't pursue and agenda. Climate change should not be political be people think it should. No doubt there are some elements of politics but it's not the sole factor.

# Works Cited

"Five Forest Figures for the International Day of Forests." *World Bank Blogs*, World Bank, https://blogs.worldbank.org/open-data/five-forest-figures-international-day-forests.

"The Effects of Climate Change." *NASA*, NASA, 30 Sept. 2019, https://climate.nasa.gov/effects/.

Ocko, Ilisa. "9 Ways We Know Humans Triggered Climate Change." Environmental Defense Fund, October 1, 1969. https://www.edf.org/climate/9-ways-we-know-humans-triggered-climate-change.

http://www.petitionproject.org/signers_by_state_main.php

Mooney, Chris, and Brady Dennis. "U.S. Greenhouse Gas Emissions Spiked in 2018 - and It Couldn't Happen at a Worse Time." The Washington Post. WP Company, January 8, 2019. https://www.washingtonpost.com/national/health-science/us-greenhouse-gas-emissions-spiked-in-2018--and-it-could-nt-happen-at-a-worse-time/2019/01/07/68cff792-12d6-11e9-803c-4ef28312c8b9_story.html.

"U.S. Energy Information Administration - EIA - Independent Statistics and Analysis." Fossil fuels still dominate U.S. energy consumption despite recent market share decline - Today in Energy - U.S. Energy Information Administration (EIA). Accessed November 20, 2019. https://www.eia.gov/today-inenergy/detail.php?id=26912.

Ritchie, Hannah, and Max Roser. "Renewable Energy." Our World in Data, December 17, 2017. https://ourworldindata.org/renewable-energy.

"Why Do Some People Think Climate Change Is a Hoax? - Best Value Schools." *BestValueSchools.com*, Bestvalueschools.com,

1 July 2019, https://www.bestvalueschools.com/faq/why-do-some-people-think-climate-change-is-a-hoax/.

# THE UGLY TRUTH OF FAST FASHION
## By Bernice Langali

Shopping is considered an event, with studies showing that people can even get a physical high from the experience, style is a way to say who you are without having to speak. The revolution of fast fashion began in the 80s and has quickly dominated the fashion industry keeping us on our toes on what's "in" and what's "out". Japanese fashion designer Kenza Takado once said, "fashion is like eating, you shouldn't stick to the same menu," but this same notion has created a surplus demand to stay on trend which leads to detrimental effects on our environment. Problems begin from how the textiles are made, to how we dispose of unwanted clothing which increases our carbon footprint and contributes to the controversial topic of climate change.

When shopping, the cheaper or better a discount is, the more enthusiastic and impulsive we get damming all the consequences and most times going over budget. We all want to look "fit" with the trends but for most people, it really is a means for expression. It's funny how much an outfit can really say about your mood; For example, if someone wears big sweatpants and an oversized hoodie, what does that say about their current mood? They are probably having a lazy, the kind of day where you just want to listen to music through your headphones and kick back but wait, I know what you're thinking? Some people would wear the same outfit but with a different interpretation. It could just be the way they view fashion, or the trendiest look from their perspective, not necessarily because they're mood is correlated to the outfit in some type of way proving the point that, style can be interpreted differently and that's where fast fashion comes in; the diversity in style keeps consumers engaged and wanting more. Will Kenton says, "Fast fashion became common because of cheaper clothing, an increase in the appetite for fashionable clothing, and the increase in purchasing power on the part of consumers." We all admire to look good and the idea of getting a similar look like the ones you see on models or on runways at a reasonable price, has captivated our society immensely. After all, freedom of expression gives us that spark of individuality in what seems like a blended society.

Social media has played a huge role in this new revolution. Likes and how you are perceived on Instagram or twitter floods a consumers conscious and therefore we find different ways to portray ourselves perfectly. For many of us, the last post on our profile correlates to our new posts and little things like what you are wearing cannot be the same which is why we result to the cheaper option. In an article on the CBCNews titled, *Our Fast Fashion Habit Is Killing the Planet,* Graham Duggan states, "We are producing over 100 billion new garments from new fibres every single year," and making these fabrics causes huge environmental damage. Cotton, for example, it is one of the most popular fabrics in our society, yet cotton is also one of the world's thirstiest crops. Victoria Cernoch states, "The fashion industry produces 20% of all global wastewater" and producing and shipping these products out to consumers "produces 10% of all global carbon emissions. That's more than all international flights and maritime shipping combined." Just think about that for a second, the clothes you put in our suitcase left a bigger carbon footprint than the flight you put them on.

As fashion evolves, different fabrics emerge as a new cost-effective way to produce clothes. Cotton is bad for our environment considering how much water is used to grow them, but synthetic fibers like spandex and polyester are even worse. In an article on the New York Times by Tatiana Schlossberg, "More than 60 percent of fabric fibers are now synthetics, derived from fossil fuels, so if and when our clothing ends up in a landfill (about 85 percent of textile waste in the United States goes to landfills or is incinerated), it will not decay." Synthetic fabrics use substances like oil but there's something about the shine of a leather jacket that appeals to most of us. Another perhaps even worse way of making fabrics is viscose. Viscose is often touted as a sustainable alternative to cotton or polyester and is popular in the fashion industry as a cheaper and more durable alternative to silk. It is made from "the 'cellulose' or wood pulp from fast growing, regenerative trees such as euca-lyptus, beech and pine, as well as plants such as bamboo, soy and sugar cane. Clendaniel, Morgan states, "they're often made from old-growth trees from endangered rainforests" and the process involves a huge amount of waste. It's almost at every turn, the concept of fast fashion only gets shittier. From man-ufacturing the fabrics, to processing, dying, and finishing, you have to use a lot of toxic chemicals which often times just get dumped near villages.

Getting rid of clothes poses a perhaps even bigger threat and I know what you are thinking, I recycle my clothes so in some way, I am helping the environment but in an article by Elizabeth Cline, "One salvation army in New York creates 18 tons of unwanted clothing every three days" and "the aver-age American throws away 80 pounds of clothes a year." This means that the clothes you donate are mostly still trash and end up in landfills or incinerated affecting the air quality globally. Fast fashion competitors know this is a problem which is why greenwashing has been on the rise.

Greenwashing is when companies market themselves as being greener than they really are and use words like "sus-tainable" which have no set legal definitions therefore the ambiguity of the word sells you the feeling of responsibility. Sophie slater states, "It's hard to make informed choices about our consumption. In part, this is because the literature of ethics and sustainability is notoriously hard to navigate. Just because a brand instigates a better workers' code, doesn't mean that they're not polluting by the bucketload, and vice versa." For example, Zara's mid-rise jeans claim that they are made in a way that reduces water consumption in the dyeing process but in fact the dyeing process only uses one percent of all the water used to make the pants. The notion of greenwashing deceives consumers to believe that they are being greener when purchasing these clothes because we live in a society where people actually care about the environment. Take H&M for example, they're recycling bins get you to spend more buying clothes by giving you a discount, so you are getting the feeling of responsibility recycling clothes but are still fueling their economy by buying more. It like as a community we are taking one step towards saving the future but simultaneously taking two steps back damming our environment.

Fashion is a lifestyle and the high that comes with shopping is undeniable. Whether used as a way of expression or just because it is a fun event, having new clothes excites us all and quickly we think of different ways we can style a piece. A mixture of the fast fashion's business model and our desire to want more at a cheaper price, continue is derange our environment in unbelievable ways. In a Forbes article titled *'Fashionopolis' Author Dana Thomas On How Fast Fashion Is Destroying The Planet And What You Can Do About It,* "In the 1980's the average person brought about 12 new articles of clothing, today, that number is 68 per year half of which are worn three times or less." Look no one is saying don't shop, we all enjoy the thrill, but being aware of the effect's only sheds light on the fast-growing issue. 68 new pairs of clothing a year is just ridiculous, and consumers are the biggest contributors. If more of us are aware and only shop when needed, buying clothes that aren't made from cheap and fast fabrics, a huge step will be taken towards environmental change.

# Works Cited

Cernoch, Victoria. "Fast Fashion Has Been Ruining Your Life and Destroying the Environment: How a Circular Economy Can..." *Medium*, Medium, 29 Mar. 2019, https://medium.com/@victoriacernoch/fast-fashion-has-been-ruining-your-life-and-destroying-the-environment-how-a-circular-economy-can-b6346a50eaf5.

Clendaniel, Morgan. "Your Clothes Might Be Destroying The Rainforest." *Fast Company*, Fast Company, 7 Sept. 2017, https://www.fastcompany.com/40448774/your-clothes-might-be-destroying-the-rainforest.

Cline, Elizabeth L. "The Salvation Army Probably Can't Use Your Clothes." *Slate Magazine*, Slate, 18 June 2012, https://slate.com/human-interest/2012/06/the-salvation-army-and-goodwill-inside-the-places-your-clothes-go-when-you-donate-them.html.

Duggan, Graham. "Our Fast Fashion Habit Is Killing the Planet." *CBCnews*, CBC/Radio Canada, 25 Aug. 2019, https://www.cbc.ca/passionateeye/m_features/our-fast-fashion-habit-is-killing-the-planet.

Kenton, Will. "How Fast Fashion Works." *Investopedia*, Investopedia, 18 Nov. 2019, https://www.investopedia.com/terms/f/fast-fashion.asp.

Schlossberg, Tatiana. "How Fast Fashion Is Destroying the Planet." *The New York Times*, The New York Times, 3 Sept. 2019, https://www.nytimes.com/2019/09/03/books/review/how-fast-fashion-is-destroying-the-planet.html.

Shatzman, Celia. "'Fashionopolis' Author Dana Thomas On How Fast Fashion Is Destroying The Planet And What You Can Do About It." *Forbes*, Forbes Magazine, 27 Sept. 2019, https://www.forbes.com/sites/celiashatzman/2019/10/04/fashionopolis-author-dana-thomas-on-how-fast-fashion-is-destroying-the-planet-and-what-you-can-do-about-it/#52b788463b97.

Slater, Sophie. "The 'Greenwashing' Hiding the Truth of Your Favourite Fashion Brands." *Vice*, 1 May 2019, https://www.vice.com/en_uk/article/kzmw5a/the-greenwashing-hiding-the-truth-of-your-favourite-fashion-brands.

Argument Essays

# Violence In Video Games
## By Jonathan Moreci


Not too long ago in August, after mass shootings that killed 31 people and left countless more in critical condition, many politicians (including the president) were quick to blame video games and their violent content as a root cause for the shootings. Though the argument that video games cause violence has long been scepticized in America at large, it has been a common talking point since video games have been around. When games like DOOM and Wolfenstein 3D came out in the 1990's, politicians scapegoated the titles for violence in society, and have continued to do so ever since. The largest school shootings, like Columbine High School in 1999 and Marjory Stoneman Douglas in 2018, were blamed on violent video games and how they affected the minds of the shooters involved. Social psychologists have long studied this idea of video games causing real world violence, and though there has not been a clear and concise consensus on the issue, there's a common agreement that there is not a correlation between the two. Yet it doesn't seem like such a far out idea to think that the horrific, graphic images shown in video games could have an adverse effect on the minds of the average everyday American. It actually sounds perfeclty reasonable.  In fact, Deborah L. Davis Ph.D. of Psychology Today says that children who are exposed "to violence in the media and video games showed reduced levels of cognitive brain function(Davis). This means that certain areas of the brain used for thinking, reasoning, learning and control of emotions were less active than in adolescents who were xposed more frequently to violence and graphic images. Brain function is negatively affected when presented with violent images at adolescence due to kids not being adept to handling graphic scenes. This is a big reason why the Video Games Rating Act of 1994 was enacted, in order to make sure these types of images do not get into the wrong hands. This is important to understand because though these rating systems are in place, many of the times they do not work in stopping children from possessing mature video games that have a long lasting impact on their mental health. So if violent video games are detrimental to our minds, what are the consequences of this in our day to day lives? A study review by Craig A. Anderson says for children "the evidence strongly suggests that exposure to violent video games is a causal risk factor for increased aggressive behavior, aggressive cognition, and aggressive affect and for decreased empathy and prosocial behavior"(Anderson). It is clear that children are more vulnerable mentally and emotionally to these types of images portrayed in video games, and it can be concluded that exposure to such images would create some sort of desensitivity to violence and graphic images shown. And though it is a small and casual risk for aggression, it is still a risk that many Americans are not willing to take today as it seems everywhere we turn we are confronted with violence and tragedy on the news and media.

What we have discussed so far has shown us that no explicitly violent and gory images go without consequence on our minds and attitudes. Everything has a risk to harm us, yet I believe that shouldn't stop people from consuming this type of media. The fact of the matter when it comes to video games is that it does not cause children to act more aggressively than any other form of media, and cannot be linked back to root causes of violence and mass shooting that politicians love to claim. Researchers at The University of York worked diligently on a case study to find a link between violent video games and violent behavior early last year. In the series of experiments done, with over 3,000 participants tested and studied, the team looked at whether video games primed players to violence, and whether increasing realism of a video game's violent graphics contributed to aggressive behavior. The study showed that video games did not "'prime' players to behave in certain ways and that increasing the realism of violent video games does not necessarily increase aggression in game players"(University of York). This study, along with many others like it, have been referenced to counteract the claims of businesses and politicians who hold a need to scapegoat violent video games. Take in account the 2010 Supreme Court case BROWN v. ENTERTAINMENT MERCHANTS ASSOCIATION, about banning the sales of certain violent video games in retail stores. In the monumental case, Judge Scalia made the decision that "violent video games and harmful effects on children do not prove that such exposure causes minors to act aggressively. Any demonstrated effects are both small and indistinguishable from effects produced by other media"(Scalia). The Supreme court take from the most true and credible of sources, which helps build the validity of these statements and sources used to make the judgment call.

Video games might be more useful than one would realize and can contribute positively to people's everyday lives. According to Sheila Eugenio, video games can actually improve coordination, build problem solving skills, enhance your attention span and help you learn about the world around you (Eugenio). Video games help immerse yourself in these skills and practices, like hand eye coordination, that many people have and will take for granted. These skills are very important and video games are prime exerciers of them. Beyond skill building, I would make the case that video games help with releasing some of the human's more primitive instincts in a less destructive manner. Though we cannot always act out in aggression when the weight of the world is holding us down, we do have the outlet of video games to help get some of the frustration out. I surely can't go a kill a hooker with a rocket launcher in real life when I cannot find my car keys, but with games like Grand Theft Auto.. well, I can!

## Work Cited

Davis, Deborah L. "Protect Your Brain from Images of Violence and Cruelty." *Psychology Today*, Sussex Publishers, www.psychologytoday.com/us/blog/laugh-cry-live/201312/protect-your-brain-images-violence-and-cruelty.

"Violence in the Media-Pyschologists Study Potential Harmful Effects." *American Psychological Association*, American Psychological Association, www.apa.org/action/resources/research-in-action/protect.

"BROWN v. ENTERTAINMENT MERCHANTS ASSN." *Legal Information Institute*, Legal Information Institute, 27 June 2011, www.law.cornell.edu/supct/html/08-1448.ZS.html.

"No Evidence to Support Link between Violent Video Games and Behaviour." *University of York*, www.york.ac.uk/news-and-events/news/2018/research/no-evidence-to-link-violence-and-video-games/.

Eugenio, Sheila. "Public Access - 8 Cognitive Benefits of Playing Video Games for Kids." *Engadget*, 9 Feb. 2017, www.engadget.com/2017/02/09/8-cognitive-benefits-of-playing-video-games-for-kids/.

Define Social, Asking for a Friend
By Nya Avelina Bautista

In the sixth grade, I downloaded my first social media app, Instagram. I thought of it as a great getaway to share my photos and to share any of my artistic abilities that I found through editing. Then came in the multitude of applications such as Twitter and Snapchat. I found different ways to attempt in being prominent in social media at such a young age that it distorted my perception of life itself. I began to have the mindset that everytime I hung out with friends, the little I had at the time, I had to take a picture and share it. It came to the point where I felt like my only life was online and to show everyone at my school someone I wanted to be outside of school. Since I barely had any friends at the time, I started to become lonely and drowning in the hashtags. Despite the name, social media created a gap between my social skills and my own mental health in believing that I was lonely because of the amount of followers and likes I would receive on a post. And even though I didn't realize it at the time, I let social media corrupt my mindset to want to become someone I wasn't and although it began at middle school, it was just the beginning. There are multiple reasons why social media can be good for some people, but in today's society social media has shaped young adults' mental health, communication skills, and introducing social comparisons. Social media has detrimental effects on one's self identity and distorts their reality.

Social Media makes a big impact on the way people see themselves. It is through media trends such as what to wear, what to eat, or how a person should look that manipulates a person's persona. In times social media is bombarded by unavoidable advertisements and created the concept of "Instagram models" that get thousands of likes just due to the booming business of social media. In this day and age, it is difficult to avoid the mainstream control of how social media perceives us to be. Those who spend most of their time on social media are affected because it creates an unrealistic nearly unreachable life at the age they're in. This audience is typically the young adults in this generation.

Katie Hurley from Psycom found studies where social media was found detrimental saying, "One study out of the University of Pittsburgh, for example, found a correlation between time spent scrolling through social media apps and negative body image feedback. Those who had spent more time on social media had 2.2 times the risk of reporting eating and body image concerns, compared to their peers who spent less time on social media. The participants who spent the most time on social media had 2.6 times the risk." With the idea of body image concerns, it leads to the idea that some one should "eat less" to look "skinnier". Without the correct idea of a good maintenance of one's body, there are different ideas that lead to these risks. Today's advanced technology allows people to present themselves in unreal ways. Whether it'd be by narrowing their waist, creating a smaller nose on Facetune, the fake character they create takes away from their authentic selves. Nobody wants to show themselves, they would rather show what social media wants them to look like or rather show themselves in a way where they feel they'll be accepted by others and society. The more one scrolls on social media, the more one builds up these perceptions in how they would want to change themselves, not for the better, but for acceptance. Social comparison begins with this constant scrolling and "stalking" to drive a need to be accepted in the social media society, and that is the controlling effect social media has on society.

Communication was different before the birth of technology and social media. Society began where people would go out to play, walking to the front door to pick someone up on a date, or getting to know someone over a cup of coffee. Now society created a world where a visual "bio" of a person can be easily shown and now have the opportunity to scroll past a person they didn't like just from what a person said they were in a description. The benefits of meeting face-to-face has been ruined by the way social media damaged the way people have communicated so they don't have to head on deal with the possibility of rejection. On someone's profile a person can make it seem like they have the best communication skills and have great relationships with people through the internet, but when in reality a person's communication skills can turn into a complete whole different spectrum. Some individuals have become so out of tune with reality that they would much rather meet a person online and talk through a screen than to ever do it organically.

The avoidance of problems head on is also developed with the downfall of communication with the rise of social media. They are not forced to publicly be expressive, they are not used to talking to people head on without the help of an app deciding whether they are compatible. This makes people scared of human interaction. A Youngstown State University study by Megan Sponcil and Priscilla Gitimu share the effects of college students on social media and how convenient it is to communicate on social media rather than in reality. They say, "Since this social media phenomenon is continuing to grow at a fast pace, it is important to understand the effects it has on personal communication. Social media networks offer a straightforward way to converse with peers and get peer feedback, as well, which may influence a young adult's self-esteem" (Sponcil & Gitimu). With the convenience of social media and the simplicity to reach someone at a touch of a screen, college students tend to communicate more on social media than making time to meet someone one-on-one.

With these introductions to social comparisons and the lack of communication evolving, these young adults begin to have detrimental effects on their mental health. From the constant scrolling and shifting from app to app, lack of sleep creates possible routes to depressions and different behaviors.

Katie Hurley found another study saying, "...a separate study from the University of Pittsburgh School of Medicine showed that the more time young adults spent on social media, the more likely they were to have problems sleeping and report symptoms of depression." Come to think about it, whether it is from social media or from just pulling all nighters to finish homework assignments, the following day my mood progressively gets worse and worse until I get a nap. With the amounts of stress young adults now begin to develop from school, now there are developments with social media bringing their self esteem down furthermore leading to lack of sleep. Additionally with a lack of sleep, Christopher Barnes created a study saying, "We argue that low levels of sleep will hinder the restoration of the resources needed for cognitive self-control. In turn, this leaves employees less able to overcome impulses to engage in unethical behavior." Without those eight needed hours of sleep, restlessness may overturn on a teenage body leading to behavioral problems at home, school, and in one's social life.

With the new age of technology, screen time can waste a detrimental amount of time on one's life. Tagging along to screen time, I came to think of the idea of social media does transform our society and current businesses. Social media promotes the idea of sharing information through these applications or websites with pictures or information. Social media creates a world where people can electronically communicate, share, and upload. Within these social media applications, it makes it easier to communicate to family members that you may not be able to see whether they are a state away or living in a different country. The benefits of social media are that one can reconnect with others at the touch of their fingertips. Additionally, it makes it easier for companies to market their goods and communicate it to other users on the internet. There are many accounts on different social media platforms where new businesses can be created and from that there are even different social media apps that allow other people to create their own business to sell clothes or other items.

Yes, there are benefits within the growth of social media, but society needs to understand that it shouldn't be a topic to look over. The developments that social media can make on one person is detrimental enough, but on a whole generation there needs to be solutions. People's self worth are being put on the line based off of "likes" or "followers". Though it seems unfathomable to make a solution, it is actually quite simple. It is what we take, as a society, to make that change you want to make. It is up to us to know our limits and to know our own solutions rather than to complain. Make a business account. Share the love throughout the applications. It is what you make out of these applications in order to create a better society rather than loathing on someone else's life, body, or pictures.

## Works Cited

Barnes, Christopher M., et al. "Lack of Sleep and Unethical Conduct." *Organizational Behavior and Human Decision Processes*, vol. 115, no. 2, 2011, pp. 169–180.,

Hurley, Katie. "Social Media and Teens: How Does Social Media Affect Mental Health?" Psycom.net - Mental Health Treatment Resource Since 1986, 2019,

Sponcil, Megan, and Priscilla Gitimu. "Use of Social Media by College Students: Relationship to Communication and Self-Concept ." *Journal of Technology Review.* Pp. 2. AABRI,

Vallejo, Camila. "Instagram Will Soon Hide Likes. Here's What It Means for Connecticut-Based Businesses and Influencers." *Courant.com*, Hartford Courant, 15 Nov. 2019.

# Against the Electoral College
## By Jasleen Brayana

Our Founding Fathers considered many methods for the president's election during the Constitutional Convention of 1787. They hoped for an efficient way to elect the president that would give more power to the people and the state over the federal government; the Electoral College was created. In the Electoral College, each state is apportioned a certain number of electors based on the state's population. It also provides a way of voting in which a presidential candidate could still win if they gained less popular votes than the other candidates. Though in some cases, states with smaller populations were being overrepresented and presidential candidates targeted specific states for electoral college votes.

Electoral College consists of 538 electors which are allocated by the number of senators and members in the House of Representatives for each state. To win the Electoral College, the presidential candidate needs at least 270 electoral votes. Usually, when a person votes for their presidential candidate, they are actually voting for the presidential candidate's electors who in return will vote for president and vice president. In a way, the electoral college allows populous states not dominate the election just by popular votes. However, over the years, there has been an inconsistency in representation whether it be over- or underrepresentation. According the article, "Is the Electoral College Fair?" by Denise Lu, the author discusses imbalance in representation in the Electoral College. Lu states, "In 2016, California was the most misrepresented in the electoral college. The state is home to 12 percent of Americans, but holds only 10 percent of electoral votes. Its share of the total U.S. population is 2 percentage points more than its share of electoral votes. A similar pattern repeats in the country's largest states," (Lu, Par. 6-7). In this case, many Californians who voted won't feel represented enough because two percent of the American population is distributed amongst other states instead the state that resides those two percent Americans.

The reason why Californian voters are underrepresented is the ratio to one elector to Californian voting population. In the article, the ratios stated are, "1 elector represents 712,000 people in California [and] 1 elector represents 195,000 people in Wyoming," (Lu, Figure 1). The number of voters is greater in California to have one elector vote for their candidate whereas in Wyoming representation of voters to one elector is smaller. The disparity in the ratios show that some states that there are more people being represented in the electoral college where-as some states aren't. And those differences in percentage or ratio counts because every vote matters in electing the president.

The Electoral College is known for winner-takes-all system in forty-eight states expect Nebraska and Maine. This is when the all the electoral votes will go to the presidential candidate that won the popular vote in that state. In an article, "The "winner-take-all" Electoral College system used by 48 states, including Colorado, sees court challenges" by Steven LeBlanc, the author discusses the 2016 election and aftermath of the election. LeBlanc states, "Vera said the group deliberately chose two Democratic-leaning states and two Republican-leaning states — Clinton won about 61 percent of the vote in Massachusetts, while Trump won about 55 percent in South Carolina — to argue that the winner-take-all system harms voters of both parties," (LeBlanc, Par. 6). Because of this system, voters have to give the winning candidate all of their electoral votes when there is a slight difference in popular votes to which candidate the electoral votes will go to. Trump won South Carolina by fifty-five percent and Clinton lost by forty-five percent yet all the votes went to Trump, similar how all the votes went to Clinton for Massachusetts. With the state population being equally separated, the voter population isn't able to have their vote count for their choice of the presidential candidate based on the winner-takes-all system.

When states are equally separated between the pres-idential candidates or political ideologies, there are known as "swing" states because they can easily be switch political ide-ologies. In the article, "'Can't Take Any of Them for Granted':

Meet the Key Voters Who Could Decide If Trump's Reelected"
by Todd Spangler and his colleagues discuss swing states in
the 2016 election. They stated, "In 2016, Donald Trump demol-
ished the Democrats' vaunted blue wall in the Midwest by winning Michigan, Wisconsin and Pennsylvania by the slimmest of
margins. And he flipped Florida red again after it had gone for
Barack Obama in both of his runs for the White House," (Spangler, et al., Par. 1). The candidates focus on swing states,
states that switch between the two political parties, so they
get the electoral votes. Whereas safe states tend to vote one
certain political ideology. It makes sense to campaign in swing
states for their potential winning. It puts power in a handful of
swing states on deciding on which candidate would win the
election. Thus, defeating the purpose of the people equally
voting with informed decisions. It gives candidates automatic
win rather than allowing the representatives to vote in their
choice of the candidate and instead vote in population's favor
with belief that state is only democratic or republican.

However, the Electoral College does have benefits
to settle recounts and presidents winning by a slight margin
in the popular vote. According to the article, "Why Was the
Electoral College Created?" by Dave Ross explains why the
Electoral College was created.  Roos explains, "'John F. Kennedy's popular vote margin over Richard M. Nixon was just
118,574,' writes Will. 'If all 68,838,219 popular votes had been
poured into a single national bucket, there would have been
powerful incentives to challenge the results in many of the
nation's 170,000 precincts,'" (Roos, Par. 21). In the 1960, both
presidential candidates were nearly tied, and the voters may
have wanted a recount if it weren't for the Electoral College in
which President Kennedy won. Nonetheless, if recounting for
the popular vote were to occur then the winning presidential
candidate for the 1960 election would have been the same
regardless of the slight margin in winning.

In conclusion, the electoral college was created by our
Founding Fathers to try to accurately represent the state's or
the people's opinions in the present. Though, there are powers given to other states because of strategic campaigning

by presidential candidates. Perhaps, it is because of strategic campaigning or winner-takes-all system that voters are mis-represented in the electoral votes. Every system has room for improvement and our government was made in a way to allow change to occur as time passes.

## Work Cited

Del, Jose A. "Should the Electoral College Be Eliminated? 15 States Are Trying to Make It Obsolete." *The New York Times*, The New York Times, 22 May 2019, www.ny-times.com/2019/05/22/us/electoral-college.html.

LeBlanc, Steve. "The 'Winner-Take-All' Electoral College System Used by 48 States, Including Colorado, Sees Court Challenges." *The Denver Post*, The Denver Post, 27 Mar. 2018, www.denverpost.com/2018/03/26/elector-al-college-challenge/.

Roos, Dave. "Why Was the Electoral College Created?" *History.com*, A&E Television Networks, 15 July 2019, www.history.com/news/electoral-college-founding-fathers-con-stitutional-convention.

Spangler, Todd, et al. "'Can't Take Any of Them for Grant-ed': Meet the Key Voters Who Could Decide If Trump's Reelected." *USA Today*, Gannett Satellite Information Network, 6 Dec. 2019, www.usatoday.com/story/news/politics/elections/2019/12/02/election-2020-swing-states-will-rely-on-these-key-voters/4298609002/.

Science Essays

The start of the Pandemic
By Arian Wahidi

What is a Virus? Many ask and wonder. A virus is a small, microscopic agent that spreads quickly only inside a living organism. Viruses can spread person to person very quickly without them even knowing. Viruses spread through droplets, for example if someone were to sneeze and cough the virus it could transfer to another. The one thing that many don't understand about viruses is that for the most part they aren't even alive. They are made of genetic material, DNA and RNA covered in a protective coat. Their only job is to make and spread more viruses. So when the virus enters a living cell, they attach themselves to the host, then penetrate itself on it. Once they make their replica they go another to another. So, how is this related to today's pandemic you ask?

COVID-19, also known as coronavirus 2019 is a deadly virus that attacks your respiratory system. So in this case, the virus attaches it's spiky proteins onto the healthy receptors that are on your lungs. With the coronavirus spreading so quickly into the body, it hijacks every healthy cell in your body which ends up killing it. Since the virus affects mostly the respiratory system, symptoms vary person to person according to studies now. According to the CDC website, "symptoms may appear 2-14 days after exposure to the virus"(CDC). Meaning after coming in contact with the virus without any protective gear or caution, you won't know that you have the virus after a few weeks.

Symptoms to look out for are fever, coughing, shortness of breath, chills/shaking, headache, muscle pain, sore throat, and a new symptom which is loss of taste or smell. But symptoms like trouble breathing, pain in the chest, confusion or bluish lips or face are emergency signs that a person needs to call 911 as soon as possible. Although these are the symptoms they have found, few symptoms could also be found as well.

So, how did this all start or spread around the world? The start of the Covid-19 outbreak came from a food market in Wuhan, China. This wasn't also the first time this had happened in China. There were more Coronavirus cases throughout the years but nothing as effective as the Covid-19. According to the Vox video called "How wildlife trade is linked to coronavirus", the "first case of SARS was in 2002, which originated in mainland China"(Vox). It was said in the video that the "coronavirus had emerged at a very similar market, southern China, which eventually reached 29 countries and killed nearly 800 people"(Vox). In the Vox video, a Professor and expert on China's animal trade named Peter Li explains that possibly the start of the coronavirus came from animals, possibly the animals that were being sold and bought for food at the Wuhan food market. He explains that "the cages are stacked one over another, and the animals at the bottom are often soaked with all kinds of liquid such as pus, blood, or animal excrement"(Peter Li). This is an example of how viruses can jump to one animal to another just by the physical contact and liquids of another. Which ends up to the human who ends up buying those animals for food and consuming that virus that came from those animals.

Testing for Covid-19 is still going, and research as well. But recent studies have found that the virus was linked to bats, which was also sold in the market. In the Scientific American article called "How China's "bat woman" hunted down viruses from SARS to the new coronavirus", states that a Wuhan virologist Shi Zhengli, "have identified dozens of deadly SARs like viruses in bat caves and warns there is more" (Jane Qiu). The article goes into detail of how after the first 2002 coronavirus case, Shi Zhengli and her team went on the hunt to find bat caves in China in relation to the Coronavirus case. Her efforts finally paid off after finding a cave called the Shitou Cave, in the capital of

Yunnan, China. There she conducted another test with catching the bats and collecting their blood and saliva. There she found " "bat-borne coronaviruses with incredible genetic diversity"( Jane Qiu). She says that " the majority of them are harmless, but dozens of them belong to the same group as SARS" (Shi Zhengli"). Although there are many rumors and theories that the Covid-19 is not from animals and did not start in Wuhan, China, the science and research says otherwise. This is where politics comes in and tries to deny the science.

With the Coronavirus creating panic and worry around the world, many try to argue with the science and logic around it. For example, rumors went out in the society that face masks weren't as effective as they thought. In reality the U.S itself was struggling to provide all hospitals with face masks and proper equipment for the frontline workers that were in need of supplies. A new mandated rule issued last week, stated that New York, LA and Contra Costa County and more were to wear some kind of face shield or face mask to cover furthermore spreading of the virus. In recent news, protests broke out in Michigan arguing against the order "stay safe, stay home". Due to the new rule of anti-social distancing and the stay at home order, many are angry to find that their businesses are suffering and the economy is dropping very low. In the Washington post article called "Both public health and politics played a role in Trump's coronavirus decision" states that "The president initially spent weeks downplaying the threat of the virus, in a large part because he is worried about the effect of the economy"(Ashley Parker, Josh Dawsey, Yasmeen Abutaleb). The President's initial thought was opening one day for the people on Easter, but after many polls and discussion to find that the death rate might significantly increase due to the lack of social distancing and spreading of the virus. Public health keeps advising Trump the strict lockdown rules and to extend it furthermore due to the increasing deaths in many states. In the it states that "Throughout the coronavirus crisis, Trump has at times maintained an uneasy relationship with the public health and scientific communities, frustrated with their advice and directives that essentially have forced the economy to shut down"(Ashely Parker, Josh Dawsey, Yasmine Abutaleb). As a President who advocates for business and a well going economy, Trump has faced "3 million Americans who have already filed for unemployment". This throws many politicians and the President into huge worry, due to the massive amount of Americans who aren't working making money and are losing their jobs due to the outbreak of the virus. In recent news, Trump has released a 3 step phrase plan in order to slowly open back the economy. This not only puts many Americans into worry but the health care workers who are trying to decrease the number of deaths rate. In the article Newsweek article called "Trump's 3 phrase plan to reopen America's economy explained" goes in detail stating "An East coast group, made up of Massauchusetts, New York, New Jersey, Delaware, Connecticut, Pennsylvania, and Rhode Island will also work together to evelop a reopening plan"(Seren Morris). This puts many into worry, considering the fact that the East coast is suffering the most cases of Covid-19. Ranking New York first and New Jersey second into having the most death rates and cases in the entire country. This let alone, a huge risk for many Americans once this lockdown is open.

So what can we do to prevent furthermore? After knowing all the facts and information about viruses and Covid-19, the best thing that we can do for ourselves and each other is social distancing, respecting the stay at home order, washing your hands/ not touching your face and so much more. During a Pandemic like this, it is also important to understand the facts, keep up to news  and take your health and self being serious to prevent furthermore spreading.

# Works Cited

CDC. "Coronavirus Disease 2019 (COVID-19) – Symptoms." Centers for Disease Control and Prevention , 14 Mar. 2020, www.cdc.gov/coronavirus/2019-ncov/symptoms-testing/symptoms.html.

EDT, Seren Morris On 4/17/20 at 8:19 AM. "This Is What Trump's Three-Phased Plan to Reopen America's Economy Means." Newsweek , 17 Apr. 2020, www.newsweek.com/donald-trump-opening-america-again-lockdown-coronavirus-guidelines-14 98518. Accessed 20 Apr. 2020.

Parker, Ashley, et al. "Both Public Health and Politics Played a Role in Trump's Coronavirus Decision." Washington Post , www.washingtonpost.com/politics/both-public-health-and-politics-played-a-role-in-trumps-coro navirus-decision/2020/03/30/f2912acc-729e-11ea-a9bd-9f8b593300d0_story.html. Accessed 20 Apr. 2020.

Qiu, Jane. "How China's 'Bat Woman' Hunted Down Viruses from SARS to the New Coronavirus." Scientific American , 11 Mar. 2020,

# What Do Black Holes Do?
## By Jacqueline Wong

For the first time ever we have seen a black hole in action. At least 55 million lightyears away, Pōwehi is located in the galaxy called Messier 87 and has a mass of 6.5 billion times more than the sun, according to Daniel Clery in sciencemag.org. The picture NASA took has bright orange surrounding a dark void in the center. Voids like these can eat a star, or even a whole galaxy! Scientists still are puzzled by their workings and what is on the other side of them. But with the work they've done and in finding the proper data, we may answer these questions: Where do they come from? How do they form? What is inside a black hole? Will our star become a black hole?

Black holes are mysterious vortexes that wander around space, leaving nothing in it's path except darkness. But don't be mistaken, these vortexes aren't just plain emptiness. According to NASA, "A black hole is a place in space where gravity pulls so much that even light cannot get out". Black holes are made up of nothing but pulling gravity and squeezing matter until it is unable to be seen. Not even light can escape it! They shred a star to pieces, giving off a dark vibe as the matter and light from dying stars are sucked into them, creating nothing except more darkness.

To understand what a black hole is, we must understand the life of a star and what paths it takes, since black holes were once one of them. A star is born in a nebulae that is made up of gas and dust. Nebulae are able to make stars because of their dense concentration of gases. The star will try to reach equilibrium between gravity and pressure, and if the settings are right, the star will grow. After about 10 million years, stars can either become a small star, an average sized star, or a massive star. In order to become a black hole, however, you need to become a black hole, however, you need to become a massive star. When a massive star is unable to hold itself any longer, it may not be able to sustain nuclear fusion. Nuclear fusion of a star is how a star makes its energy, fusing hydrogen with helium. When the star runs out of hydrogen, it creates an unstable environment and either supernovas (explodes), or directly becomes a black hole. While becoming a black hole, matter in a star is pushed to its limits compressing itself into the smallest mass as gravity wins.

So far, we encountered what a black hole is and then how it becomes a black hole. To further understand what it does, we can ask this question, "what's inside a black hole?" According to Paul Sutter, an astrophysicist at SUNY Stony Brook and the Flatiron Institute in New York City, he tells us what black holes do quite well: "Because all the mass of the black hole is concentrated into an infinitely tiny point, the differences in gravity are extreme. You are stretched head to toe in an aptly named process known as spaghettification." Spaghettification is an astrophysics term meaning that something is being squeezed into a noodle-shape, long and thin strand, and is largely referred to with black holes.

We see the singularity, the infinity tiny point, the point in which the black hole swallows you up. Everywhere you go, the singularity is with you and you continue to fall in the black hole. Because of this, there is an event horizon. The event horizon is ultimately invisible because it isn't really anything at all. But here's the catch. When you're outside the event horizon, you can move anywhere you want. The black hole is still pulling you in, but you haven't gotten to the singularity yet. When you're inside it, you can't escape the singularity. This is when space and time are twisted and turned as it enters the black hole. If you're inside the event horizon, you could see that everything from outside the black hole and the light from other stars, is bending and twisting.

At this point, we may ask what is inside a black hole. Is it another universe? Or do they lead to a hidden world we never knew of? Hah, probably not. The singularity, as said above, is the point in which a black hole devours you and bends you until nothing is left. But the thing is, no human has ever been inside of a black hole before, and I don't think we want to go in. However, I believe that there isn't anything on the other side, since everything is pulled, spaghettified, and ripped to shreds in a million times smaller than we are now. Scientists have taken their guesses too. One of them is something that caught my eye-they're called white holes.

White holes are the complete opposite of black holes, meaning they spew out matter and light. A journalist of physical scientist named Charlie Wood writes, "While a black hole's event horizon is a sphere of no return, a white hole's event horizon is a boundary of no admission- space-time's most exclusive club. No spacecraft will ever reach the region's edge." So basically, Whatever comes near them, they push it away. The gravity flows outwards rather than inwards like a black hole, and the white hole is probably more visible than a black hole. White holes look exactly like black holes except in the event horizon, all that light comes pouring out of them.

However, no one knows if they even exist or not. "A black hole cordons off its bit of space when a star collapses into a tiny volume, but playing this video backwards doesn't make physical sense," says Wood. However, if we someday find a white hole, we will have all the answers in the palm of our hands to say what is on the other side of black holes.

There is a question in which some of us non-astronomers might have. That is if our sun will become a black hole. As NASA says,

"The Sun would need to be about 20 times more massive to end its life as a black hole" as in a red giant. Someday our sun will expand to become a red giant, but it will not have enough energy to become a black hole. That is because the pressure building up in a star does not work well with the gravitational pull that the star also has. So The sun expands, becoming a red giant and destroying planet Earth. But this red giant faze will last only a billion years (and that's a short time for a star) until it collapses once again, leaving only a white dwarf behind.

There is so much more we don't know about black holes, and much of them are very confusing to humanity. But scientists have made theories and have come upon their guesses. Even to know these simple things, like black holes having so much gravity pulling towards its singularity, are still questioned so deeply as to "why" they do so. But for us humans, we do not need to worry. As stated by scientists, not any black hole is near us at this very moment, and we are in a very safe place in the galaxy. It is up to the future us to decide what we will do if that happens…

# Work Cited:

"Black Hole Facts - Interesting Facts about Black Holes." Space Facts, space-facts.com/black-holes/.

CleryApr, Daniel, et al. "For the First Time, You Can See What a Black Hole Looks Like." Science , 19 Apr. 2019, www.science-mag.org/news/2019/04/black-hole#.

Dunbar, Brian. "What Is a Black Hole?" NASA , NASA, 21 May 2015, www.nasa.gov/audience/forstudents/k-4/stories/nasa-knows/what-is-a-black-hole-k4.html.

Sutter, Paul. "Take a Fun Trip into a Black Hole: What's It Like Inside?" Space.com , Space, 18 Nov. 2019, www.space.com/into-a-black-hole-whats-inside.html.

Wood, Charlie. "White Holes: Black Holes' Neglected Twins." Space.com , Space, 10 June 2019, www.space.com/white-holes.html. Garner, Rob. "NASA Visualization Shows a Black Hole's Warped World." NASA , NASA, 25 Sept. 2019, www.nasa.gov/feature/goddard/2019/nasa-visualization-shows-a-black-hole-s-wa rped-world.

The interesting Social Psychology that is in Leadership, Psychology, and Casual Instances by Ajani Viray

Social psychology is defined by Merriam Webster as: "the study of the manner in which the personality, attitudes, motivations, and behavior of the individual influence and are influenced by social groups." This study of psychology applies to us in many different ways, with some examples being a family reunion, an outing with your friends, and/or a date with the person you like. And when we analyze and dissect all these situations, we realize that there are an unbelievably copious of different paychological factors and reasoning within one interaction that will blow anybody's mind. Some examples we will look into are leadership, debates, and casual instances.

Let us take Donald Trump for example: disregarding that the 45th president is a very controversial figure, there are so many examples of psychological moves he does to assert his dominance. Some examples that show this is the interactions between himself and French president Emmanuel Macron. During the joint press that was held in April 2018, there was a moment when both President Trump and Macron were about to prepare to take pictures. Trump was speaking saying how he and Macron have a great friendship, saying it is not "fake news." He then brushes Macron's shoulder and says, "... In fact, let me brush that little piece of dandruff off... you had a little piece... We have to make him perfect. He is perfect" even though he did not actually have dandruff on his shoulder. According to social coach Barron Cruz, in this particular situation, Trump creates the image that Macron has dandruff to make him look lower than he is in several ways. Trump saying that Macron has dandruff creates an unappealing image of him. However, Macron can not come back with many effective options to use on Trump. If Macron had denied the fact, he would look very defensive and inferior to Trump. However, not saying anything would also prove that Trump was right about the dandruff and that Macron has no defense because he will not speak up. Trump pulled a power card on Macron that leaves little to no room for Macron to snap back. Another factor is that Trump knew that so many people were watching this event, so it was the perfect time to pull something like that, as lots of eyes are on them and it's a great chance to get other people to try to make Macron look interior. Another example that Trump has pulled multiple times (Like during the April 2018 joint press and Trump's visit to France) is when he shakes Macron's hand, Trump firmly grasps his hand and whips/drags him around. This also is a huge power move, as this shows that Macron is physically inferior to Trump (Cruz).

This is important to understand because one key quality a leader (in this case, President Trump) needs to be respected is dominance. A strong leader cannot be walked all over, as this shows weakness. This stems from our biology, as animals, including humans. Lots of animals do this for survival and to be "top dog." According to Marc Bekoff, a professor emeritus of Evolutionary Biology at the University of Colorado, some reasons for this include protection (such as family, territory, etc.) or attention.

For the debate aspect, let us use a former member of the Harvard debate team and co-founder of The Daily Wire Ben Shapiro. Ben Shapiro is a conservative commentator who has gotten into intense debates with many people and is popularly known for "destroying" his opponents during debates. How was he able to do so, you may ask? According to Lewis

Howes, a New York Times bestselling author and lifestyle entrepreneur who has interviewed Shapiro before, Ben does a good job of disconnecting his emotions from his arguments. A lot of people tend to argue with emotions, which tends to lead to more flawed arguments and personal attacks, which in contrast Shapiro tends to avoid. Another thing Shapiro does is put his opponent on the same level as he is and shows his opponents respect. According to Susan Krauss Whitbourne, a Professor Emerita of Psychological and Brain Sciences at the University of Massachusetts Amherst debates at the end of the day are based on our own perspectives in life and that there is not exactly a "right" or "wrong" answer, so you should show your opponent respect and not put yourself above them. Another example that Shapiro does is present hard facts. When it comes to debates, one thing you need to do in order to win is present strong evidence (aka facts) for the claims you make on why you are right. And he always does this by being able to present cases of past events and strong statistics, which in turn make his arguments more concrete. You will more likely lose the argument if the claim and facts you present is wrong or not as solid (Whitbourne).

Now for the more casual aspect of social psychology, what is the goal? The goal is to be able to get along with others, whether you intend your bond is platonic, romantic, business, etc. The desired outcome is that people like you, which according to Shana Lebowitz, a correspondent for Business Insider who had studied psychology at Brandeis University, is possible in a multitude of ways. One way that is possible is mirroring the other person, which is a method that mimics the other person's posture and behavior. Researchers showed in an experiment that included 72 men and women working together on a task, those who mimicked their partner had a higher likelihood of liking their partner compared to those who did not. Another way to do this is by showing more positivity and interest in the other person. This refers to engagement in the conversation and staying positive throughout, doing things like smiling, complimenting them, and making the conversation one they will look fondly back on and smile at. When showing interest, asking them questions to try and get to know them helps tremendously, especially when it comes to deep and personal topics. The person will feel more welcomed that they have the ability to be able to share something they do not share so easily, and sharing things yourself will give the other person a more "human" view of you rather than an "unflawed caricature" A third and important way, especially for a platonic and romantic relationship, is by finding common values. Known as the similarity-attraction effect, people are more attracted to those who are very similar. These values can refer to many things, such examples as morals, politics, and sex. This can be towards things that are positive or negative (Lebowitz).

Looking at things such as Donald Trump's tactics in leadership, Ben Shapiro's tactics in a debate, and different studies in casual bonding, there are many factors when it comes to social psychology. Stemming from our biological roots, there are a lot of factors of how we interact in different social situations and how it affects how we think and act today.

# Works Cited

Bekoff, Marc. "Social Dominance Is Not a Myth: Wolves, Dogs, And." *Psychology Today*, 15 Feb. 2012, www.psychologytoday.com/us/blog/animal-emotions/201202/social-dominance-is-not-myth-wolves-dogs-and. Accessed 19 Apr. 2020.

Cruz, Barron. "Trump Brushes FAKE Dandruff (High-Status PowerPlay) Watch Macron's Reaction!" *YouTube*, 3 May 2018, www.youtube.com/watch?v=X-WPhoI45dN8&t=. Accessed 19 Apr. 2020.

Howes, Lewis. "Ben Shapiro: Problem-Solving in Life and Business." *Lewis Howes*, 7 Jan. 2019, lewishowes.com/podcast/ben-shapiro-problem-solving-in-life-and-business/. Accessed 19 Apr. 2020.

Whitbourne, Susan Krauss. "6 Ways to Win Any Argument." *Psychology Today*, Sussex Publishers, 16 Aug. 2014, www.psychologytoday.com/us/blog/fulfillment-any-age/201408/6-ways-win-any-argument.

Mindwalk Essay

Mindwalk: Technology

By Cooper Perry


Technology is advancing at a rate no one thought to be possible. So many things that seemed impossible a decade or two ago can be done from your cell phone. But technology is more than just phones and computers. It's everywhere, from the most crowded cities to the vastest fields. With humankind becoming more and more infatuated with technology as time goes on, people have developed many different views on it. Is it something that should be embraced or rejected? Will the evil robot overlords overtake the Earth someday? Only time will tell. In this paper I want to explore different points of view of technology, more specifically how it impacts people with scientific, artistic, and political backgrounds.


When searching for artistic views on technology, I found a poem that resonated with me. It's called *Ode to Technology*, written by Tien Dang.

You've brought us closer,

Then made us more distant.

Made us more aware,

Then made us doubtful of ourselves.

Introduce us to more friends,

Then invited more enemies.

Save us more time,

Now it's spent to be more busy.

This poem shows that a lot of things technology has done for us as a species are double-edged swords. The first two lines read "You've brought us closer, Then made us more distant." By allowing us to communicate with each other from anywhere, physical get-togethers are less common (even more so now). The next two lines, "Made us more aware, Then made us doubtful of ourselves." The internet has made all information extremely accessible to anyone with an internet connection. With such a large database of intelligence constantly available, it took a lot of weight off of our minds to remember necessary things like our schedules and to-do lists. Next, the poem reads "Introduce us to more friends, Then invited more enemies." By being able to easily connect with anyone around the world, it of course includes people who may not be as friendly as others. I resonate with this personally, once I sent a friend request on Steam to a youtuber, thinking they'd just accept it for no reason, just like a few others had done for me, but he seemed very impatient, asking what I wanted. This experience that happened years ago still has me scared to engage in any digital conversation with someone I don't know personally. The next lines read "Given us more publicity, Then exploited us." People have the ability to put themselves out there through social media, but some people don't realize that putting too much personal information out into the world can put themselves in serious danger. Finally, the last two lines read "Save us more time, Now it's spent to be more busy." Technology, by making it easier for us to perform tasks, has drastically increased our workload. Since we can use technology to work more quickly and efficiently, we are now expected to be able to complete more work in a day, and as a result are given more work. This has become *VERY APPARENT* in the recent switch to online classes due to the coronavirus pandemic. One of my classes is practically assigning 3x the daily work as we had in normal class.

Technology has both positive and negative influences on politics. On one hand, the internet can act as a whole world of real estate for advertising and campaigning. On the other, technology may not be as reliable as hard paper when it comes to things like ballots. The internet is the most impactful piece of technology when it comes to politics, so for this part of the paper I'm going to stick to the internet as a whole. On the subject of how the internet can influence the publicity of political figures, a man from Mexico says, "We become numb to the news, like the presidential campaigns in Mexico. A term ago, we were struggling to get more political awareness, and now everything is made a meme and laughed at. It defeats the purpose of the internet." While this is true, I disagree with the last thing he says. The creation of memes from political subjects is the best way to appeal to the younger generations today. Depending on how much the meme spreads, it could sway opinions of tens of thousands of people across the country. Memes, at least the ones I've seen, don't usually portray any one person in a negative light. I'm sure there are many memes about bashing political figures, but certain memes don't reach all demographics. For example, older people on

Facebook probably spread memes about hatrid for a political figure, but for younger people, memes are just silly, and usually don't make too much sense on their own. The part that makes a meme good and reusable is the ability to give it context to make it humorous. A good example of this is a video of Bernie Sanders hitting a desk. It became popular for a bit due to how it could be modified to make a joke. The origin of the meme was from a comedy skit starring Bernie, so there wasn't any negativity towards him or his campaign. Memes, by definition, are some form of media that can be reused to the point that they are widespread across the internet. A meme mocking someone, especially a politician wouldn't get far, since not everyone is a fan of downplaying another person for amusement.

Scientists of every field use technology to gather the most accurate data possible. But for this section, I'm going to talk about something more topical; how scientists are using technology to combat the ongoing pandemic. Programmers have developed AIs in response to the COVID-19 outbreak. One of these AIs was made to take existing recorded data and use it to predict future outbreak locations. The data it analyzes consists of news reports, social media platforms, and government documents. A similar AI was used by the Canadian service known as BlueDot. BlueDot was able to predict an outbreak several days before the Centers for Disease Control and Prevention or the World Health Organization issued public warnings. Technology is also being used to speed up delivery of medical supplies. Drones are being used to transport supplies quickly from point A to point B. A company called Terra Drone has been lending its drones to Xinchang County's disease control centre and the People's Hospital to transport supplies safely while maintaining reasonable distancing and disinfecting measures. Drones are also being used to survey public spaces to spot people not abiding by the quarantine rules. In regard to the virus itself, companies such as Tencent, DiDi, and Huawei are lending their supercomputing centers to researchers to find a vaccine for the coronavirus quickly. The rate that these supercomputers can parse models and make calculations is far superior to any normal computer. As well, Google is developing a website to help people identify symptoms of the Coronavirus and direct them to the nearest place they can be tested.

Technology has impacted everyone's lives. Whether or not it's for the better is up to the individual. There are just as many people who worship technology as there are people who demonize it. Personally, I think technology is amazing, I can type up this paper and turn it in digitally, instead of writing multiple pages by pencil and sending it through the mail. Of course, I can recognize the cons of technology becoming as prominent as it has, we're definitely getting closer and closer to all those sci-fi films showing a future where technology can do seemingly impossible things like teleportation. Whether or not that sci-fi future turns out to be utopia or dystopia is entirely up to us as a species. Robots will only take over the world if we program them to do as such.

# Works Cited

Tien, Tim. "Ode to Technology." 2013. Hello: Poetry, https://hellopoetry.com/poem/417758/ode-to-technology/. Accessed 4 May 2020.

Smith, Aaron, et al. "People Think Technology Impacts Politics Positively and Negatively." Pew Research Center: Internet, Science & Tech, Pew Research Center, 31 Dec. 2019, www.pewresearch.org/internet/2019/05/13/publics-think-technology-impacts-the-political-environment-in-both-positive-and-negative-ways/.

Marr, Bernard. "Coronavirus: How Artificial Intelligence, Data Science And Technology Is Used To Fight The Pandemic." Forbes, Forbes Magazine, 21 Apr. 2020, www.forbes.com/sites/bernardmarr/2020/03/13/coronavirus-how-artificial-intelligence-data-science-and-technology-is-used-to-fight-the-pandemic/#462591135f5f.

The End

Made in the USA
Las Vegas, NV
03 September 2021

29530857R00218